On Freud's "Remembering, Repeating and Working-Through"

In *On Freud's "Remembering, Repeating and Working-Through"* international contributors from a range of psychoanalytic backgrounds reflect on this key 1914 paper.

Each chapter considers an aspect of Freud's original work, addressing both the theoretical and clinical dimensions of the paper and incorporating contemporary perspectives. Bringing out all three aspects of the paper's title, the contributors consider the issues raised by the so-called change in psychoanalytic paradigm, from the classic central concern of remembering to a clinical experience which prioritises enactment and repetition. The reflections on this important paper demonstrate how it goes beyond technique to open new vistas on the conception of psychoanalysis as a whole.

On Freud's "Remembering, Repeating and Working-Through" will be essential reading for psychoanalysts and psychoanalytic psychotherapists in practice and in training. It will also be of interest to readers seeking a deeper understanding of current Freudian thinking.

Udo Hock, PhD, is a psychoanalyst based in Germany. He is the editor and translator of the work of Jean Laplanche into German. He is co-editor of the psychoanalytic journal *Psyche*. He has published widely on topics of classical psychoanalysis including drive, infantile sexuality, transference, repetition compulsion, *après-coup*, and, in particular, the notion of 'Entstellung' (distortion, disfigurement).

Dominique Scarfone is honorary professor at the Université de Montréal, Canada. He is member emeritus of the Société Psychanalytique de Montréal and honorary member of the Italian Psychoanalytic Society. He is the author of several books and articles, and co-editor of *Unrepresented States and the Construction of Meaning* (Routledge).

The International Psychoanalytical Association Contemporary Freud Turning Points and Critical Issues Series
Series Editor: Silvia Flechner

IPA Publications Committee
Natacha Delgado, Nergis Güleç, Thomas Marcacci, Carlos Moguillansky, Rafael Mondrzak, Angela M. Vuotto, Gabriela Legoretta (consultant)

On Freud's "Remembering, Repeating and Working-Through"

Edited by Udo Hock and
Dominique Scarfone

Routledge
Taylor & Francis Group

LONDON AND NEW YORK

Designed cover image: Freud by Julia Kotulova, Charcoal & digital, 2019

First published 2024
by Routledge
4 Park Square, Milton Park, Abingdon, Oxon OX14 4RN

and by Routledge
605 Third Avenue, New York, NY 10158

Routledge is an imprint of the Taylor & Francis Group, an informa business

British Library Cataloguing-in-Publication Data
A catalogue record for this book is available from the British Library

ISBN: 9781032602486 (hbk)
ISBN: 9781032602479 (pbk)
ISBN: 9781003458340 (ebk)

DOI: 10.4324/9781003458340

Typeset in Palatino
by KnowledgeWorks Global Ltd.

Contents

Contributors

Elias Mallet da Rocha Barros is a Training and Supervising Analyst at the Brazilian Psychoanalytic Society of São Paulo (SBPSP), Distinguished Fellow of the British Psychoanalytic Society (BPS) and the 1999 recipient of the Mary Sigourney Trust Award.

Alberto Rocha Barros is an affiliated member at the Durval Marcondes Institute of the Brazilian Psychoanalytic Society of São Paulo (SBPSP). He holds a bachelor's degree and a Ph.D. in Philosophy.

Rachel Blass is a Training and Supervising Analyst at the Israel Psychoanalytic Society and a member of the British Psychoanalytical Society. She has published and taught widely on the foundations of psychoanalytic thinking and practice, with a special focus on Kleinian psychoanalysis and its Freudian roots.

Lawrence Friedman, M.D., is Clinical Professor of Psychiatry at the Weill-Cornell Medical College in New York, where he is a member of the DeWitt Wallace Institute of Psychiatry: History, Policy, and the Arts. He is in private practice and on the faculty of the Psychoanalytic Association of New York.

Riccardo Galiani is a psychoanalyst and a full member of the Italian Psychoanalytic Society and the International Psychoanalytical Association. He is also an associate professor in the Department of Psychology of the Luigi Vanvitelli University. He is the author of numerous articles and has published six books, including *Hamlet and Hamlet in psychoanalytic culture* (1997), and *Holding Seduction Anticipation* (2010, 2017). He is an editor of the *Rivista di psicoanalisi*.

Roberta Guarnieri, psychiatrist and psychoanalyst, lives and works in Venice, Italy. She works as a psychoanalyst with adults and adolescents, and is also a supervisor in the training institute of the Italian Psychoanalytic Society. She was part of the editorial board of two Italian journals: *Psiche, rivista di cultura psicoanalitica* and *Notes per la psicoanalisi*. She has a special interest in psychoanalysis and culture.

Udo Hock, Dr. phil, psychoanalyst. He is the editor and translator of Jean Laplanche into German, and co-editor of the psychoanalytical journal 'Psyche'. Publications on the classical topics of psychoanalysis: drive, infantile sexuality, transference, repetition compulsion, *après-coup*, and in particular on the notion of 'Entstellung' (distortion, disfigurement). He is the vice-president elect of the European Psychoanalytical Federation (EPF).

Laurence Kahn is a Training and Supervising Analyst of the French Psychoanalytical Association. Before being a psychoanalyst, she worked as an historian and anthropologist. She was the co-editor of the *Nouvelle Revue de Psychanalyse* from 1990 to 1994, President of the APF from 2008 to 2010, and editor in chief of *L'Annuel de l'APF* from 2010 to 2015. She has written several books, including *What Nazism did to psychoanalysis*, and numerous articles.

Josef Ludin is a Training analyst of the Association Psychanalytique de France (IPA), and works as a psychoanalyst in private practice in Berlin. He is a doctor of neurology and psychiatry.

Ilka Quindeau, Dr. phil., Training Psychoanalyst (DPV/IPV), Professor for Clinical Psychology, is currently fellow at Center for Research on Antisemitism at the Technische Universität Berlin. She also runs her own practice. Her research interests include: memory, trauma, gender, sexuality; anti-Semitism; psychoanalytical film interpretations.

Avgi Saketopoulou, originally from Cyprus and Greece, trained and now practices in New York City. She is a member of the faculty at the New York University Postdoctoral Program in Psychotherapy and Psychoanalysis. She is the author of the monograph *Sexuality Beyond Consent Risk, Race,* Traumatophilia and, with Dr. Ann Pellegrini, co-author of *Gender Without Identity*.

Dominique Scarfone is honorary professor at the Université de Montréal, member emeritus of the Société psychanalytique de Montréal and honorary member of the Italian Psychoanalytic Society. He is the author of articles and books, among which *Laplanche: An introduction* and *The Unpast: The Actual Unconscious,* and co-editor of *Unrepresented States and the Construction of Meaning* (Routledge).

Robin Verner, a Swiss American, born in New York City, currently works in Berlin as a clinical psychologist, teaching analyst, supervisor, and incidental translator. Her fields of interest include a fundamental understanding of psychoanalytic processes as translation.

Series Editor's Foreword

On Freud's "Remembering, Repeating and Working-Through", edited by Udo Hock and Dominique Scarfone
This significant series, "Contemporary Freud: Turning Points and Critical Issues" was founded in 1991 by Robert Wallerstein and subsequently edited by Joseph Sandler, Ethel Spector Person, Peter Fonagy, Leticia Glocer Fiorini and, most recently, by Gennaro Saragnano. Its important contributions have highlighted varied approaches to psychoanalysis in different regions and it has succeeded in creating a new modality of exchange among psychoanalysts. It is therefore my great honor, as Chair of the Publications Committee of the International Psychoanalytic Association, to continue the tradition of this most successful series.

The objective of this series is to approach Freud's work from a historical and contemporary point of view. On the one hand, this means highlighting the fundamental contributions of his work that constitute the axes of psychoanalytic theory and practice. On the other, it implies learning about and spreading the ideas of present psychoanalysts about Freud's *oeuvre*, both where they coincide and where they differ.

The study of Freud's theory has expanded and taken new directions, and this has led to a theoretical, technical, and clinical pluralism that must be worked through. It is necessary to avoid a comfortable and uncritical coexistence of concepts, to consider systems of increasing complexity that entail both the convergences and divergences of the categories at play.

In this volume, Udo Hock and Dominique Scarfone bring together contributors from different regions of the IPA, whose papers are a testimony to the importance of Freud's publication: "Remembering, Repeating and Working-Through". Revisiting this historical work is consistent with the expectations of an IPA series which addresses "turning points" in Freud's thinking as well as in contemporary psychoanalysis.

While Freud's paper is considered as one of his publications on technique, the editors appropriately propose a useful distinction between the psychoanalytic method that aims at accessing the repressed unconscious and the psychoanalytic technique, which addresses the means by which one gains access to it and the obstacles that interfere with it.

An example of an obstacle is the phenomenon of repetition compulsion. This is an obstacle to the goal of the analysis, that which repeats itself and tends to manifest itself in action. It is important to underline that Freud used the notions of repetition and remembering with a metapsychological lens; that is, phenomena that are associated with unconscious processes. The notion of repetition compulsion is again taken up by Freud in 1920, when he proposed that the repetition compulsion is related to the death drive.

Udo Hock and Dominique Scarfone offer an interesting and original reflection in regard to the contiguity of many of Freud's texts on remembering and the theme of disfigurement in Freud's thinking. Freud's theory, in every phase of his work, is inextricably linked to this concept of disfigurement. As the editors state: "The German word, *Entstellung*, has an interesting, almost contradictory double meaning: it simultaneously means 'masking' and 'unmasking' or 'covering' and 'uncovering'. This means that the unconscious can only show itself veiled or masked: deformation is, paradoxically, what gives form to the unconscious".

The notion of remembering is addressed in detail by the editors. They highlight that in "Remembering, Repeating and Working-Through", Freud defines remembering as the "reproduction in the psychical field." We are reminded that the way that Freud considered remembering had a metapsychological dimension; it is not simply recalling or retrieving something from what may be thought as a basin of memories. Reproduction in the psychic field is related to the linking of memory traces to language, to speech—that is, in the symbolic realm.

The individual chapters of this book reflect on Freud's paper from different angles. One of these is the perspective of traumotophilia, developed by A. Saketopoulou, who underlines, for the purposes of working through, the importance of taking the risk of being exposed in a repetitive manner in general, and, in the analysis, to experiences that are at the limit of the bearable.

Another perspective is offered by R. Blass who elaborates in depth on a notion put forward by Freud, regarding the curative impact in analysis of having access to one's own truth. She argues that for this idea to be useful and make sense, a conceptual framework is needed that includes notions of emotional knowing (as opposed to intellectual ones) and notions of the dynamic forces at play in primarily mental states as well as a desire for truth. R. Guarnieri, in her chapter, underlines the notion of remembering as a process that takes place in a psychic realm, which involves a passage to a symbolic process, a transformative path that converts the excitement associated with the drives, into representations, which allow the passage from thing presentation to word presentation.

The richness and originality of the contributions to this volume clearly achieve the goal of this series. It is evident that Freud's "Remembering, Repeating and Working-Through" continues to offer ideas for discussion and questioning but also for elaboration. The expansion of Freud's work offered by the authors is a testimony to the richness of his legacy with its originality, creativity and, at times, provocative thinking. This book is a demonstration of the way in which Freud's work has become a breeding ground from which new ideas and developments have arisen.

The Publications Committee is pleased to publish this book *On Freud's "Remembering, Repeating and Working-Through"*, which constitutes the 21st volume of the IPA "Contemporary Freud, Turning points and critical issues" series. Udo Hock and Dominique Scarfone have brilliantly and skillfully edited this new volume. The result is this important book, which will surely encounter the favor of every psychoanalytic student as well as others who are interested in Freud's work and its evolution as well as in the complexity of mental life. I want to thank wholeheartedly the editors and contributors of this new volume that continues the tradition of the successful IPA book series.

Gabriela Legorreta Series Editor
Chair, IPA Publications Committee

1 An Introduction to Revisiting Freud's "Remembering, Repeating and Working-Through"

Udo Hock and Dominique Scarfone

The paper "Remembering, Repeating and Working-Through" is not very long and is written in a quite straightforward manner. But an index of its importance for Freud himself is that it begins with a reminder of the changes in psychoanalytic technique over the years. One can easily imagine that Freud is, thus, announcing some innovation in this regard. As we shall see, however, the novelty in the present case is not limited to questions of technique, or perhaps we should say that, as always, Freud's reflections of technique are here again tightly linked with metapsychological novelty.

Psychoanalytic technique

Let us first look at James Strachey's editor's introduction (1958) to the so-called "papers on technique" that Freud had written between 1911 and 1915 and were included in Volume 12 of the *Standard Edition*.[1]

These "papers on technique" include the following six titles: "The Handling of Dream-Interpretation in Psycho-Analysis" (1911e), "The Dynamics of Transference" (1912b) "Recommendations to Physicians Practising Psycho-Analysis" (1912e), "On Beginning the Treatment" (Further recommendations on the technique of psychoanalysis I) (1913c), "Remembering, Repeating and Working-Through" (Further recommendations on the technique of psychoanalysis II) (1914g) and finally, "Observations on Transference-love" (Further recommendations on the technique of psychoanalysis III) (1915a). Freud himself made it clear, both by a remark in the first edition of his text "On Beginning the Treatment" and by the consecutive counting of the last four essays, that they belonged together; accordingly, he published them in 1918 under the title *On the Technique of Psychoanalysis*.

In his commentary, Strachey emphasizes Freud's reticence, indeed his reluctance, towards publishing papers on the technical aspects of psychoanalysis: on the one hand, Freud had published a relatively small number of texts on this topic. Only in his later texts from the 1930s—"Analysis Terminable and Interminable" (1937c), "Constructions in Analysis" (1937d), for example—had he turned again to questions of technique. On the other hand, he had shown great skepticism towards any "Guidelines for young

DOI: 10.4324/9781003458340-1

analysts," for he was of the opinion that the psychological factors at play in psychoanalysis were too complex and variable to be pressed into a compendium of psychoanalysis. No book reading could replace the clinical experience that the psychoanalyst had both with his own patients and, even more so, in his own analysis. Freud's comparison of a psychoanalytic treatment with a chess game has become famous. It is worth re-reading the relevant passage with which he begins his text "On Beginning the Treatment":

> Anyone who hopes to learn the noble game of chess from books will soon discover that only the openings and end-games admit of an exhaustive systematic presentation and that the infinite variety of moves which develop after the opening defy any such description. This gap in instruction can only be filled by a diligent study of games fought out by masters. The rules which can be laid down for the practice of psycho-analytic treatment are subject to similar limitations.
>
> (Freud, 1913c, p. 123)

Precisely because of the fundamental indeterminacy of the various factors that affect psychoanalytic treatment, Freud subsequently refrains from demanding an "unconditional acceptance" of clearly fixed rules over and above the basic rule of free association, preferring instead in the same passage of his essay to speak of "recommendations" (*ibid.*); this is also the expression that appears in the title of four of the six essays mentioned above. In this way, however, Freud distances himself from discourses on psychoanalytic technique that place too much emphasis on unambiguity and clarity (and in the history of psychoanalysis, we have witnessed quite different currents with such settings), and indeed he formally delegitimizes them. Probably the discrepancy between the openness of the Freudian text and the feeling of having to acquire a very specific technique with its associated terms (transference interpretation, abstinence, etc.) is greatest in the training situation. Often the only way out for candidates is to adopt a supposed institutional treatment "style" with the corresponding names and terms in order to get through the training period as unscathed as possible.

The history of psychoanalysis shows sufficiently that what is in vogue today will be shelved tomorrow: who would still profess the strict, even rigid, treatment rules of ego psychology and who would profess the early aggressive transference interpretations of Melanie Klein? Perhaps it should be added here that the diversity of technical treatments is not an invention of the present, but instead has accompanied psychoanalysis from the beginning. A quotation from Lacan from his seminar on Freud's technical writings may illustrate this as an example for the 1950s:

> Observing today (1954) the manner in which various practitioners of psychoanalysis think, express, conceive of their technique, one considers that things are in such a state that it would not be exaggerated

to call it a state of general confusion. Let me tell you that presently, there are possibly not two analysts who, in the end, hold the same idea regarding what we do in analysis, what we aim for, what is obtained and what analysis is about.

(Lacan, 1975, pp. 16–17, translated for this edition)[2]

What seems more important to us in the present context is that Freud left no technical set of rules on which his successors could have based themselves; this seems to apply no less to Freud's reception in the 1950s than to the present situation. Against this background, it can be said without exaggeration that any form of technical orthodoxy springs less from the spirit of Freud than from a particular group identification with its specific leading figures.

What, then, distinguishes Freud's technical writings, to which "Remembering, Repeating and Working-Through" undoubtedly belongs? In order to answer this question, it is perhaps first necessary to define more precisely what is meant by "technique," as distinct from "method." Unfortunately, studying Freud's texts is not very helpful in this regard; his use of the two terms seems somewhat arbitrary. For example, catharsis and hypnosis are referred to as methods in one case (Freud, 1904a[1903]), but as techniques in the other, and especially in "Remembering, Repeating and Working-Through." We propose, therefore, the following, somewhat simple, distinction: while the psychoanalytic *method* seeks ways of accessing the repressed unconscious, the psychoanalytic *technique* is concerned with the question of how these ways of access are created, that is, how obstacles can be identified and overcome in order to reach the goal. In other words, technique concerns the many ways by which the method of psychoanalysis can be implemented and its fundamentals aims pursued.

Freud's technical writings have in store a whole list of obstacles to such implementation: what to do, for example, when the dream material becomes overflowing in the treatment and seems to displace all recent material (Freud, 1911e)? How to deal with the fact that transference takes over during the cure and seems to condition all the patient's expressions and ideas (Freud, 1912b)? Or when—comparable to a fire during a theatre performance—actual transference-love breaks out during the analysis, which completely engulfs the patient, so that he loses all understanding and interest in the treatment (Freud, 1915a)?

"Remembering, Repeating and Working-Through" also belongs in this series, as Freud is dealing here with the problem that the analysand does not remember anything at all of what has been forgotten and repressed, but expresses it in action: "He reproduces it not as a memory, but as an action" (Freud, 1914g, p. 150. In many of the contributions to the present volume, we shall be reminded how Freud dealt with this difficulty. For now, we shall anticipate only this much: in this particular paper, we get a clearer view of how Freud deals with the ever-new hurdles and obstacles emerging during the analytical process. From his perspective, these are, as it were, lines of conflict that are inherent to the analytical game of chess; hence, the game should not be broken off because the opponent has not kept to the rules. It is a matter of facing a new situation: "the master" (i.e., the unconscious of the patient), has rather created a new form of resistance that makes it even more difficult for the analyst to reach his goal, which is to unearth the forgotten and repressed. This is why a special "tactic" is needed (*ibid.*, p. 153). In other words, this new resistance, which Freud will call repetition compulsion a few lines down, is initially nothing other than a new mode of manifestation of the unconscious itself and not a power external to the analytic process. One can see very clearly here how an initially technical obstacle (patients repeating, acting in treatment) is right away granted by Freud the dignity of a metapsychological problem, one that has to do with the essence of the unconscious, a stance that will be prolonged in subsequent texts such as "The 'Uncanny'" (1919h) and even more so in *Beyond the Pleasure Principle* (1920g).

Remembering

At this point, it is worth noticing that "Remembering, Repeating and Working-Through" is not a text dealing with problems of technique alone, it is also a text about remembering, or more precisely, about failing to remember. Thus, the essay belongs not only to Freud's ensemble of technical writings, but to the rather long series of texts that have to do with distorted forms of remembering. The proximity of very different texts on remembering via the common theme of disfigurement had struck one of us long ago (Hock, 2000[2012], 56f.); it also appears in two French publications devoted to Freud's texts on remembering. One is the collection of eight essays by Freud, edited by Pontalis, on the problem of remembering under the title *Huit études sur la mémoire et ses troubles* [Eight studies on memory and its disturbances], (Freud, 2010), with a very interesting preface by the editor. The other is Gribinski's book, *Portes ouvertes sur Freud* [Open doors on Freud], 2021, in which the author translated into French a large number of Strachey's introductory texts to Freud's essays and added his own comments. Here again, there is a section on memory, "La mémoire et ses troubles" ("Memory and its disturbances, *ibid.*, pp. 367–398), gathering ten other introductions by Strachey to Freudian essays, also annotated by Gribinski. Many of the Freudian texts selected by Pontalis are also cited here, most of which were cited as examples of memory gone wrong in Hock's (2000[2012]) study. It goes without saying that "Remembering, Repeating and Working-Through" appears in all three publications.

However, the two French authors remain reserved in their explanations as to why Freud was ultimately only ever interested in disorders of memory. But at least they concur in considering that acting out or repeating is a special form of memory disorder, which, as is well known, led Freud to an expansion and even a new conceptualization of the psychic apparatus in the further course of his thinking.

In answering the question of why Freud dealt exclusively with forms of disordered remembering, the magic word is "distortion." Freud's theory of memory, in every phase of his work, from the early theory of seduction to the late text on the biblical figure Moses, is inextricably linked to this concept of disfigurement. It is a common link between all of Freud's texts. For non-German-speaking readers, the term is not easy to recognize: in Strachey's translation it is regularly rendered as "distortion", while in French *déformation* is the current choice, though *défiguration* is also acceptable. The German word, *Entstellung*, has an interesting, almost contradictory double meaning: it simultaneously means "masking" and "unmasking" or "covering" and "uncovering." This means that the unconscious can only show itself veiled or masked: deformation is, paradoxically, what gives form to the unconscious. Accordingly, in "Remembering, repeating and working-through" repetition/acting is memory in disguise, and this is precisely what allows the unconscious to be uncovered or unmasked. The 1914g paper thus joins the long list of Freudian texts that deal exclusively with distorted forms of remembering. And this is by no means fortuitous. Rather, these distortions (forgetting, repeating, misremembering, transferring, dreaming, *fausse reconnaissance*/false recognition, hallucinatory memories, and so on) indicate repressions that have taken place and come back in the present in a distorted form. The converse also applies: where no distortion has taken place, psychoanalysis has no business, for it means that the unconscious has not intruded. One cannot marvel enough at Freud's extraordinary sensitivity for language, insofar as he inscribed these forms of distortion as titles to the various essays on memory.

Incidentally, one realizes that the first three pages of "Remembering, Repeating and Working-Through" are devoted equally to questions of treatment (pp. 1 and 2) and to questions of memory (pp. 2 and 3). For the technical questions, dealt with in the various pre-analytical or analytical procedures (1. hypnosis and catharsis, 2. psychoanalysis as an art of interpretation, 3. psychoanalysis as an analysis of resistance) revolve fundamentally around the problem of access to repressed memories. Perhaps one may go so far as to say that the whole psychoanalytic setting is geared toward uncovering these memories according to all the rules of the art, that is, by tracing the distortions to which the conscious material was submitted via dream-work, transference, acting, malfunctioning and so on. The psychoanalytic rules themselves aim to grasp these particularities of the analytic process. It is a struggle for the right tactics to overcome the resistance by means of which the unconscious makes itself known. Distortion is not only the decisive term describing the transformation of latent dream thoughts into the manifest dream content, the term also names the transformations that memories undergo when they are contaminated, so to speak, by the unconscious. In this respect, distortions represent the material *par excellence* to which the psychoanalytic process is attuned.

Repeating

More than technique or memory, the aspect *"Remembering, Repeating and Working-Through"* strikes us most with is its introduction of repetition as a major feature of what is at work in psychopathology *and* during the treatment. Remembering serves mainly, in this regard, as a backdrop against which to highlight repetition.

Repetition was implicitly present in Freud's considerations on psychopathology in the *Project* (1895a). There, he established that one such characteristic was the compulsive nature of neurotic preoccupation. The compulsive insistence of a given thought or image necessarily involved the repeated return of such representation. In fact, as early as in his book, *On Aphasia* (1891), Freud had referred to the recurrent utterances of motor aphasic patients just after the stroke that impaired their speech apparatus. He sided with the British neurologist Jackson, who considered that such utterances should not be mistaken for real speech: they were "the last words produced by the speech apparatus before the injury, or even at a time when there already existed an awareness of the impending disability" (Freud, 1891, pp. 61–62).

An observation such as this already puts us on the Freudian track regarding repetition. The last words produced as the injury was impending can indeed be put on a par with the last horrific scene witnessed by the severely traumatized soldier and which shall thereafter keep intruding in his mind, or the last part of the female body that was visible to the future fetishist before the terror caused by the sight of the female genitalia, which led to the choice of the fetish that must be compulsively used in the future (Freud, 1927e; Katan, 1969; Scarfone, 2018).

Freud's reflection on repetition, however, did not take shape immediately. While the seeds are noticeable in retrospect, fully appreciating the importance of repetition in psychic life was a slow process. In this progressive discovery, repetition, in fact, took different values, if not different meanings.

The present book looks at "Remembering, Repeating and Working-Through" as representing what could be termed the intermediate stage of Freud's thinking on repetition. We are in the year 1914 and Freud has, by now, established a rather standard analytic procedure. He has been gathering extensive clinical material from cases that are now familiar to us and which had helped him to put together the psychoanalytic method. Therefore, he seems in a position to effectuate, in what are called his papers on technique, more granular descriptions of what goes on during the treatment sessions and, in the process, to remark that there is more than one way of remembering in analysis.

Already in the *Project*, Freud had formulated an important distinction between the mnemic *sensorial image* of the desired object and the mnemic *image of the movement* (*Bewegungsbild*) whose reactivation makes the desired view available again (Freud, 1895a, pp. 328–329). He then already had a sense that action was indeed one way of remembering. Yet, the 1914g paper is not simply a statement regarding this piece of knowledge. Freud is now writing a deeply clinical paper in which action—always a basic feature of his conception of psychic functioning—is described under the specific light of repetition.

Obviously, all repetition is action, for how can one observe repetition if not in remarking that something presents itself again to the observer's perceptual apparatus. But here, in the course of analysis, the reverse is also true: wherever we see action instead of remembering, we can calmly state that we are witnessing repetition. This is counterintuitive, but it starts making sense if we do not merely describe repetition as "the same thing occurring again" but keep in mind the *Project*'s view that every action leaves a *motor* trace in memory. This, therefore, immediately distinguishes it from the other, *sensorial* mnemic traces—visual images, sound images etc.—and even more so from abstract semantic memories. In other words when a motor mnemic trace is not fully psychical (i.e., not fully connected to symbolic thinking), it can be considered an actual or potential repetition.

This means that, just like action, repetition is omnipresent. How, then, can we usefully separate the generic repetition occurring all the time from a kind of repetition so salient that Freud felt it necessary to write a specific paper about it? For this, Freud seems to think that we must address the contrast between repetition in action and repetition in remembering. At a closer look, indeed, remembering itself is a form of repetition, as Hans Loewald (1973) pointed out. In the *Project,* Freud spoke of "reproductive thought." And. indeed, in "Remembering, Repeating and Working-Through," he defines remembering as the "reproduction in the psychical field" (1914g, p. 153). Hence, we see the word "remembering" itself take a slightly different meaning in metapsychology than in ordinary parlance. Remembering is not simply recalling, recollecting or evoking, and it is also not retrieving something in some "memory bank." One may still wonder, however: what does "reproduction in the psychical field" actually mean? Clearly, this has something to do with connecting the mnemic trace, or image, to speech (inner speech included). In Freud's view, therefore, before such connection takes place, repetition in action is not fully psychical, or is at best proto-psychical. What we have then is the introduction of yet another way of thinking about the unconscious: it may be conceived of as that which repeats itself without being really, psychically, represented; so much so that it tends to manifest itself essentially *in action*. In the analytic setting, we meet this manifestation all the time in the transference, which, Freud remarks, is a resistance and, yet, our best ally in getting the unconscious on a track that will lead to this other form of remembering: the reproduction in the psychical field, that is, a reproduction (hence, a repetition) that can be expressed through speech.

In view of what precedes, we would be looking in vain into the patient's verbal utterances for the memories (mnemic traces or images) they are supposed to contain. Remembering does not function in that way. It does not consist in the capture of discrete memories; it rather means reorganizing the whole pre-conscious–conscious structure in a way that allows for speech to find a freer movement, a more widely open perspective so that the energy of the sensory and motor traces can be transferred to the "psychical domain," i.e., can be put to symbolic usage.

Remarkably, this aspect of Freud's thinking was already present in *The Interpretation of Dreams*, where he established, for instance, a clear distinction between the "sensorial intensity" of a dream content and its "psychical intensity" (1900a, p. 330). A remark suggesting that, for him, a dream content becomes fully psychical to the extent that it connects with the dream-thoughts an—implicitly—with language. As for the "sensorial intensity," it refers to the apparent importance of a dream image in the manifest content. As we know, the whole idea of dream analysis requires not taking the apparent importance of manifest elements at face value and deconstructing instead the manifest dream in order to document the work of displacement and condensation that presided over its formation. These primary processes, indeed, made it so that the thoughts that presided over the dreaming (latent content) are hidden from view in the manifest dream. Yet, the analysis of the dream is not simply about unearthing these thoughts for themselves. In a famous footnote near the end of Chapter VI in *The Interpretation of Dreams*, Freud insists that what matters most is neither the manifest nor the latent content of dreams, but the *dream-work* occurring in between. We could say that the same applies to psychoanalysis in general. What truly matters is not merely finding the isolated meaning of a dream, slip or symptom, but helping the psyche start moving ahead again, finding its forward thrust, evolving rather than going in circles of repetition.

Hence, the meaning of "reproduction in the psychical field" could be to put whatever is gathered from the sterile process of repetition onto a path open to elaboration, to *becoming*. The resulting speech acts of the analysand may, therefore, not patently map onto the isolated translation of the act into words; the result is, rather, that speech and thinking benefit from the energy that was freed by the analytic unbinding of a repetitive transferential pattern. To paraphrase a famous Freudian dictum: "Where repetition was, there thinking and symbolization shall be." With these remarks in mind, we see the notion of *working-through* making an implicit entrance, even before Freud resolves to write two short paragraphs on this third element at the end of "Remembering, Repeating and Working-Through" (more on this later).

*

Knowing that some five years after the writing of "Remembering, Repeating and Working-Through," repetition will take on an even greater importance in the context of *Beyond the Pleasure Principle* (1920g), Freud's highlighting of repetition in the present paper clearly looks in retrospect like an intermediate step. Repetition does have greater salience in Freud's thinking of 1914, but it is still just an alternative to remembering proper, not yet revealing all its secrets. Freud even writes that "in drawing attention to the compulsion to repeat we have acquired no new fact but only a more comprehensive view" (1914g, p. 151). Nevertheless, it proves a powerful means for guiding psychoanalytic understanding and practice. Freud realizes that repetition is part of a triad formed by repetition, resistance, and transference, a triangle from which he extracts precious clinical indications. For one thing, it opens the way to a brilliant juggling with the time dimension, between present and past:

> We have only made it clear to ourselves that the patient's state of being ill cannot cease with the beginning of his analysis, and that we must treat his illness, *not as an event of the past, but as a present-day force.* This state of illness is brought, piece by piece, within the field and range of operation of the treatment, and while the patient experiences it as something real and contemporary, we have to *do our therapeutic work on it, which consists in a large measure in tracing it back to the past.*
>
> (*ibid.*, pp. 151–152, emphasis added)

Transference is what brings the state of illness "piece by piece, within the field and range of operation of the treatment." When this occurs, the apparent linear form of time that the patient brought under scrutiny as his/her past is totally upset: what seemed to be the past is now operating as a "present-day force." In turn, what the patient experiences during the treatment "as something real and contemporary" must be "tra[ced] back to the past." This is made possible thanks to transference:

> The main instrument (…) for curbing the patient's compulsion to repeat and for turning it into a motive for remembering lies in the handling of the transference. *We render the compulsion harmless, and indeed useful, by giving it the right to assert itself in a definite field.* We admit it into the transference as a playground in which it is allowed to expand in almost complete freedom and in which it is expected to display to us everything in the way of pathogenic instincts that is hidden in the patient's mind.
>
> (*ibid.*, p. 154, emphasis added)

All the same, the importance of repetition should not cast a shadow over the two other components of the triad announced in the title: remembering and working-through. We saw that, by contrast with repeating, remembering itself takes on a new profile. Staying a little longer with this concept as addressed by Freud in this paper, we saw that he is formulating a truly *metapsychological definition of remembering* that is not merely a question of retrieving memories. As early as in the paper on "Screen memories," Freud (1899a) had warned that memories do not *emerge from* the past but are *about* the past; even so, they are formed according to the needs of the present (p. 322). Hence, having or retrieving memories was never about obtaining a faithful picture of the past, although Freud sometimes gives the impression that this is what analysis is about: for instance, when he assigns to it the task of lifting infantile amnesia or when, as late as 1937, he writes that "The path that starts from the analyst's construction ought to end in the patient's recollection" (Freud, 1937, p. 265). Yet—Strachey's choice of the word "recollection" for *Erinnerung* notwithstanding—if we take into consideration the rest of Freud's remarks on what it is to remember in analysis, it is clear that he gives analysis the mandate to uncover the "historical truth," which is not exactly an objective picture, but the truth about infantile wishes and fantasies and the defensive struggle against them. In that sense, "historical truth," which assumes paramount importance in Freud's last major work, *Moses and Monotheism* (1939a), is quite close to this other vaguely defined, yet central psychoanalytic notion: psychical reality.

4 Working-Through

A most striking aspect of "Remembering, Repeating and Working-Through" is that Freud seems to give short shrift to the third element of the trilogy. He even starts the third limb of his paper by writing: "I might break off at this point but for the title of this paper, which *obliges me* to discuss a further point in analytic technique" (*ibid.*, p. 155, emphasis added). It's as if the title had been forced on him by someone else. This may well be a rhetorical strategy, as if Freud was eschewing the problem of working-through after discovering that he had little to say about it. Yet, in those two final paragraphs, he says things that, in the reader's mind, should have inspired him to rather long developments. His last remarks are indeed that "[working-through] is *a part of the work which effects the greatest changes in the patient* and which distinguishes analytic treatment from any kind of treatment by suggestion" (*ibid.*, pp. 155–156, emphasis added).

One would, then, expect to see Freud say a little more. Yet, the other thing he says about working-through is that "The doctor has nothing else to do than to wait and let things take their course, a course which cannot be avoided nor always hastened" (*ibid.*, p. 155)

Noticeably, just as he had "juggled with time" regarding repetition, Freud defines working through not as a technical innovation but again as a specific way of dealing with time. A good example of this is the comparison between the "beginner" and the experienced analyst. While the beginner mistakenly believes that when the patient's resistance has been exposed the analyst's work is done, the experienced analyst knows that the patient needs more time, the time to deepen and work through the resistance. Identifying with the patient, the "beginner" takes the patient's resistance as the last word, hence the cure seems to stall. Freud introduces instead a change of perspective, for, whereas "the treatment seemed to make no headway, [t]his gloomy foreboding always proved mistaken. The treatment was as a rule progressing most satisfactorily" (*ibid.*) The novelty is that the time of repetition had imperceptibly become the time of working through. To overcome resistance, the analyst must not only help the patient discern it, but also "allow the patient time," "wait and let things take their course," endure the "trial of patience." Freud's vocabulary here clearly refers to dealing with time.

Still, Freud's way of dealing with working-through is rather astonishing. On the one hand, working-through appears as just a brief addendum to remembering and repeating, apparently possessing no form of its own and being allotted but two paragraphs. On the other hand, however, Freud ends this apparently small part of his essay by giving it an extraordinary importance: "Nevertheless it is a part of the work which effects the greatest changes in the patient and which distinguishes analytic treatment from any kind of treatment by suggestion" (*ibid.*, pp. 155–156). The contrast with the space given to such a tremendous component could not be sharper.

One of us (Scarfone, 2004) suggested that Freud's rather laconic description of working-through is actually consistent with the process it describes: just as the analyst in session must leave the process of working-through essentially to the patient and, accordingly, should give no directions about how to proceed, so Freud leaves to the analyst–reader the task of "working-through" their understanding of the concept and not expect a more precise guidance than the one just offered. For patients and analysts alike, there is no positive description possible of how working-through is achieved. Every analysand does it in a unique manner, and every analyst must discover by him/herself what particular form working-through may take in each different analysis.

◆

As editors, we were impressed by the fact that many of our guest authors chose to write about working-through. It is as if a need was felt to compensate for Freud's parsimony on the matter. A second, smaller group of authors concentrated on repetition. Remembering was not forgotten, but the reflections concerning this element of the trilogy are interspersed among the papers on repeating and working-through.

The contributions gathered here were carefully scrutinized, subjected to critical assessment and eventual revision by their authors. A broad categorization of the papers guided our grouping of them. Thus, we ordered the papers in terms of their main focus into linguistic and terminological, conceptual and clinical categories. Obviously, there are overlaps, as is to be expected in our field. Our hope is that going through this collection of papers, readers will rediscover the significance and the importance of this pivotal work by Sigmund Freud.

Notes

1 The German version can be found in the Freudian *Studienausgabe* in the volume *Schriften zur Behandlungstechnik* (145–148). A French translation has recently been produced by Michel Gribinski (2020, pp. 467–471) and supplemented with its own commentary, which is well worth reading (*ibid.*, pp. 359–366).

2 "Quand, pour l'heure – je parle de maintenant, 1954 (…) on observe la façon dont les divers praticiens de l'analyse pensent, expriment, conçoivent, leur technique, on se dit que les choses en sont à un point qu'il n'est pas exagéré d'appeler la confusion la plus radicale. Je vous mets au fait qu'actuellement, parmi les analystes (…) il n'y en peut-être pas un seul qui se fasse, dans le fond, la même idée qu'un quelconque de ses contemporains ou de ses voisins sur le sujet de ce qu'on fait, de ce qu'on vise, de ce qu'on obtient, de ce dont il s'agit dans l'analyse." (Lacan 1975, 16–17)

References

Freud, S. (1891b[1953]) *On Aphasia. A Critical Study*, (E. Stengel, translator) New York: International Universities Press.

Freud, S. (1895a) *Project for a Scientific Psychology. S.E.*, 1: 283–397. London: Hogarth Press.

Freud, S. (1899a) Screen memories. *S.E.*, 3: 301–322. London: Hogarth Press.

Freud, S. (1900a) *The Interpretation of Dreams. S.E.*, 4 and 5. London: Hogarth Press.

Freud, S. (1904a[1903]) Freud's Psycho-Analytic Procedure. *S.E.*, 7: 247–254. London: Hogarth Press.

Freud, S. (1911e) The Handling of Dream-Interpretation in Psycho-Analysis. *S.E.*, 12: 89–96. London: Hogarth Press.

Freud, S. (1912b) The Dynamics of Transference. *S.E*, 12: 97–108. London: Hogarth Press.

Freud, S. (1912e) Recommendations to Physicians Practising Psycho-Analysis. *S.E.*, 12: 109–120.

Freud, S. (1913c) On Beginning the Treatment. *S.E.*, 12:123–144. London: Hogarth Press.

Freud, S. (1914g) Remembering, Repeating and Working-Through. *S.E.*, 12: 147–156. London: Hogarth Press.

Freud, S. (1915a) Observations on Transference-Love. *S.E.*, 12: 157–171. London: Hogarth Press.

Freud, S. (1918) *On the Technique of Psychoanalysis.* (Unavailable today, but see *Papers on Technique, S.E.*, 12: 85–173.) London, Hogarth Press.

Freud, S. (1920g) *Beyond the Pleasure Principle. S.E.*, 18: 7–64. London: Hogarth Press.

Freud, S. (1927e) Fetishism. *S.E.*, 21: 147–158. London: Hogarth Press.

Freud, S. (1937d) Constructions in Analysis. *S.E.* 23: 255–269. London: Hogarth Press.

Freud, S. (1939a) *Moses and Monotheism. S.E.*, 23: 3–137. London: Hogarth Press.

Freud, S. (2010) *Huit études sur la mémoire et ses troubles.* Préface de J.-B. Pontalis. Paris: Gallimard.

Gribinski, M. (2020) *Portes ouvertes sur Freud*. Paris: Fario.

Hock (2012 [2000]) *Das Unbewußte Denken. Wiederholung und Todestrieb*. Gießen: Psychosozial-Verlag.

Katan, M. (1969) The link between Freud's Works on Aphasia, Fetishism and Constructions in Analysis. *International Journal of Psycho-Analysis, 50*: 547–553.

Lacan, J. (1975) *Le séminaire I: Les écrits techniques de Freud (1953-1954)*. Paris: Seuil.

Loewald, H. (2000[1973]) Some Considerations on Repetition and Repetition Compulsion. In: *The Essential Loewald: Collected Papers and Monographs* (pp. 87–101). Hagerstown, MD: University Publishing Group.

Scarfone, D. (2004) À quoi œuvre l'analyse. *Libres cahiers pour la psychanalyse, 9*: 109–123. Also in *Quartiers aux rues sans nom*, Paris, Éditions de l'Olivier, 2012.

Scarfone, D. (2018) Foreign Bodies. The Body-psyche and its Phantoms. In: V. Tsolas and C. Anzieu-Premmereur (Eds), *On the Body. A Psychoanalytic Exploration of the Body in Today's World* (pp. 146–158). London: Routledge.

2   Remembering, Repeating and Working-Through (Further Recommendations on the Technique of Psycho-Analysis II)

Sigmund Freud

It seems to me not unnecessary to keep on reminding students of the far-reaching changes which psycho-analytic technique has undergone since its first beginnings. In its first phase—that of Breuer's catharsis—it consisted in bringing directly into focus the moment at which the symptom was formed, and in persistently endeavouring to reproduce the mental processes involved in that situation, in order to direct their discharge along the path of conscious activity. Remembering and abreacting, with the help of the hypnotic state, were what was at that time aimed at. Next, when hypnosis had been given up, the task became one of discovering from the patient's free associations what he failed to remember. The resistance was to be circumvented by the work of interpretation and by making its results known to the patient. The situations which had given rise to the formation of the symptom and the other situations which lay behind the moment at which the illness broke out retained their place as the focus of interest; but the element of abreaction receded into the background and seemed to be replaced by the expenditure of work which the patient had to make in being obliged to overcome his criticism of his free associations, in accordance with the fundamental rule of psycho-analysis. Finally, there was evolved the consistent technique used today, in which the analyst gives up the attempt to bring a particular moment or problem into focus. He contents himself with studying whatever is present for the time being on the surface of the patient's mind, and he employs the art of interpretation mainly for the purpose of recognizing the resistances which appear there, and making them conscious to the patient. From this there results a new sort of division of labour: the doctor uncovers the resistances which are unknown to the patient; when these have been got the better of, the patient often relates the forgotten situations and connections without any difficulty. The aim of these different techniques has, of course, remained the same. Descriptively speaking, it is to fill in gaps in memory; dynamically speaking, it is to overcome resistances due to repression.

We must still be grateful to the old hypnotic technique for having brought before us single psychical processes of analysis in an isolated or schematic form. Only this could have given us the courage ourselves to

DOI: 10.4324/9781003458340-2

create more complicated situations in the analytic treatment and to keep them clear before us.

In these hypnotic treatments the process of remembering took a very simple form. The patient put himself back into an earlier situation, which he seemed never to confuse with the present one, and gave an account of the mental processes belonging to it, in so far as they had remained normal; he then added to this whatever was able to emerge as a result of transforming the processes that had at the time been unconscious into conscious ones.

At this point I will interpolate a few remarks which every analyst has found confirmed in his observations.[1] Forgetting impressions, scenes or experiences nearly always reduces itself to shutting them off. When the patient talks about these 'forgotten' things he seldom fails to add: 'As a matter of fact I've always known it; only I've never thought of it.' He often expresses disappointment at the fact that not enough things come into his head that he can call 'forgotten'—that he has never thought of since they happened. Nevertheless, even this desire is fulfilled, especially in the case of conversion hysterias. 'Forgetting' becomes still further restricted when we assess at their true value the screen memories which are so generally present. In some cases I have had an impression that the familiar childhood amnesia, which is theoretically so important to us, is completely counterbalanced by screen memories. Not only some but all of what is essential from childhood has been retained in these memories. It is simply a question of knowing how to extract it out of them by analysis. They represent the forgotten years of childhood as adequately as the manifest content of a dream represents the dream-thoughts.

The other group of psychical processes—phantasies, processes of reference, emotional impulses, thought-connections—which, as purely internal acts, can be contrasted with impressions and experiences, must, in their relation to forgetting and remembering, be considered separately. In these processes it particularly often happens that something is 'remembered' which could never have been 'forgotten' because it was never at any time noticed—was never conscious. As regards the course taken by psychical events it seems to make no difference whatever whether such a 'thought-connection' was conscious and then forgotten or whether it never managed to become conscious at all. The conviction which the patient obtains in the course of his analysis is quite independent of this kind of memory.

In the many different forms of obsessional neurosis in particular, forgetting is mostly restricted to dissolving thought-connections, failing to draw the right conclusions and isolating memories.

There is one special class of experiences of the utmost importance for which no memory can as a rule be recovered. These are experiences which occurred in very early childhood and were not understood at the time but which were subsequently understood and interpreted. One gains a knowledge of them through dreams and one is obliged to believe in them on the most compelling evidence provided by the fabric of the neurosis. Moreover, we can ascertain for ourselves that the patient, after his resistances have been overcome, no longer invokes the absence of any memory of them (any sense of familiarity with them) as a ground for refusing to accept them. This matter, however, calls for so much critical caution and introduces so much that is novel and startling that I shall reserve it for a separate discussion in connection with suitable material.[2]

Under the new technique very little, and often nothing, is left of this delightfully smooth course of events.[3] There are some cases which behave like those under the hypnotic technique up to a point and only later cease to do so; but others behave differently from the beginning. If we confine ourselves to this second type in order to bring out the difference, we may say that the patient does not remember anything of what he has forgotten and repressed, but acts it out.[4] He reproduces it not as a memory but as an action; he repeats it, without, of course, knowing that he is repeating it.

For instance, the patient does not say that he remembers that he used to be defiant and critical towards his parents' authority; instead, he behaves in that way to the doctor. He does not remember how he came to a helpless and hopeless deadlock in his infantile sexual researches; but he produces a mass of confused dreams and associations, complains that he cannot succeed in anything and asserts that he is fated never to carry through what he undertakes. He does not remember having been intensely ashamed of certain sexual activities and afraid of their being found out; but he makes it clear that he is ashamed of the treatment on which he is now embarked and tries to keep it secret from everybody. And so on.

Above all, the patient will begin his treatment with a repetition of this kind. When one has announced the fundamental rule of psycho-analysis to a patient with an eventful life-history and a long story of illness and has then asked him to say what occurs to his mind, one expects him to pour out a flood of information; but often the first thing that happens is that he has nothing to say. He is silent and declares that nothing occurs to him. This, of course, is merely a repetition of a homosexual attitude which comes to the fore as a resistance against remembering anything [p. **138**]. As long as the patient is in the treatment he cannot escape from this compulsion to repeat;[5] and in the end we understand that this is his way of remembering. What interests us most of all is naturally the relation of this compulsion to repeat to the transference and to resistance. We soon perceive that the transference is itself only a piece of repetition, and that the repetition is a transference of the forgotten past not only on to the doctor but also on to all the other aspects of the current situation. We must be prepared to find, therefore, that the patient yields to the compulsion to repeat, which now replaces the impulsion to remember, not only in his personal attitude to his doctor but also in every other activity and relationship which may occupy his life at the time—if, for instance, he falls in love or undertakes a task or starts an enterprise during the treatment. The part played by resistance, too, is easily recognized. The greater the resistance, the more extensively will acting out (repetition) replace remembering. For the ideal remembering of what has been forgotten which occurs in hypnosis corresponds to a state in which resistance has been put completely on one side. If the patient starts his treatment under the auspices of a mild and unpronounced positive transference it makes it possible at first for him to unearth his memories just as he would under hypnosis, and during this time his pathological symptoms themselves are quiescent. But if, as the analysis proceeds, the transference becomes hostile or unduly intense and therefore in need of repression, remembering at once gives way to acting out. From then onwards the resistances determine the sequence of the material which is to be repeated. The patient brings out of the armoury of the past the weapons with which he defends himself against the progress of the treatment—weapons which we must wrest from him one by one.

We have learnt that the patient repeats instead of remembering, and repeats under the conditions of resistance. We may now ask what it is that he in fact repeats or acts out. The answer is that he repeats everything that has already made its way from the sources of the repressed into his manifest personality—his inhibitions and unserviceable attitudes and his pathological character-traits. He also repeats all his symptoms in the course of the treatment. And now we can see that in drawing attention to the compulsion to repeat we have acquired no new fact but only a more comprehensive view. We have only made it clear to ourselves that the patient's state of being ill cannot cease with the beginning of his analysis, and that we must treat his illness, not as an event of the past, but as a present-day force. This state of illness is brought, piece by piece, within the field and range of operation of the treatment, and while the patient experiences it as something real and contemporary, we have to do our therapeutic work on it, which consists in a large measure in tracing it back to the past.

Remembering, as it was induced in hypnosis, could not but give the impression of an experiment carried out in the laboratory. Repeating, as it is induced in analytic treatment according to the newer technique, on the other hand, implies conjuring up a piece of real life; and for that reason it cannot always be harmless and unobjectionable. This consideration opens up the whole problem of what is so often unavoidable—'deterioration during treatment'.

First and foremost, the initiation of the treatment in itself brings about a change in the patient's conscious attitude to his illness. He has usually been content with lamenting it, despising it as nonsensical and under-estimating its importance; for the rest, he has extended to its manifestations the ostrich-like policy of repression which he adopted towards its origins. Thus it can happen that he does not properly know under what conditions his phobia breaks out or does not listen to the precise wording of his obsessional ideas or does not grasp the actual purpose of his obsessional impulse.[6] The treatment, of course, is not helped by this. He must find the courage to direct his attention to the phenomena of his illness. His illness itself must no longer seem to him contemptible, but must become an enemy worthy of his mettle, a piece of his personality, which has solid ground for its existence and out of which things of value for his future life have to be derived. The way is thus paved from the beginning for a reconciliation with the repressed material which is coming to expression in his symptoms, while at the same time place is found for a certain tolerance for the state of being ill. If this new attitude towards the illness intensifies the conflicts and brings to the fore symptoms which till then had been indistinct, one can easily console the patient by pointing out that these are only necessary and temporary aggravations and that one cannot overcome an enemy who is absent or not within range. The resistance, however, may exploit the situation for its own ends and abuse the licence to be ill. It seems to say: 'See what happens if I really give way to such things. Was I not right to consign them to repression?' Young and childish people in particular are inclined to make the necessity imposed by the treatment for paying attention to their illness a welcome excuse for luxuriating in their symptoms.

Further dangers arise from the fact that in the course of the treatment new and deeper-lying instinctual impulses, which had not hitherto made themselves felt, may come to be 'repeated'. Finally, it is possible that the patient's actions outside the transference may do him temporary harm in his ordinary life, or even have been so chosen as permanently to invalidate his prospects of recovery.

The tactics to be adopted by the physician in this situation are easily justified. For him, remembering in the old manner—reproduction in the psychical field—is the aim to which he adheres, even though he knows that such an aim cannot be achieved in the new technique. He is prepared for a perpetual struggle with his patient to keep in the psychical sphere all the impulses which the patient would like to direct into the motor sphere; and he celebrates it as a triumph for the treatment if he can bring it about that something that the patient wishes to discharge in action is disposed of through the work of remembering. If the attachment through transference has grown into something at all serviceable, the treatment is able to prevent the patient from executing any of the more important repetitive actions and to utilize his intention to do so in statu nascendi as material for the therapeutic work. One best protects the patient from injuries brought about through carrying out one of his impulses by making him promise not to take any important decisions affecting his life during the time of his treatment—for instance, not to choose any profession or definitive love-object—but to postpone all such plans until after his recovery.

At the same time one willingly leaves untouched as much of the patient's personal freedom as is compatible with these restrictions, nor does one hinder him from carrying out unimportant intentions, even if they are foolish; one does not forget that it is in fact only through his own experience and mishaps that a person learns sense. There are also people whom one cannot restrain from plunging into some quite undesirable project during the treatment and who only afterwards become ready for, and accessible to, analysis. Occasionally, too, it is bound to happen that the untamed instincts assert themselves before there is time to put the reins of the transference on them, or that the bonds which attach the patient to the treatment are broken by him in a repetitive action. As an extreme example of this, I may cite the case of an elderly lady who had repeatedly fled from her house and her husband in a twilight state and gone no one knew where, without ever having become conscious of her motive for decamping in this way. She came to treatment with a marked affectionate transference which grew in intensity with uncanny rapidity in the first few days; by the end of the week she had decamped from me, too, before I had had time to say anything to her which might have prevented this repetition.

The main instrument, however, for curbing the patient's compulsion to repeat and for turning it into a motive for remembering lies in the handling of the transference. We render the compulsion harmless, and indeed useful, by giving it the right to assert itself in a definite field. We admit it into the transference as a playground in which it is allowed to expand in almost complete freedom and in which it is expected to display to us everything in the way of pathogenic instincts that is hidden in the patient's mind. Provided only that the patient shows compliance enough to respect the necessary conditions of the analysis, we regularly succeed in giving all the symptoms of the illness a new transference meaning[7] and in replacing his ordinary neurosis by a 'transference-neurosis'[8] of which he can be cured by the therapeutic work. The transference thus creates an intermediate region between illness and real life through which the transition from the one to the other is made. The new condition has taken over all the features of the illness; but it represents an artificial illness which is at every point accessible to our intervention. It is a piece of real experience, but one which has been made possible by especially favourable conditions, and it is of a provisional nature. From the repetitive reactions[9] which are exhibited in the transference we are led along the familiar paths to the awakening of the memories, which appear without difficulty, as it were, after the resistance has been overcome.

I might break off at this point but for the title of this paper, which obliges me to discuss a further point in analytic technique. The first step in overcoming the resistances is made, as we know, by the analyst's uncovering the resistance, which is never recognized by the patient, and acquainting him with it. Now it seems that beginners in analytic practice are inclined to look on this introductory step as constituting the whole of their work. I have often been asked to advise upon cases in which the doctor complained that he had pointed out his resistance to the patient and that nevertheless no change had set in; indeed, the resistance had become all the stronger, and the whole situation was more obscure than ever. The treatment seemed to make no headway. This gloomy foreboding always proved mistaken. The treatment was as a rule progressing most satisfactorily. The analyst had merely forgotten that giving the resistance a name could not result in its immediate cessation. One must allow the patient time to become more conversant with this resistance with which he has now become acquainted,[10] to work through it, to overcome it, by continuing, in defiance of it, the analytic work according to the fundamental rule of analysis. Only when the resistance is at its height can the analyst, working in common with his patient, discover the repressed instinctual impulses which are feeding the resistance; and it is this kind of experience which convinces the patient of the existence and power of such impulses. The doctor has nothing else to do than to wait and let things take their course, a course which cannot be avoided nor always hastened. If he holds fast to this conviction he will often be spared the illusion of having failed when in fact he is conducting the treatment on the right lines.

This working-through of the resistances may in practice turn out to be an arduous task for the subject of the analysis and a trial of patience for the analyst. Nevertheless it is a part of the work which effects the greatest changes in the patient and which distinguishes analytic treatment from any kind of treatment by suggestion. From a theoretical point of view one may correlate it with the 'abreacting' of the quotas of affect strangulated by repression—an abreaction without which hypnotic treatment remained ineffective.[11]

Notes

1 In the first edition only, this and the following three paragraphs (which make up the 'interpolation') were printed in smaller type.

2 This is, of course, a reference to the 'Wolf Man' and his dream at the age of four. Freud had only recently completed his analysis, and he was probably engaged in writing the case history more or less simultaneously with the present paper, though it was only published some four years later (1918b). Before that time, however, Freud entered into a discussion of this special class of childhood memories in the later part of Lecture XXIII of his *Introductory Lectures* (1916–1917).

3 Freud picks up his argument from where he left it at the beginning of the 'interpolation' on the previous page.

4 This had been made plain by Freud very much earlier, in his postscript to his analysis of 'Dora'(1905e), *Standard Edition*, 7, p. 119, where the topic of transference is under discussion.

5 This seems to be the first appearance of the idea, which, in a much more generalized form, was to play such an important part in Freud's later theory of the instincts. In its present clinical application, it reappears in the paper on 'The "Uncanny"' (1919h), *Standard Edition*, 17, p. 238, and is used as part of the evidence in support of the general thesis in Chapter III of *Beyond the Pleasure Principle* (1920g), *Standard Edition*, 18, p. 18 ff., where there is a reference back to the present paper.

6 See examples of this in the case histories of 'Little Hans' (1909b), *Standard Edition*, 10, p. 124, and of the 'Rat Man' (1909d), *Standard Edition*, 10, p. 223.

7 'Übertragungsbedeutung.' In the editions before 1924 this read 'Übertragungsbedingung' ('transference-determinant').

8 The connection between this special use of the term and the usual one (to denote the hysterias and obsessional neurosis) is indicated in Lecture XXVII of the *Introductory Lectures* (1916–1917).

9 In the first edition only, this read 'repetitive actions'.

10 '... sich in den ihm nun bekannten Widerstand zu vertiefen.' Thus in the first edition only. In all the later German editions 'nun bekannten' was altered to 'unbekannten'. This, however, seems to make less good sense: 'to become more conversant with the resistance that is unknown to him.'

11 The concept of 'working-through', introduced in the present paper, is evidently related to the 'psychical inertia' which Freud discusses in several passages. Some of these are enumerated in an Editor's footnote to a paper on a case of paranoia (1915f), *Standard Edition, 14*, p. 272. In Chapter XI, Section A (a) of *Inhibitions, Symptoms and Anxiety* (1926d), Freud attributes the necessity for 'working-through' to the resistance of the unconscious (or of the id), a subject to which he returns in Section VI of 'Analysis Terminable and Interminable' (1937c).

3 Remembering, Repeating and Working-Through—A Comparative Approach

Understanding Freud's language working through translation

Udo Hock, Ilka Quindeau, and Robin Verner

Introduction

A hallmark of the series *Contemporary Freud* is giving voice to colleagues from a wide variety of cultural backgrounds and psychoanalytic schools, writing in several different languages. In the present volume, for example, English, French, German, Italian, Spanish, and Portuguese are the native languages of the individual authors. So, most of the texts have been translated into English from other languages. Consequently, they have undergone significant transformation, perhaps even distortion (*Entstellung*).

In this chapter, we take this tacit and often unthought transference into consideration, specifically working along the nominal concepts of Freud's essay "Erinnern, Wiederholen und Durcharbeiten" ("Remembering, Repeating and Working-through"). We pursue some significant changes the German text has undergone through its translation into English and French. Our group has a good basic knowledge of these three languages: Robin Verner, a native New Yorker has lived in Germany for forty years and works analytically in both English and German; Udo Hock, a German author and experienced translator from the French since the mid-1990s, is known especially for his work with Jean Laplanche; and Ilka Quindeau is a renowned author, former president of the International Psychoanalytic University Berlin and a pivotal advocate for a comparative psychoanalysis.

So, equipped with an understanding of translation and detranslation central to psychoanalytic work itself and a certain methodology of philosophy, where it is not uncommon to sharpen one's concepts (truth, being, etc.), by comparing terminological equivalents in other languages, including Greek and Latin, we believe that a translation comparison between the German original and the English or French versions should be helpful for the understanding of both the Freudian text and its translations into other languages. In doing so, we do not indulge in linguistic ontology, nor do we believe that, by analyzing language or words alone, meaning can be ascertained.

DOI: 10.4324/9781003458340-3

We are, however, convinced that such an analysis has heuristic value, leading not only to new hypotheses or understandings about certain terms, which must then be tested on clinical material, but must also consider the understanding and specific usage of the author, the cultural background and *"l'épreuve de l'étranger"* (Berman, 1984). Freud's paper "The 'Uncanny'" (1919h) seems exemplary in this respect: he employs a meticulous analysis of the word itself and derives from it a certain hypothesis, which he then seeks to verify or even falsify.

Further, in comparing translations and their vicissitudes, some external factors must be taken into consideration. The international complications of publishing rights, copyright laws, institutional and personal politics as well as academic and doctrinal competition all affect the work of translation and have played a key role from the very beginning in the dissemination of Freud's theories.

For our textual comparisons in the English translation, we necessarily used the Jones/Strachey *Standard Edition* and quoted accordingly, but also considered the work of Joan Riviere in the first English translation of "Further Recommendations in the Technique of Psychoanalysis: Recollection, Repetition and Working Through" which appeared in the *Collected Papers, Vol. II* of 1924. For many years there was no standardized edition of Freud's work in French and articles appeared in various translations. "Remémoration, répétition, et élaboration" first appeared in 1953, more than forty years after it was written, a vastly different time in psychoanalysis compared with 1924 or 1914. Eventually, the *Oeuvres Complètes de Freud/Psychanalyse* (1993), a collective work under the direction of Jean Laplanche became definitive. The title became *"Remémoration, répétition et perlaboration."* From their French perspective, with "a demand for fidelity to the German text" and independent of all institutional oversight or influence, Bourgignon, Laplanche *et al.* translated deliberately maintaining the "strangeness" of the foreign text, as well as its stylistic and conceptual particularities: *"Remémoration, répétition et perlaboration."*

Note for example the differences in the translations of the title itself. Comparing the morphology and inflection of either the English noun "recollection" or the gerund "remembering" to the German, we find quite a discrepancy in the theoretical understanding and interpretation of the psychic procedure. These translation choices open, *inter alia*, a discussion about the process: occurrence or operation, and questions of participatory activity, in describing the psychic event. In German, the three words of the title function both as verbs and nouns without derivation, leaving open to interpretation the reference with regard to the act, the action, or the concept (e.g., to remember, the act of remembering, or the term remembering).

In the English translation the choice made between "repetition" and "repeating" introduces an interpretation and one that assumes a non-finite temporality. Another example is the hyphenation of "working(-)through", which underscores a specific terminological distinction while retaining the vernacular. By contrast, the French colloquial noun *élaboration* is replaced by the neologism *perlaboration*, giving precedence to the concept over the action. The difference in prefix further changes the emphasis. "É" usually marks the action of removing or moving something, whereas "per" stresses not only the idea of "through" (*durch*) but also suggests the notions of intensity, scalarity, and deviation.

It is understood that this approach to the text entails a close reading of the Freudian essay. Other texts of Freud and post-Freudian authors should serve only the clarification of passages that come across as all too cryptic and puzzling in "Remembering, Repeating and Working-through".

Erinnerung—remembering (recollection)—*remémoration*

Let us begin with Freud's definition of *Erinnern/Erinnerung* (remembering/ remembrance or memory), which he explicates in the first three and a half pages, continuing with the juxtaposition of the subsequent repetition (*Wiederholen*) and working-through (*Durcharbeiten*). The German expression *Erinnerung* literally means that something from the past ostensibly reappears in memory, with an emphasis on locality: inside, in the interior of the psychic apparatus something reappears that triggers a "sense of familiarity" (Freud 1914g, 147/G.W., X, 127). In Strachey's English translation, two closely related terms appear side by side: on the one hand, remembering for *erinnern*, and memory for the substantivized form, the memory/*die Erinnerung*. In the French text, the verb to remember/*erinnern* is translated both as *remémorer* and (the self-reflective) *se souvenir*; for the noun the memory/*die Erinnerung*, one finds *la remémoration* on the one hand, and *le souvenir* on the other. Here, the pair *remémorer/remémoration* emphasizes the ability to remember, while *se souvenir/le souvenir* accentuates a specific memory. We would like to mention one more difference between the three languages. The English "memory" means not only *"die Erinnerung,"* but also *"Gedächtnis,"* i.e., a substantification of *denken* (to think) derived from the past participle (*gedacht*/thought), indicating a place of storage, which, incidentally, is a word not at all used in Freud's essay. A French equivalent for "memory" is *"la mémoire,"* which is also not used in the translation. Finally, it should be noted that neither "remembering" nor "memory"—nor their equivalents in other languages— belong to the specific psychoanalytic vocabulary or terminology. Rather, they are colloquial and the subject of all sorts of disciplines of knowledge that need have nothing to do with the assumption of an unconscious: philosophy, cultural theory, psychology, neuroscience, etc.

Verdrängungswiderstand—repression-resistance—*résistance de refoulement*

How can it be that Freud begins his famous essay with a word, remembering/*Erinnern*, which, as a term, does not belong to the specific terminology of psychoanalysis, but nevertheless has radically changed our conceptual understanding?

Freud's essay does provide an answer to this question. In fact, in the first pages Freud discusses a fundamental problem of his patients, which he tries to resolve over time with the help of various techniques: specifically, they *cannot remember* anything related to the symptom formation. Whether through hypnosis, psychoanalysis as an "art of interpretation" (Freud, 1920g, 18/G.W., XIII, 16), or the analysis of resistance or, perhaps better, "resistance analysis" as the three successive stages of psychoanalytic technique might be called, the aim is to achieve the same goal by new means: "Descriptively: the filling in of the gaps of memory, dynamically: the overcoming of the resistances due to repression" (Freud, 1914g, 148/G.W., X, 127). The concept of "repression-resistance"/*Verdrängungswiderstand* (i.e., the resistance due to repression) in the present context can, therefore, be very precisely defined: it is the patient's resistance to certain situations, i.e., "impressions, scenes, experiences" (*ibid.*), which remain recalcitrantly repressed and, thus, to which he has no direct access. The repression-resistance is primarily a resistance against remembering, or, in other words, the analysand is unwilling to succeed in remembering something.

Freud, then, is interested in the problem of memory because his patients "fail" to remember, or present memory lapses, a clear sign that the unconscious has interfered. Consequently, the crucial terms explaining these phenomena have in common that they are about "memory failures (lapses)", expressed in their very name: *Deckerinnerung* (screen-memory) and *Reminiszenz* (reminiscence), *Vergessen* (forgetting) and *Déjà vu*, *Erinnerungstäuschung* (*pseudo-memory; memory deception*), *Erinnerungsstörung* (*memory disturbance, fausse reconnaissance, déjà raconté*), *Konstruktion* (construction), etc., to name just a few of an infinitely long series to which Freud devoted entire articles—not least the essay under discussion here. Freud writes in the second half of the first part of his text, which begins with the sentence "At this point I will interpolate some remarks" (Freud, 1914g, 148/G.W., X, 127), to limit the most radical version of memory lapses, *forgetting*, by pointing out various forms of forgetting and remembering: forgetting can be reduced to "shutting them [memories] off" (*ibid.*) or can be compensated, as it were, via screen memories, as Freud exemplified with his own screen memory (1899a), but also with reference to Leonardo da Vinci's vulture fantasy (Freud, 1910c). Then there are the cases in which the patient's "conviction" about a biographical connection seems more important than any memory of it; Freud later devoted the essay "Constructions in Analysis" (1937d) to this problem (cf. also Freud, 1920g, 18/G.W., XIII, 16). And finally, Freud cites the most remarkable instance in which only through dream experiences from early childhood can "subsequently (…) understanding and interpretation be found (1914g, 149/G.W., X, 129), without the analysand invoking the absence of any memory of them or a 'sense of familiarity' as a ground for refusing to accept them". Here, the influence of the Wolf-man's case history and his wolf dream is unmistakable (cf. Freud, 1918b, 51/*G.W.*, *XII*, 80).

Let us once again consider the comparativist perspective and review the English and French translations. Most striking is certainly the English translation of **nachträglich** [boldface in the original] to "subsequently." Although we do not wish to resume the decade-long debate about an accurate understanding of *Nachträglichkeit* (cf. e.g., Birkstedt-Breen, 2003; Laplanche, 2017[2006]), we nonetheless consider this translation inadequate. It assumes a linear determination, a sequence of scenes, which, in the present context, is precisely called into question by the German adverb *nachträglich* (here meaning *ex post facto*, retrospectively, afterward). For it is the same "after the fact"/*après coup* that structures the whole story in the Wolf-man and makes it especially interesting. The current preference of adopting the French *après-coup* for Freud's *nachträglich* seems to have become commonplace. Laplanche's proposal to use "afterwards" or "afterwardsness" did not catch on.

The translation of *Deckerinnerung* into screen-memory and *souvenir-écran* rather than the literal translation of the original cover-memory and *souvenir-couverture* also seems worth discussing. The German word *Deckerinnerung* makes the connection visible between *decken* (cover or *couvrir*) and *entdecken* (discover or *découvrir*), which is lost in the translation into "screen" or "*écran*". Freud's memory does not function at all like a screen onto which one's fantasies are projected; in the *Deckerinnerung*, rather, an alleged "childhood memory" is utilized for the representation of one's fantasies. Freud illustrates this with an interpretation of his own screen-memory (*Deckerinnerung*). "Just think: to take a girl's flowers away, for example, means yes: to deflower" (Freud, 1899a, 316; *G.W.*, *I*, 546f.; Hock, 2003).

Finally, a word about the translation of memory/*Erinnerung* itself into French. Lacan repeatedly attempts to apply *remémoration* for his concepts of the signifier and of the symbolic by distinguishing it from a Platonic tradition of *réminiscence imaginaire* (Lacan, 1966, pp. 431 and 519; Lacan, 1973, p. 47). In doing so, he runs the risk of overlooking the fact that, for Freud, it is not memory but reminiscence presenting the decisive problem of his hysterics. Laplanche, on the other hand, wants to distinguish psychoanalysis from any psychological theory of memory and writes:

> … Hysterics suffer not from memories [*souvenirs* orig.] whether forgotten or not, but from 'reminiscences'. This term could of course be reduced to memory, but a memory cut off from its context, equally one could give it that sense of extravagance also found in Platonic doctrine: the sense of something that returns as if from elsewhere, a pseudo memory, perhaps, coming from … the other."
>
> (Laplanche, 2020[1992], p. 25)

Crucial to understanding Freud's conception appears to be the idea that the *Erinnerung*/memory, under the influence of the unconscious, undergoes multiple forms of *Entstellung*/distortion, and is, thus, continuously taking different forms; a kaleidoscope, as it were, composed of all the enigmatic memory phenomena to which Freud turned his interest throughout his life.

Wiederholen—repetition—*répétition*

Freud devotes most of his paper to the problem of repetition. The German word *wiederholen* consists of the prefix *wi(e)der*/again, and the root word *holen*/to get or fetch.

Holen is etymologically related to the English word *hale*, which, as an adjective, describes health and as a verb means to haul or drag. Lacan alludes to the related French verb *haler* and the burden that the subject drags behind him in the compulsion to repeat (Lacan, 1973, p. 50). The prefix *wieder* means roughly "again" or "once more" and is regularly translated into both English and French as "re-", admittedly a very ambiguous prefix in both languages.

To understand the German prefix, it seems important to differentiate between *"wieder-"*/again and *"zurück-"*/back. In English we use the prefix "re." *Zurück*-connotes a linear movement within a continuous and homogeneous conception of time and space, most clearly exemplified in the term "regression": it means "go back to an earlier state." The "again," on the other hand, is prior to any position of the subject in space or time, there is no where, no whence and no whither here, it takes place in the dialectic of presence and absence, paradigmatically staged in the Fort-Da game.

The English translation "to repeat, repetition" and the French *"répéter, répétition"* both derive from the Latin *repetere* and connote a different semantic field, referring to *petere* meaning "to go to;" e.g., *per Romam petere* (going to Rome), as well as *repetere*, going again toward or going back again. Moreover, there is a petition/*demande* that never ceases; this is what "repetition" literally means.

Agieren, acting out, enacting, *mise en acte, agir*

Freud introduces the problem of repetition into his text by linking the new with the old. For the pair "remembering/forgetting" continues to be at issue, but in a new form:

> ...the patient does not remember anything of what he has forgotten and repressed but acts it out. He reproduces it not as a memory but as an action; he repeats it, without, of course, knowing that he is repeating it.

> (Freud, 1914g, 149/*G.W.*, X, 129)

Immediately it becomes clear that enacting/acting out is a form of remembering, but without any "sense of familiarity;" therefore, Freud also speaks of reproduction as an act (or action) unbeknown to the patient; this is, as it were, the minimal definition for acting-out.

The term has given rise to a complicated translational debate, as discussed in Laurence Kahn's contribution to this volume, among others. First rendered in French as *mise en acte*, it later becomes, in the translation of Bourgignon *et al.*, literally *agir* (1989, 176). In Strachey's translation it appears as "acting out", although it remains unclear to the German-speaking reader why simply "acting" is not used instead; also what the distinction between "acting" and "acting-out" might be. For, in acting, the world becomes a stage on which the subject presents his or her own conflicts.

In the anglophone world, however, the term "enactment" has become common (Sandler, 1970; cf. Bohleber *et al.*, 2013) as a rule reserved for "acting in" the analytical setting.

In fact, Freud's text makes it clear that acting-out takes place both inside and outside the analytic space:

> We must be prepared to find, therefore, that the patient yields to the compulsion to repeat [a synonym for enactment; U.H.], which now replaces the impulse to remember, not only in his personal attitude to his doctor but also in every other activity and relationship which may occupy his life at the time—if, for instance, he falls in love or undertakes a task or starts an enterprise during the treatment.
>
> (Freud, 1914g, 150/G.W., X, 130)

For this, in the English-speaking world, the term "acting out" gradually prevailed (cf. Kahn's chapter in this volume, including endnote 35). On the other hand, within the French tradition, "acting out" is used when the analytic frame is endangered, even to the point of collapse, as in the case of Dora (cf. on this, in addition to Kahn's text, Mannoni, 1969, pp. 156 ff.; Laplanche, 1987, pp. 182f. and pp. 240f.).

It is also worth mentioning the word chain for *Agieren* (*agir*, acting-out)— *Akt* (*acte*, act)—*Aktualisieren* (*actualiser*, actualize) across all three languages, clearly acting-out is at the same time and always an act-ualizing. It knows— just as the dream—only one time, the actual (*l'actuel*, *l'actual*, cf. Scarfone, 2014 and Kahn, 2015) and proceeds—just as the dream—via actions. In this respect, acting-out can be described as dreaming while awake.

Important for the understanding of acting-out is finally its connection to "abreacting" (French: *abréagir*): this is to be understood as the release/*Abfuhr* of trapped affects (Freud).

Übertragung—transference—*transfert*

Let us now look at how Freud conceives of the relation between acting-out and transference. Beyond what Freud remarks about it: "… the transference is itself only a piece of repetition …" (Freud, 1914g, 151/*G.W.*, *X*, 130), what seems most important is that, in acting-out, the analysand is addressing the analyst. Freud's brief clinical examples all point in this direction: the acting-out takes place within the transference. The text, on the other hand, leaves it open whether the choice of a love object during the cure also happens within the transference or whether it can happen independently of it. What does seem certain, however, is that acting-out also occurs outside of any treatment and, thus, outside of any transference relationship. One has only to think of manic acting-out: love or sexual objects are changed restlessly, purchases are made, ventures undertaken, and so on. Here, acting-out is a part, even the most prominent part, of the symptomatology and, as we will see in more detail, proves to be a mode of being of *par excellence* for the unconscious. Conversely, not every form of transference has to do with acting-out. It can just as well show itself through seemingly banal expressions: "You have new curtains, your trousers remind me of my father, etc." There is an intersection between transference and acting-out, which, following Aulagnier and Ponta-lis (1963) we could call *transfert agi* (cf. on this Kahn, this volume).

Übertragungswiderstand—transference-resistance—résistance de transfert

Let us go a step further into the relation between acting-out and resist-ance, which Freud sets in direct correlation: "The greater the resistance, the more extensively acting out (repetition) will replace remembering" (Freud, 1914g, 151/*G.W.*, *X*, 130). Freud also explains this connection in relation to transference; the *transfert agi* thus appears to him here as a transference-resis tance/*Übertragungswiderstand*, without using this expression in the present context. The compound word in German contains within itself two possible meanings that fall apart in translation: on the one hand, it could mean resist-ing the transference, that is, that the patient refuses to give into the transfer-ence. In this case, the translation would have to be *résistance au transfert* or resistance *to* transference. On the other hand, it means resistance through the transference, that is, resistance that employs the transference, and would then have to be rendered as *résistance de transfert* or resistance *of* transfer-ence. In fact, Strachey translates *Übertragungswiderstand* as *transference-resistance* (cf. *G.W.*, *VIII*, 369, 373, *S.E.*, *12b*, 103, 106); without a preposition the specific relationship of one word to the other remains open. Freud, on the other hand, is clearly concerned with the resistance that comes from transference. The "*transfert agi*" even appears to him as the form of resist-ance *par excellence*, because the patient, through the unconscious expres-sion of his hostility (negative transference) or his desire for love (positive transference), attacks the frame of the cure itself (no more ideas, no more openness to interpretation, sessions are cancelled and missed, holidays are planned, a termination is threatened, etc.) as well as rejecting any in-sight into a connection between the current situation and the past. Conse-quently, there is no more willingness to cooperate and no more interest in remembering. It is no longer the real-life situation and the corresponding symptoms that are unbearable, but, rather, the treatment situation itself and its facilitating agent, the analyst.

Let us conclude this section with a comparison of repression-resistance (*Verdrängungswiderstand*) and transference-resistance (*Übertragungswiderstand*): while repression-resistance is about all possible forms of memory lapses/*Entstellungen* that can be traced back to the influence of repression, transference-resistance is about the analytical situation and the analyst himself coming under the influence of the unconscious via transference. In repression-resistance, the difficulty in remembering is intrapsychic or intrasubjective, whereas in transference-resistance it is interpsychic or intersubjective.

Acting-out in the cure is understood, after all, as an extreme form of transference-resistance that can make speaking about the situation impossible. A third perspective is in danger of being lost here, because everything appears to take place temporarily in a here-and-now dynamic between analyst and patient, experienced as real and immediate. The analyst, then, no longer represents, but, rather, *is* the disappointing father or the beloved object. Acting-out is nevertheless also a form of distorted memory, completely replacing any memory, so that a very peculiar version of the forgotten and repressed is now produced, which the patient is no longer able to represent intrapsychically.

Übertragungsneurose—transference neurosis—*névrose de transfert*

But how to handle this new circumstance that the repressed can also just return *in actu*? What "*tactics*" (Freud) should be chosen? Freud is initially explicit in his answer: for him, "remembering in the old manner—reproduction in the psychical field"—is the aim to which he adheres (1914g, 153/G.W., X, 133). Incidentally, in this context Freud suggests obliging the patient "not to make any important decisions" affecting his life during the time of his treatment—for instance, not to choose any profession or definitive love-object—but to postpone all such plans until after his recovery (*ibid.*), a recommendation that is difficult to implement in view of the length of analyses today.

If one reads carefully the passage on dealing with acting-out, it is notable that Freud's remarks all revolve around the concept of transference. It is said that "attachment through transference" must be "serviceable" in order to prevent important repetitive actions (*ibid.*), then the "the reins of the transference" should be put on "untamed instincts" (*ibid.*/G.W., 134), and finally Freud's reflections culminate in the realisation: "The main instrument, however, for curbing the patient's compulsion to repeat and for turning it into a motive for remembering lies in the handling of the transference" (*ibid.*). What then follows appears to be quite unique in Freud's work, for he acknowledges that the power of the unconscious is too strong not to have to offer major concessions. Therefore, he opens the transference to the repetition compulsion (to which we will return) as a "playground" where it can freely romp. However, the patient is obliged to comply with the frame-work of the treatment. *Faute de mieux*, then, Freud advocates for tolerating acting out/repetition within the treatment as long as the framework itself is not attacked, that is, as long as the agreements about space, time, and money are respected. In this way it is possible to give "all the symptoms of the illness a new transference meaning and in replacing his ordinary neuro-sis by a 'transference-neurosis' of which he can be cured by the therapeutic work" (*ibid.*, 153–154/*ibid.*, 134f.).

"*Übertragungsbedeutung*" (transference meaning) is a hapax in Freud's work, the word occurs only once—as does, for example, "*Vorstellung-srepräsentanz*"—but in post-Freudian discourse it has achieved some notice. In English it is rendered by Strachey as "transference meaning," in French as "*signification transférentielle*." Freud does not specify an exact meaning, but it seems obvious that transference meanings are considered a consequence of transference-interpretations (incidentally, a term that Freud never uses), as practiced especially in post-Kleinian discourse. In other words, the ana-lyst interprets the symptoms and other forms of his patient's unconscious expression as if addressed to him. This gives them a new meaning, a mean-ing in the transference, and the much cited "intermediate region between the illness and real-life" (*ibid.*, 154/*ibid.*, 135) emerges, within which the analyst holds the significance of a primary object. The famous "transference neurosis"/*Übertragungsneurose* (*ibid.*), although it does not really appear very often in Freud's work, nevertheless has become significant as a psycho-analytic term: "transference neurosis" or "*névrose de transfert*" are the Eng-lish and French versions, respectively (cf. Laplanche & Pontalis 1973[1967], 462–464). The great advantage of transference-meaning and transference neurosis, however, is that the patient's illness is now, as it were, an actual, real condition and, thus, directly accessible to the analyst's interventions:

> The new condition has taken over all the features of the illness; but it represents an artificial illness which is at every point accessible to our intervention. It is a piece of genuine experience, but one which has been made possible by especially favourable conditions, and it is of a provisional nature. From the repetitive reactions exhibited in the transference we are led along the familiar paths to the awakening of the memories, which appear without difficulty, after the resistance has been overcome.
>
> (Freud, 1914g, 154/*G.W.*, X, 135)

Once again, we can see Freud's dialectical thinking in this passage: what previously appeared to be the greatest hurdles to analytic work: repression-resistance, transference-resistance, and, of course, acting out, he reinterprets one after the other in the course of his text and, in further work, declares them to be indispensable components of said process. For they contain the essential material for gaining access to the patient's unconscious. All these hurdles, however, do not stop him—at least in this text—from holding fast to the ideal of remembering.

Durcharbeiten—working-through—*perlaboration*

The concept/term of working-through appears for the first time in this paper and forms the last note in the trichord of analytical technique "Remembering, Repeating, Working-Through." In this text, however, Freud devotes only a single page to the idea, and the concept of working- through hardly appears anywhere else in the rest of his work (see Freud, 1926d, 159/*G.W.*, *XIV*, 192). This is surprising, especially since Freud sees working-through as the *differentia specifica* of psychoanalysis and attributes to it significant transformative power:

> Nevertheless it is a part of the work which effects the greatest changes in the patient, and which distinguishes analytic treatment from any kind of treatment by suggestion. From a theoretical point of view, one may correlate it with the 'abreacting' of the quotas of affect strangulated by repression—an abreaction without which hypnotic treatment remained ineffective.
>
> (Freud, 1914g, 155f/*G.W.*, *X*, 136)

Interestingly, in the current discourse on the various schools of psychotherapy, neither a discussion of suggestion nor the significance of its absence plays much of a role; psychoanalysis has turned to advantage the fact that, unlike other therapeutic approaches, it manages without suggestion. Psychological changes then, i.e. changes in experience and behavior, are not a result of suggestion in the analytical cure, but of working-through. What does this mean exactly?

Let us look at the Duden dictionary and consider the meanings of the German word "durcharbeiten." Notice that, in psychoanalytical discourse, only the substantivated verb is used and not the noun "Durcharbeitung", which emphasizes the procedural moment. Several context relevant meanings can be found; "to work through (durcharbeiten)" means: 1. A continuing work process; 2. to read completely, thoroughly and evaluate and elaborate; 3. To knead through; 4. painstakingly make one's way through something.

This emphasizes both the moment of thorough and careful immersion as well as the confrontation with resistance. Both are condensed into the wording with which Freud introduces the concept:

> One must allow the patient time to become more conversant with this resistance with which he has now become acquainted, *to work through it,* to overcome it, by continuing, in defiance of it, the analytic work according to the fundamental rule of analysis.
>
> (Freud, 1914g, 155/*G.W.*, *X*, 136, emphasis in original)

Freud establishes it is resistance that necessitates working-through. It is not enough to simply uncover it and communicate it to the analysand. Rather, overcoming resistance further requires psychic work on the part of the patient. Only then would the "repressed instinctual impulses" (*Triebimpulse*) become accessible (*ibid.*), and the memories would "appear without difficulty" (*ibid.*, 154/*ibid.*, 135). Freud determines, subsequently, that, prior to this text, resistance was located in the ego. It was formed to defend against objectionable impulses and served to protect repression, as he proposes after the introduction of the second topical model (Freud, 1926d, 157/*G.W.*, *XIV*, 189). The resistance proceeds from the ego, which clings to its anticathexes:

> It is hard for the ego to direct its attention to perceptions and ideas which it has up till now made a rule of avoiding, or to acknowledge as belonging to itself impulses that are the complete opposite of those which it knows as its own.
>
> (*ibid.*, 159/*ibid.*, 192)

In this context, working through resistance means the dissolution of the anticathexes. In this way, drive energy, or libido, becomes available for new cathexes and the repressed impulses become accessible through the sublation/*Aufhebung* of the repression.

In the later addenda to *Inhibitions, Symptoms and Anxiety*, Freud further differentiates the concept of resistance and distinguishes five distinct types, emanating from the ego, the id, and the superego (*ibid.*, 160/*ibid.*, 193). For working-through the resistance of the id or the unconscious is of crucial importance and finds its expression in repetition compulsion. Here, Freud refers to a dynamic moment that is still effective after the ego resistance has been sublated/*aufgehoben* and has yet to be overcome: "the power of the compulsion to repeat—the attraction exerted by the unconscious prototype upon the repressed instinctual process..." (*ibid.*, 159/*ibid.*, 192).

The editors of the *Studienausgabe* point out that the concept of working-through would also be necessary because of psychic inertia, a psychic incidence Freud referred to in various texts (*Studienausgabe*, Ergänzungsband, fn. 2, p. 215). This phenomenon is also called the "adhesiveness of the libido" (Freud, 1937c, 241/*G.W.*, *XVI*, 87). Thus, in certain individuals, as in a case of hysteria, he observed a greater difficulty in withdrawing libidinous cathexis from one beloved object and shifting it to another. This adhesiveness of the libido, he said, frequently leads to delays in the cure. It is precisely in these cases, where an object cathexis is so stubbornly held on to, that working-through is particularly important. This is a form of engagement, a psychic work aimed at resolution and transformation.

This psychic work is found within psychoanalysis in various forms. Dream work seems hereby paradigmatic, that is, in the forms of regression, condensation, displacement, and secondary processing. These modii are also evident in the work of remembering and formed in a similar model. The work of mourning, on the other hand, aims less at transformation than at detachment or dissolution, which seems in this respect more like working-through. Economically speaking, working-through serves the withdrawal of cathexis, be it from an object, an activity, or a symptom. Laplanche gives key importance to the concept of dissolution in Freud's work. Unlike Freud—in whose remarks on mourning (1917e, 249–263/G.W., XI, 428–446) this detachment appears in a problematic comparison to the simple severing of an attachment or loosening of a fixation—Laplanche sees this "loosening" as "analysis" itself. He refers to the meaning of the Greek word *"ana-lyse,"* which denotes both untying and analyzing. Analysis is not a detaching but an untangling of threads (Laplanche, 2020[1992], fn. 24, 87). The idea that the work of mourning/*Trauerarbeit* is not like severing, but is more an unravelling, seems essential to understanding the productive aspect of mourning(work) in a sense of transformation—rather than of destruction. In this sense, the work of mourning is well suited to illustrate the idea of working-through.

The release of libidinous cathexis in the mourning process essentially takes place in memories: "Each single one of the memories and expectations in which the libido is bound to the object is brought up and hypercathected, and detachment of the libido is accomplished in respect of it" (Freud, 1916–1917g, 245/G.W., X, 430). Laplanche vividly describes the process of constructive mourning as an act of translation:

> Bereavement forces me, through the agony of thinking, to start unraveling the fabric of my existence, a fabric woven on the loom of the lost other. But in this process, even as I detach a single thread [...] from the whole, that thread is not, as Freud thought, broken. It is, on the contrary, overinvested, set apart, and thought over, linked back to its history [...] and, beyond everyday history such as that of a couple, related to a larger and far longer history.
>
> (Laplanche 2020[1992], 80)

With Laplanche, we can also ascribe a translational dimension to working-through, in addition to the economic dimension: working-through consists in a dissolution of the structures of meaning and renewed translations. Here, the moments of *Nachträglichkeit*, posteriority, or afterwardsness, and the primacy of the other play a special role.

Roussillon (2010) refers to another form of working-through, which is not about the dissolution of structures of meaning and new translations, but about the initial assignment of meaning to what is called the "primarily repressed." For example, traumatic experiences can become accessible to symbolization for the first time in the course of an analysis. This complex and lengthy process can also be described in terms of working-through. While Freud uses the metaphor of work, Roussillon associates this process with play in the sense of Winnicott. Like play, working-through serves to bring threatening content under control, thus defusing it and enabling sub-jective appropriation. In this context, the compulsion to repeat plays an important and constructive role in that, fragment by fragment, piece by piece, these experiences can be actualized and processed, "just as children play" (Roussillon, 2010, 1412).

References

Aulagnier, P. & Pontalis, J.-B. (1963) *Réflexions sur l'action et l'agir dans leur relation au transfert analytique*. Paris: Jacques Dupont.

Berman, A. (1984) *L'épreuve de l'étranger*. Paris: Gallimard.

Birkstedt-Breen, D. (2003). Time and the Après-coup. *International Journal of Psychoanalysis, 84*(6): 1501–1515.

Bohleber, W., Fonagy, P., Jiménez de la Jara, J. P. *et al.* (2013). Für einen besseren Umgang mit Konzepten, modellhaft illustriert am Konzept "Enactment". *Psyche, 67*(12): 1212–1250.

Bourguignon, A., Cotet, P., Laplanche, J., & Robert, F. (1989) *Traduire Freud*. Paris: PUF.

Freud, S. (1975) Ergänzungsband: Schriften zur Behandlungstechnik. In: *Studienausgabe*. Frankfurt am Main: Fischer.

Freud, S. (1899a). Screen Memories (Über Deckerinnerungen, *G.W., I*: 531–554). *S.E., 3*: 299–322. London: Hogarth Press.

Freud, S. (1910c). *Leonardo da Vinci and a Memory of his Childhood (Eine Kindheitserinnerung des Leonardo da Vinci. G.W., VIII*: 127–211). *S.E., 11*: 57–138. London: Hogarth Press.

Freud, S. (1912b) The Dynamics of Transference (Zur Dynamik der Übertragung. *G.W., VIII*: 364–374). *S.E., 12* (pp. 97–108). London: Hogarth Press.

Freud, S. (1914g). Remembering, Repeating and Working Through (Erinnern, Wiederholen und Durcharbeiten, *GW., X, 127). S.E., 12*: London: Hogarth Press.

Freud, S. (1917e). Mourning and Melancholia (Trauer und Melancholie. *G.W., X*: 428–446). *S.E., 14*: 237–258. London: Hogarth Press.

Freud, S. (1918b). *From the History of an Infantile Neurosis* (Aus der Geschichte einer infantilen Neurose. *G.W., XII*: 27–157). *S.E., 17*: 1–124. London: Hogarth Press.

Freud, S. (1919h). The 'Uncanny' (Das Unheimliche. *G.W., XII*: 229–268). *S.E., 17*: 217–256. London: Hogarth Press.

Freud, S. (1920g). *Beyond the Pleasure Principle* (Jenseits des Lustprinzips. *G.W., XIII*: 1–69). *S.E., 18*: 7–64. London: Hogarth Press.

Freud, S. (1926d). *Inhibitions, Symptoms and Anxiety* (Hemmung, Symptom und Angst. *G.W., XIV*: 113–205). *S.E., 20*: 77–174. London Hogarth Press.

Freud, S. (1937c). Analysis Terminable and Interminable (Die endliche und die unendliche Analyse. *G.W., XVI*: 59–99). *S.E., 23*: 209–254. London: Hogarth Press.

Freud, S. (1937d). Constructions in Analysis (Konstruktionen in der Analyse. *G.W., XVI*: 41–56). *S.E., 23*: 255–270. London: Hogarth Press.

Hock, U. (2003). Die Zeit des Erinnerns. *Psyche, 57*(9/10): 812–840.

Kahn, L. (2015). *L'écoute de l'analyste. De l'acte à la forme*. Paris: PUF.

Lacan, J. (1966). *Écrits*. Paris: Seuil.

Lacan, J. (1973). *Le séminaire XI. Quatre concepts fondamentaux de la psychanalyse*. Paris: Seuil.

Laplanche, J. (1987). *Problématiques V. Le baquet – Transcendance du transfert*. Paris: PUF.

Laplanche, J. (2017[2006]). *Après-coup*. New York: The Unconscious in Translation.

Laplanche, J. (2020[1992]). *The Unfinished Copernican Revolution. Selected Works 1967–1992*. New York: The Unconscious in Translation.

Laplanche, J. & Pontalis, J.-B. (1973[1967]). *The Language of Psychoanalysis*. London: Hogarth Press.

Mannoni, O. (1969). *Clefs pour l'imaginaire ou l'Autre Scène*. Paris: Seuil.

Roussillon, R. (2010). Working Through and Its Various Models. *International Journal of Psychoanalysis, 91*(6): 1405–1417.

Sandler, J. (1970). Basic Psychoanalytic Concepts. VI. Acting Out. *British Journal of Psychiatry, 117*(538): 329–334.

Scarfone, D. (2014) L'impassé, actualité de l'inconscient. *Revue française de psychanalyse, 78*: 1357–1428.

4 Note on Acting-out and *Agieren*

Udo Hock

Agieren

Particular attention needs to be paid to the translation of the word *Agieren*, since it is central to the middle section of Freud's essay, which is focused on repetition. It has found its way into the psychoanalytic vocabulary in numerous forms derived from it: active *versus* passive or activity *versus* passivity, specific action, (actual) neurosis, act (Lacan), reaction, abreaction, etc.

A first remark applies to the semantics of *Agieren* outside psychoanalysis: the German word derives from the Latin *agere* and has two meanings, both of which Freud intends in his use of the word: (1) to act, to be active, and (2) to appear, to play a role. Freud therefore does not invent it, but makes use of it.

A second remark concerns the occurrence of the word in Freud's own work. Even before his essay 'Remembering, Repeating and Working-Through, Freud refers to *Agieren* on various occasions, for example in the Afterword to the Dora case (Freud, 1905e/G.W., V, p. 283) and especially in the 1912–1914 essays, which are devoted to the technical problems of psychoanalysis and here, in particular, to transference. Incidentally, the word also appears in Freud in the conventional, non-analytical sense, for example in the essays "The 'Uncanny'" (Freud, 1919h, S.E., 17, cf. G.W., XII, p. 242) and "Femininity" (Freud, 1933, S.E., 22, cf. G.W., XV, p. 143). In these contexts, *Agieren* does not take place in the context of psychoanalytic treatment, but simply means "taking on someone's role" or even "putting on a show". Freud rarely uses the word even after writing "Remembering, Repeating and Working-through"; it is not one of the regularly recurring technical terms in his teaching.

The translation of *Agieren* into English in particular led to major difficulties of understanding, which have still not been resolved. Strachey repeatedly renders it as *"acting* out", and so it also appears in the vocabulary of psychoanalysis and more recently in the glossary of the EPF/FEP. This translation proposal has been taken up again and again and also criticized (cf. in particular Laurence Kahn's contribution in the present volume). Strachey, by the way, was able to rely on Freud's agreement. For, in a letter

DOI: 10.4324/9781003458340-4

written in English to Ferenczi on 4 February 1924, he himself had spoken of "acting out" and added "acting" in brackets. Nevertheless, the "out" added to the "acting" caused several problems for the readers of the *Standard Edition*:

- The "out" suggests that in *Agieren* there is, as it were, a release of tension, that it is therefore comparable to acting out. However, this is by no means the case in Freud's essay; rather, acting out is defined here as a special form of remembering mistakes, in which the repressed is enacted through action.
- With the accentuation supplied by "out", one runs the risk of not focusing sufficiently on what is decisive about *Agieren*: patients bring their unconscious conflicts, awakened by the analytical cure, to the stage of life, as it were.
- "'acting out' or 'acting in'" (cf. Lacan, 1978, p. 246)?
  The question arises as to whether the *Agieren* takes place outside or inside the session. As is well known, Freud allows all possibilities here, but his concept of *Agieren* in the context of "Remembering, Repeating and Working-through" is necessarily tied to the treatment situation and the transference situation that goes with it. In other words, Freud also relates acting out outside the treatment room (e.g., the choice of a love object or even a spouse) to the specific dynamic between analyst and patient. It is only through this that the word acquires its special psychoanalytic meaning.
- Finally, Laurence Kahn points out in her text that in the French milieu "acting out" is related to the expression *"passage à l'acte"*. Accordingly, acting out is not so much about acting during the treatment, but about an end, even a violent termination, of the treatment: for example, by breaking it off (cf. also the contribution by Hock, Quindeau & Verner).

In view of these objections to the translation of *Agieren* to acting out, it at least seems worth considering an alternative. Both the simple "acting" and "enacting" come into question for the time being. After all, Laurence Kahn has cited a passage in her contribution in which Strachey also favors such a solution. For, in the final passage of his essay "The Dynamics of Transference" (1912b), Freud speaks of the "wanting to act" of the patient's unconscious impulses (*G.W., VIII*, p. 374) and Strachey translates this expression as "seeking to act" (*S.E., 12*, p. 108). And a few lines further up, Freud says that the patient "wants his passions to act", which Strachey translates as "he seeks to put his passions into actions" (*ibid.*). English thus offers the possibility of dispensing with the "out": "act" or "action" and seems sufficient reflection of Freud's acting.

The question of whether "acting" or "enacting" is better suited to a possible alternative translation of "acting" is certainly not easy to answer.

Acting is used much more frequently in English than the German *Agieren*, especially in connection with theater acting; therefore there is a certain resistance to ascribing a certain psychoanalytical meaning to the word. But *Agieren* is also a term that was not invented by Freud, but was already ready in the language. And "acting" certainly has the advantage that it reflects well the core idea of *Agieren*, which is that it is a "doing".

For its part, "enacting" emphasizes more strongly the character of staging that *Agieren* has in itself. The '"doing" in *Agieren* is, at the same time, a "showing" in the sense of performing or presenting. It makes explicit what is implicit in *Agieren*, especially in the psychoanalytical meaning of the word.

From here, it is only a step to "enactment", which has replaced *Agieren* in recent decades, at least in the Anglophone world (cf. Bohleber et al., 2013). Of course, this has been accompanied by a double shift in meaning.

Enactment refers electively to stagings, to forms of *Agieren* that take place in the analytical hour. This, however, ignores forms of *Agieren* that take place outside the treatment room. Freud, however, explicitly emphasizes in his essay that *Agieren* takes place inside as well as outside the analytic situation.

The "enactment" is no longer focused on the analysand as his or her way of making something repressed recur or repeat itself; it is, rather, understood as a relational event between analysand and analyst in which the analyst has an equal share. In a certain sense, this drops Freud's construction from "Remembering, Repeating and Working-through", according to which *Agieren* is a special, indeed the greatest possible, form of resistance to remembering that emanates from the id, as he will later add (*G.W., XIV*, p. 192).

These considerations are now primarily intended to bring the whole semantic–theoretical background of the term "acting" to the attention of English-speaking readers in particular, and, furthermore, to pose anew the question of its possible translation into English. For the present collection of texts, we have nevertheless decided to retain Strachey's "acting out"; this was suggested by the majority of the authors. Where the reference to the German *Agieren* is not sufficiently clear, we have added the German word in brackets.

References

Bohleber, W., Fonagy, P., Jiménez, J. P., Scarfone, D., Varvin, S. & Zysman, S. (2013) 'Towards a Better Use of Psychoanalytic Concepts: A Model Illustrated Using the Concept of Enactment'. *International Journal of Psychoanalysis* 94: 501–530

Freud, S. (1905e) *Fragment of the Analysis of a Case of Hysteria. S.E.,* 7: 1–122. London: Hogarth Press.

Freud, S. (1919h) 'The 'Uncanny''. *S.E.,* 17: 219–256. London: Hogarth Press.

Freud, S. (1933) 'Femininity'. *S.E.,* 22: 112–135. London: Hogarth Press.

Freud, S. (1952) *Gessasmelte Werke (G.W)*. London: Imago.

Lacan, J. (1978) *The Seminar of Jacques Lacan* Book I. New York: W.W. Norton.

5 The Discrete and the Continuous in Freud's "Remembering, Repeating and Working-Through"

Lawrence Friedman

Although it is a bit irregular to begin a formal essay with a declaration of personal feelings, I have learned that readers need to know my motive in order to catch the drift of my argument. Without such a declaration they are likely to imagine a grander critique than I intend, and even some sort of partisan campaign. Here, then, is how the paper came about. I have had the experience of trying unsuccessfully to convince colleagues that they are misreading Freud's comments on working through in his "Papers on Technique" (1911–1915). Since my reading seemed to me fairly plain, I was puzzled by why it was so hard to make my point.

I asked myself what might be good reasons for the "resistance." I thought I found the answer in the inherent difficulty of imagining at once both discrete units and continuous process, as Freud was demanding of analysts. That double vision is something that long ago had fascinated me in Freud's theory (Friedman, 1988.) But there was a problem with that answer. The same cinching together of units and continua was evident in an earlier part of the same paper, and analysts never balked at that. Why was the one instance accepted by all, while the other has been steadfastly ignored by many? Then I noticed that the two instances differ as to which member of the treatment couple was presenting a continuum, and which one was transmitting discrete units. It seemed that analysts can comfortably picture themselves fielding unitary messages that emerge from the continuum of the patient's activity, and yet find it uncongenial to imagine their own discretely crafted responses dissolving into a river of the patient's continuous experience. Overall, I thought, analysts were wrestling here with a fundamental philosophical problem, and I thought it would be reassuring to recognize that the difficulty is ancient and honorable, and a conundrum for all thinking beings.

Thus, I am not campaigning for or against any practice or theory. In a certain sense, my goal is to justify a common misreading. Further, I wish to make it clear that this is not a paper on technique; it is a paper about a paper on technique. I don't know how to avoid the paradox I am pointing to. I am trying to answer a question about the community's reception of an idea and dwell a little on the nature of the problem as it is written about

DOI: 10.4324/9781003458340-5

in this one text. I add some comments on the psychoanalytic literature and the philosophical background, in order to "naturalize" the conceptual difficulty, but I make no effort to trace the history of the problem in either discipline.

The context of the text

Readers might find it hard to join me if they are familiar with the Working-Through paper only as a free-standing essay, like the bulk of Freud's work. My discussion of two passages in "Remembering, Repeating and Working-Through" is based on a particular reading of the whole book in which they appear, Freud's *Papers on Technique* (1911–1915). I believe that this slight and early-conceived book is often misunderstood because analysts, when not actually discounting it as theoretically unfinished, often read back into it what we all know to be Freud's general outlook, and ask not what Freud says in a particular passage but what he must have meant there in view of what everybody knows to be his general model of the mind and treatment goal. I have argued (Friedman 1991a, 2008, 2009) that the technique book is not an application of theory. It stands alone among Freud's works as a chronicle of successive efforts to wrestle with the raw experiences that led him to adopt the principles of psychoanalytic technique, in the process layering sometimes divergent conclusions one on top of the other without retraction, each understood only by grasping a specific difficulty he was wrestling with at that moment in his practice.[1]

First example of the merger of discrete items and a continuous process

> We must still be grateful to the old hypnotic technique for having brought before us single psychical processes of analysis in an isolated or schematic form. Only this could have given us the courage ourselves to create more complicated situations in the analytic treatment and to keep them clear before us.
>
> (Freud, 1914g, p. 148)

This is a remarkable confession by Freud. Does he really mean it? "Only this could have given us the courage ..." The need for courage testifies to the dizzying dilemmas, practical and cognitive, that Freud was struggling to master in the *Papers on Technique*. But by the same token, the passage is also a tribute to *a certain kind of preliminary thinking* that one needs in order to get a purchase on those difficulties.

We can be sure that it is not a confession of cognitive weakness. Excessive modesty and fearfulness were not notable characteristics of Freud. Although it is mostly the editorial "we" and "us" (i.e., himself) that he speaks for, one suspects that he regards himself as the best of Everyman on this journey, summoning his followers along the path (the sort of thinking) that leads to the summit. And if one still suspected that Freud was confessing his personal need for a simple-minded myth to reassure him on his way to a tougher truth, that suspicion would vanish on noting that the new, complex truth *includes* the preparatory simplification, for, in the passage that leads up to what might seem a sentimental farewell to the early model, he has actually promised it lifetime employment. The old terms will remain in place forever: "The aim of these different techniques has, of course, remained the same. Descriptively speaking, it is to fill in gaps in memory; dynamically speaking, it is to overcome resistances due to repression" (Freud, 1914g, pp. 147–148).

What, then, is that simpler kind of thinking that allowed Freud to venture into the forbiddingly complex scene of the analytic encounter? It is the kind of thinking that finds "single psychical processes of analysis in an isolated or schematic fashion." The operative words are "single," "isolated," and "schematic." That's the old way. And what, by contrast, is the complexity that continues to need those single, isolated, and schematic elements as a counterpoint? It is the progressively layered "takes" on the phenomenon of analytic treatment that make up the *Papers on Technique*. As Freud's thinking develops in the pages of that book, the plot thickens: transference is a prime example. Transference morphs from the simple slippage in *Studies on Hysteria* (Breuer & Freud, 1895d) into a general human function. And yet it is not just a general human function, because, in treatment, it has certain peculiar features—or perhaps it doesn't. Analytic love is as realistic as any love but yet somehow more devious and intense. That's a typical, self-contradictory complexity in the new model. Complexity is rife in the new notion of memory. Here, memories are retrievable episodes, but yet memories are often not anecdotal, not naturally segregated, not articulated, not calling up the past, often not thoughts (just connections), frequently not incidents (but habits and character), sometimes not even actual (but just virtual). Complexity now afflicts the analyst's attention: it is *unfocused*, floating attention, but yet a laser-like *focus* on resistance. Most fateful, perhaps, is the new complexity Freud faces up to in the analytic relationship: Who is on whose side in this project; is it or isn't it a battle? These are just a few of the many examples of complexity in *Papers on Technique*.

If we position ourselves alongside Freud in 1914 and look with him at what he is facing as he writes his report, we can easily sympathize with his astonishment that he had been able to master so much complexity. We may even wonder whether he had come upon character analysis earlier than supposed, and lacked only the nosology. The true shift is that now he is not looking at a symptom (such as a stifled memory) or an avenue for its removal (like abreaction). He is seeing—or rather experiencing (and sometimes fighting)—a whole person. And that person is behaving this way and that from moment to moment, all the while claiming something personal that Freud had not originally been hired to provide. Freud could thread his way through that formidable scene only with the courage provided by a manageable earlier vision of simple parts (specific memories) and process (conscious recollection).

Analysts still find that view daunting and must, like Freud, project parts and processes into their experience of a patient's organic wholeness, conceptually freezing his slippery, variable behavior into some kind of mental portrait. Like all human beings, but more urgently because of their heavy obligation, analysts have an insatiable need for stencils to mark out simple units from the continuum in front of them. Nothing is more characteristic of the analytic literature than the drive to name things. A new term, a vivid image, a portable phrase—these are what we all hunger for and count as progress.

Such is the heritage of the many doubled visions prescribed by Freud throughout *Papers on Technique*. In imagining and conducting treatment, we must in general think two ways at once—as though looking at discrete objects "inside" the patient, and also as though confronted with a whole organism that exhibits itself in a somewhat unpredictable process.

What I want to call attention to at this point is that, although these paradoxes were so formidable that Freud needed the aid of a simple memory-retrieval model to lure him into the complex treatment event, the final, tangled vision was effortlessly adopted by generations of practicing psychoanalysts, as were many other impossible paradoxes in Freud's recipe for producing an analytic process. Daunting though it is to perceive memories and behavior as the same thing, analysts received the injunction almost without noticing its paradoxical nature. They observed behaviors, and they translated them into memories as a matter of course, and although much more went on in treatments, they felt this aspect to be perfectly natural. In practice, at least, the double vision was routine. (When this stance is criticized lately, it is more for being unrealistically pretentious than for being paradoxical.) Theorists, as we know, recognized that the whole-person aspect of the model (and, therefore, its process aspect) needed some further work, a job that was undertaken by the misleadingly named "ego psychologists." (One thinks of Hartmann [1951], Waelder [1976], and Schur [1966].)

I now ask the reader to contrast this smooth reception of a hybrid vision of discrete units and continuous process with the profession's very different reading of the last pages of the same 1914 paper, where a similar challenge is presented.

Second example of the merger of discrete items and continous process

I have often been asked to advise upon cases in which the doctor complained that he had pointed out his resistance to the patient and that nevertheless no change had set in; indeed, the resistance had become all the stronger, and the whole situation was more obscure than ever.

The treatment seemed to make no headway. The gloomy foreboding always proved mistaken. The treatment was as a rule progressing most satisfactorily. The analyst had merely forgotten that giving the resistance a name could not result in its immediate cessation. One must allow the patient time to become more conversant with this resistance with which he has now become acquainted, to work through it, to overcome it, by continuing, in defiance of it, the analytic work according to the fundamental rule of analysis. Only when the resistance is at its height can the analyst, working in common with his patient, discover the repressed instinctual impulses which are feeding the resistance; and it is this kind of experience which convinces the patient of the existence and power of such impulses.

(Freud 1914g, p. 156)

Here, Freud tells us that all the analyst need (or can) do is to prime the patient's attention with words, and then follow the patient's reported experience. Only the patient is in a position to notice and, therefore, feel acutely his *good reason* (his passionate incentive) for fudging his honesty. He meets that counterinterest for the first time as it squeezes him against his pledge of honesty, and makes brutally clear what he's giving up by being honest. Freud is neatly describing a process with two stages: one (objective) is the naming of an obstacle, presumably the behavioral evidence of interference with the process. The other (subjective) is the patient's discovery of the personal interest that is at risk, which is the specific, personal *meaning* of the phrase, "the resistance" (i.e., the *reason* for noncompliance). That discovery is made as the patient works stalwartly right through the sacrifice toward the fulfillment of analytic openness. Note that the term *working through* is expressly coined to refer to an action on a *resistance,* because the "through" depicts a rough trip under assault from a countervailing barrage. One can work *on* many things but, as the term is used here, there is nothing one can work *through* other than a resistance. The term is invented to give that activity both a name and a picture.

It is worth asking why the plain meaning of this passage is regularly ignored in favor of any and all associations that an analyst may have to the English words, "working" and "through." Admittedly, the terms and metaphors of Papers on Technique have all suffered wear and tear as guild passwords while their meaning has been assimilated to that of everyday speech. And how could it be otherwise? Having entered the general language, these terms and images can claim whatever meaning is bestowed on them by common usage, just like any other term in a natural language. Thus, one frequently hears, "On personal reflection, I think *it* means this ..." instead of "I think *Freud* meant that ..." And even when marking it specifically as Freud's invention, some analysts may start from its widespread meaning and try to imagine why the Freud they imagine *would be likely* to use such a word, rather than looking at why he *did* use it. (The metaphor of the "surgeon" in the Papers is a good example.)

But even allowing that to be the common fate of so many terms from *Papers on Technique*, in the case of "working through" the degree of resistance to Freud's actual expression is striking. Indeed, the tradition of misreading starts with the translator. An analyst who consults the main text of the *Standard Edition* will not be reading what Freud wanted him to read. There is nothing covert in Strachey's choice. His footnote (Freud 1914g, p. 155) describes and defends his act of overruling Freud.

Strachey thinks Freud wanted to say that the analyst acquaints the patient with a resistance by giving it a name. That would seem to be the implication of Freud's original versions, written before 1922. Strachey acknowledges that Freud changed this wording in a second edition (published in that year) of what I presume to be the *Sammlung* likewise *Schriften zur Neurosenlehre* (1918)—the only form of the paper that went through two editions. From then on, Strachey tells us, Freud's preferred expression (which Strachey rejects as senseless) is what we find on p. 118 of the *Gesammelte Schriften* (1925) and p. 118 of *Zur Technik der Psychoanalyse und zur Metapsychologie* (1924). In these later versions, Freud changed *nun bekannten Widerstand* (the resistance with which [the patient] is now acquainted) to *unbekannten Widerstand* (the resistance with which [the patient] is not [yet] acquainted). So Freud finally wanted the sentence to read "*Man muss dem Kranken die Zeit lassen, sich in den ihm unbekannten Widerstand zu vertiefen ...* [The patient must be allowed time to immerse himself in the resistance that is unknown to him ...]" (1925, p. 118). That seemed plainly senseless to Strachey, who wondered how Freud could say that the patient is unacquainted with the resistance after it has already been named. Unable to account for Freud's revision, and thinking to rescue him from self-contradiction, Strachey refused the new wording and substituted the one that Freud had erased.[2]

It is an unusual lapse for Strachey. Common sense says that there is absolutely no way an author can make his meaning clearer than by going to the trouble of altering an expression for a new edition. When he does that, he is saying as emphatically as possible, "I'm afraid I made you think XYZ in my first edition, and I now want to be sure you do *not* get that impression." If a word can be read in two ways, the author might let the reader fend for himself, but he would not let it rest if a substantive issue was at stake. Therefore, if an author goes to the trouble of changing his wording, it behoves the translator to try to fathom what that issue is. It wouldn't have taken much thought, either, in this case. Obviously, Freud was going out of his way to emphasize that referring to something is not the same as being acquainted with it. One thinks of Bertrand Russell's distinction (1940) between knowledge of fact, which can be learned second-hand, and knowledge by acquaintance, which cannot.[3]

Strachey can also be excused for tripping on the ambiguity of the term *resistance*. Suppose one said (just for fun), "The resistance that motivates the resistance is part of the patient's resistance." The layman would laugh but every analyst would know what was meant. In one sense, "the resistance" is an omnibus term referring to the collection of conservative forces that oppose treatment. In another sense, "resistance" is an operational term for a move in a direction opposite to the analyst's aim. In a third sense, "the resistance" refers to the highly specific, personal state inside the individual's mind that accounts for those other two. It might be said that knowledge of the existence of a resistance in the first of the meanings is beyond observation; it's an a priori, theoretical *premise* of treatment, almost the justification for undertaking treatment. In its second meaning, the analyst knows there's a resistance from his *observation* of blockage in the flow, and from that he can *infer* a resistance in the third sense that underlies it. But he would not have knowledge of resistance in that third sense (knowledge by acquaintance), since he hasn't (and cannot) personally meet the patient's internal event. Only the patient can be *acquainted* with resistance in the third sense.[4]

Freud is telling us that the patient, in order to work through the named resistance, must contribute something the analyst doesn't initially have and can't give him. The analyst can only point the way to the living experience of conflict. As already mentioned, it is a two-stage process, the first part of which is the analyst's (directing attention), and the second part—the working through part—requires the patient's struggle. As the patient becomes aware of his counter*motive* he can let the analyst know more about the particularity of the resistance, beyond the visible consequence of it that the analyst had spotted. We can see why Freud thought that the naive analysts in this passage who complained to him about the ineffectiveness of their interpretation were counting on suggestion rather than psychoanalysis to do the work. In contrast, Freud depicts the analytic mechanism of cure as the blunt, personal, conscious experience of—indeed, the forced "acquaintance" with—internal conflict:

> it is this kind of experience ... which convinces the patient of the existence and power of such impulses. ... From a theoretical point of view one may correlate it with the 'abreacting' of the quotas of affect strangulated by repression ...
>
> (Freud, 1914g, pp. 155–156)[5]

Strachey's mistranslation is a harbinger of the many arbitrary meanings later attributed to the term. As against them, and at the cost of repetition, let me summarize my reading of the concept in this paper: Working through does not mean working out an issue. Neither does it mean ironing out a resistance. It means working in the teeth of the resistance. The patient must continue to carry out his analytic duty in the face of the resistance. Then he will have the something else that is needed besides the analyst's interpretation. What would that be? He will experience the impulse that is the source of the resistance. Only the patient can feel that impulse; the analyst can only name it, and then hear about it from his patient. What is the feeling the patient will have? I think it is obvious when you consider what a resistance actually *is*: the patient will feel the interests that would ordinarily turn him away from declaring himself. Reading a thermometer is not the same as making the acquaintance of burning heat. Fidelity to the fundamental rule requires a patient to work through his resistance as one would walk through fire, and thereby feel the heat. The patient will feel both sides of a conflict at once; he will explicitly experience the incompatibility of conflicted interests. Working through a resistance, the patient will be working against half of himself, and he will not escape conscious awareness of what it is inside him that the "against" is against. Freud's reply to the inexperienced analyst is that a patient does not endure that experience no matter how plausibly informed, as long as he is acquainted only with his presented and presentable self.

From information to experience

Instead of this meaning, why has so much of the usage reduced the term *working through* to one or another tediously banal homily? Bear in mind that, along with two other terms, *working through* is the very *title* of this paper. The purpose of the paper is to transform the psychoanalytic meaning of remembering and repeating and make them the famous pillars of psychoanalytic thinking. But what of the title's third element? Should Freud have called the paper "Remembering, Repeating and Repeating?" Ask yourself how likely it is that Freud would dedicate one of his few papers on technique partly to the profound principle that analytic treatment takes a while. Or that once isn't enough for an interpretation. Or that patients should work hard. Or that treatment should be complete. Could any serious writer fill a full page with such an instruction? Why not six words? How was it possible for analysts to picture as an exercise in plodding patience what Freud found comparable to a cathartic explosion? Analysts must have some strong incentive to turn away from the gist of Freud's discussion of working through, and it is that *incentive* for misreading (not the misreading itself) that I am concerned with here. (As I will note below, there are within the Freudian tradition exceptions to this avoidance, notably Ellman [1991], Schafer [1992], although somewhat hesitantly, and Loewald [1960] in his grand scheme. But it seems to me that these have not influenced the general discussion of working through among Freudian analysts.)

I suggest that the two passages from Freud's 1914g paper present analysts the same underlying problem (discrete items *vs.* the continuum of life), but the form of the problem in the first excerpt is easily handled (how to think of a patient's continuous action as discrete memories), while that in the second (how to make discrete, repeatable interpretations inform a patient's ongoing experience) seems almost untouchable. I will look at the common problem, and then ask why they are so differently received.

The underlying problem: Islands in the stream

Analysts want to be able to target their attention and speech to specific items so they can know what they're doing and do what is best. An amorphous flow of experience threatens to undermine their control and their objectivity. (The flow literally takes the object out of objectivity.) And yet, what their patient offers them as behavior is not a text but a seamless flow of action. At first they looked at words and associations, which seemed tidy enough, but in *Papers on Technique* the material had come to embrace, in addition to not talking, talking too much, symptomatic gestures, the direction and misdirection of the patient's yearning, and, as Freud finally noted (1914g, pp. 155–156), everything about the patient that is related to his troubles.

That's at the level of practice. On the level of theory, the corresponding problem is how to squeeze together knowledge of fact and knowledge by acquaintance. Knowledge of fact can easily be captured in words and concepts. It grasps something delimited—something with borders—something nameable. It uses adjectives that can be "downloaded" into various times and places. A fact can come out of the analyst's head, so to speak, and go into the patient's head. Knowledge by acquaintance, by contrast, is gained by a unique, private experience over a stretch of time, and shares with time the quality of flow. Declarative memory is associated with the first; the second has more to do with recognition, and its description is somewhat arbitrary. I need hardly add that these are rough classifications: there is no knowledge by acquaintance that is not permeated by myriad unworded background descriptions and *vice versa*. In other words, there is no theory-free knowledge, and no purely abstract theory. Theory is always absorbed, and gets part of its meaning, from a background of the familiar world, while, from sense perception on up to thinking, the "blooming, buzzing confusion" of the familiar world is being unceasingly coded into theoretical concepts.

Why is Freud's concept of working through unwelcome?

Difficult as it is to think of description and acquaintance together, that difficulty did not keep analysts from accepting Freud's demand that they think of memory as both reportable units (discrete memories) and a continuous flow of life and behavior. But when, analogously, they were asked to equate their categorized target—an observed resistance—with the patient's flow of live experience (his inner struggle), analysts on the whole turned a deaf ear. They preferred to hear a simple encouragement to keep on urging their interpretations. Why was the tension between description and experience so much harder to accept when *making interpretations* than when *grasping phenomena*?

Freud gives us a clue in our first citation. His original confidence came from the memory-retrieval model of treatment. There, the analyst is free to follow along with the unarticulated flow of process, waiting for defined memories to emerge from the *patient* of his own accord. Without that picture to start with, Freud would have been as helpless as any other untrained beginner to parse the continuous display in front of him. When he learned that things were not that simple, Freud saw that the helpful, articulated map of memories could be accommodated to the new complexity by layering it translucently over the picture of patients' action. The resulting equivalence allowed the analyst to spot discrete memories emerging, encoded, from the patient's action. By this equation, the analyst still imagines himself "fielding" discrete information thrown out by the patient. In the notion of working through, however, the translation from a continuum to discrete units goes the other way. Freud is asking the analyst to recognize that *his own* discrete message (his interpretation of "a" resistance) is tossed into the patient's unarticulated experience, with which it must find a way to blend. The kind of "resistance" that an analyst is able to capture in a common description is just a *clue* to an intensely *individual need*, which is the resistance in its personal specificity.

Both memory-equated-to-action and interpretation-tied-to-working-through are examples of the many paradoxes that characterize *Papers on Technique*. To be sure, Freud does not present them as paradoxes. Instead, he persists in referring to "the" resistance as though it were a barricade, a *thing*—something that can be captured in a word, just as he insisted that behavior is *really* remembering. But right from the first of the *Papers*, the expressive nature of resistance was becoming more and more prominent, starting with the discovery that patients are not just *hiding* their wishes but *acting* on them. (One could say that the *Papers*, as a unified project, is a treatise on the positive aspect of resistance, in all the senses of "positive.") In Freud's depiction of working through, the resistance-as-named is just a tag—a describable, public trace of the patient's private visceral experience of wishes that are frustrated by cooperating with the analyst. Those wishes (including wishes for protection) constitute the real-time, intimately personal cost of free association.

So, now we can see why the relatively simple and commonsense conception of working through in *Papers* was nevertheless difficult to digest: on the one hand, there's the individual gut reality of a resistance inside a suffering patient. On the other hand, there's an articulated interpretation, a description so generalizable that it can be duplicated here and there, now and then, sometimes identically in hundreds of copies of a professional journal. How could such a contrast be welcome to analysts? Does an analyst really want to brood on how those two things manage to get together? On what common ground can they meet? Why even pose the bewildering question of how a detachable, generalizable, repeatable description can match up with an ongoing flow of subjective experience in time? Would it help our work in any way to start groping for subtle threads that tie the patient's inner flux to our fixed words? Is it wise to open the door to doubts about whether there is any specific connection at all between the analyst's interpretations and their intended target? It might make us think that it's all just the impact of one person on another. This is no longer a matter of contemplation; it hits the analyst where it hurts. Unlike Freud's double vision of the patient's action as being also his memory, this idea seems to insert a lot of intervening processes and variables between the analyst's words and his impact. It does not merely superimpose one *vision* on another; it raises doubts about the analyst's own *action*—his act of interpreting. It was one thing, as described in the first passage, for the analyst to tolerate a lot of continuous and variable living by the patient, since it's draped over the patient's own neat, well-articulated memories. It's a different story if we are required to picture the patient's unique, continuous, amorphous processes dissolving the analyst's neat, defined capsules of fact. And it poses a question: if patients' action is regularly translated into words by the analyst, are the analyst's words likewise received by the patient as actions? And does that mean that the analyst's interventions are not capsules of fact but mere gestures toward a patient's subjective experience, both of them being continuous processes with blurred outlines that only the patient can experience? Of course, Freud wasn't picturing such an extreme situation. But his explicit and all-too-plausible two-stage formula of "working though" is unsettling enough, and analysts would naturally feel safer fusing it into a single compound made up of the analyst's verbal gesture and the patient's phenomenological experience, thus collapsing inner fact, public name, and process function into one term: the resistance. By treating resistance as a single unit (and ignoring Freud's distinction in the passage we have examined), analysts could, like Strachey, suppose that both parties became acquainted with the resistance in the act of naming it. In other words, it was more practical to think of the process of the patient's mind as being already frozen into units. When Glover (1931) found reason to doubt the automatic identity of interpretations-made and interpretations-received, he had the saving grace to treat divergence as an exception rather than the rule, but analysts probably realized that he was opening a can of worms. To this day, the question of what is actually produced in the patient's mind as a result of an analyst's intervention (and the concomitant question of what the interpreting analyst's action actually is) is an unaskable question for some classical analysts. (For others, it can be mooted by talking about "bypassing" the ego, or by relying on the unconscious telephone metaphor.)

What, after all, *is* the nature of communication, analytic or otherwise? What, exactly, happens when you say something to somebody about himself? My conclusion is that practicing analysts have good reason to steer clear of this speculation. Start down that path and paralysis threatens (like the famous centipede's crippling self-reflection). There are enough problems to contend with in practice without such distractions. A practitioner may be well advised to turn away from that and tend to business—refuse Freud's emendation and restore his first wording. Even if Freud didn't want to let us off the hook, he had inadvertently made it possible by allowing readers of his original misphrasing to comfortably assume that the patient has become acquainted with a resistance upon hearing the analyst's interpretation. It is not that analysts require simplicity; after all, they ceaselessly and nimbly negotiate the intricate commerce between the patient's action and its meaning. But practical dangers lie in wait with Freud's concept of working through for a practitioner who wants to know what he has done to his patient.

What are the alternatives? As a very rough working model, we may prefer to think that the living experience in the depths of the patient has the same generalizable form as the analyst's generalizable description. We might wish to imagine that the patient's experience of the resistance already includes his own interpretation, as though the patient had been talking to himself without paying attention until he hears the analyst whisper the very words in his ear that he has heard inside himself. We suppose that when the patient hears his analyst's interpretation, provided that it is correct, the *sotto voce* resistance recognizes its *fortissimo* echo and swims up to meet its twin. That may sound strange, but Freudian analysts, with the usual exception of Loewald (1960), have generally learned to live with it (jettisoning topographic gradations in the process). It is a cruder model, to be sure, but not necessarily incorrect. It is, in fact, the way we manage all conversation. And if we choose the model, we can disregard Freud's 1922 revision: if the analyst's interpretation reminds the patient of his own unrehearsed interpretation, and if the resistance is a thing that analyst and patient can look at together, we can say that the interpretation has acquainted the patient with his resistance, and all that's left is to repeat it frequently in various contexts, that is, to "work it through" in the sense that Freud rejected and posterity accepted. What we lose in that option is what Freud wanted to add in this paper, which is a reminder that, besides being a name for a common obstacle, "the resistance" also names a highly individual motivation (something fed by an individual's personal "impulses"). And, in practice, we can correct for the error by following the advice of Schlesinger (2013) to focus on ensuing associations and of Faimberg (1996) to "listen to the patient's listening."

The problem: The hard-to-think-about continuum

Analysts have largely assimilated Freud's paradoxes into their peculiar workaday life with no need to engage in philosophical hairsplitting. But, in recent years, vexatious philosophical problems have buzzed into their consulting rooms. The reader will think of the mind–body problem, the question of the analyst's authority, worries about the analyst's subjectivity, and problems of free will. These are, like all philosophical problems, interwoven with one another. But the form of the problem that Freud's 1914g paper encountered overshadows them in scope and urgency. Analysts have always been aware of the tension between articulated thought, with its relatively neat definitions, and unarticulated experience that lacks a clear outline. They are aware of it because they characteristically deal in *units* of interpretations, and yet they hope to induce a transformative *process*; they engage in a cloud of relationship, but they deliver specific, propositional information. It can be argued that genuine theories of therapeutic action are rare because psychoanalysts do not want an image of transition (the *process* of change) to compromise their freedom to identify a variety of specific *forms* in the patient. Without forms to take a bead on and relate to one another in a variety of ways, an analyst might drown with his patient in the surge of shapeless process. He would prefer to stand lifeguard on the shore. Process represents change, which is therapeutic action, but it is objects that allow the multiple perspectives that bring about the change. (I have elaborated this elsewhere [Friedman, 2007].) Loewald (1960) was a master synthesizer of parts and process, so he was able to present a theory of therapeutic action by juggling continuities and states, process and structures (see Friedman, 1991b), but the hostile early reception he received shows just how threatening that project is for the working psychoanalyst.

How does the theorist work on this problem?

As Ricoeur (1970) demonstrated, Freud constructed a theory that allowed for both psychic "things" (e.g., structures) and organismic process (e.g., drives, libido). Although in many ways these views are mutually exclusive, Freud recognized that both of them must figure in any true-to-life portrait of the mind. Thus Freud (1937c) implied in his final paper that a mental "thing" (the ego) that figures so conspicuously in his model is not to be taken as more real than the process of the mind as a whole.

Nevertheless, it remains a challenge to us all, as is apparent in the resistance to Freud's corrected notion of working through. It is difficult to embrace in a single vision two disparate realities: there is the "thing" aspect of reality—items, units, foci of attention. And there is the "stream" aspect—the continuum, the unified flow of time and life, the passage rather than the stations. The problem lies in the heteronomy of such things as borders and field, the discrete and the continuous, definitions and objects, gradations and stages, parts and whole, structures and process, and (ultimately) change and identity.

The so-called ego psychologists (a better name would be holistic psychoanalysts), such as Kris (1975), Hartmann (1951), Rapaport (1960), Gill (1963), and Schur (1966), were, in effect, working on the contrast of the mental continuum with its definable contents. It should not be forgotten that Freud had already carved a place for this kind of thinking by inserting a transformative category called "sublimation" into his theory of parts. Loewald (1960) saw that sublimation was no bit-player, and he moved it to center stage (see Friedman, 1982). Kohut's "area of progressive neutralization" (1971) is another example. More recently, Donnel Stern (1997) has written about relatively amorphous, unformulated experience flowing into somewhat unpredictable explicit outcomes that are themselves open to various formulations. Wilma Bucci (2002) describes the transformation of unarticulated into articulated meanings. Bion (1962) added a "metabolic" process to Kleinian units. Fonagy *et al.* (2002) and others focus attention on a process of mentalization and reflective functioning that precipitates definable units out of continua of awareness. These new trends join older ones: George Herbert Mead (1934) referred to an unarticulated source of initiative that gets its definition from external and internalized social coding (see also Bergson, 2007; Bruner, 1990.) These theorists join an existential-phenomenological tradition (see Merleau-Ponty, 1989; Stern 2010). Gendlin (1962) typically used the gerund "experiencing" to escape from what he regarded as artificially static items of experience that analysts talk about. Loewald (1960) did the same thing for Freudian theory, putting the entire spatially visualized psychic apparatus into motion.

In the past, many Freudian analysts shunned the process outlook because it did not seem to afford them a foothold for careful treading. We know how to respond to something only if we are able to determine that it is "a" something, and that it is the sort of something to which we can call up a response. Freudian analysts wince when they hear talk about "ways of being with another" because they recognize that it opens the door to non-categorized (and therefore unmonitored) provocations and unprescribable responses. Partly for that reason, Freud wanted his followers to continue to think in terms of retrievable memories even while turning attention to living processes. For many readers of "Remembering, Repeating and Working-Through," the first injunction overshadowed the second.

In our two quotations we have seen Freud enjoin analysts to look for repeatable memories (that have some generality), on the one hand, and continuous behavior (which is an immediate happening), on the other, as two sides of the same coin. Interpretations connect abstract knowledge to transient experience. And interpretations are just a small sample of the tacit formulations inside the analyst's head. For we must remember that, in its broadest sense, theory is simply a formalization of the working hypotheses everyone frames about everyone we deal with. And the analyst has an additional mandate: it isn't sufficient for him to recognize the person on his couch; he must also have many ways of thinking about him since he is not just dealing with his patient, but trying to stay free of automatic "role responsiveness."

Newer theory, old philosophy, and recent research are struggling to complete Freud's task on a theoretical level. Some theorists clear the deck by simply abandoning discrete items of mind (see Friedman, 1988). To some extent they are reacting to the opposite simplification of thinking only in terms of static items.

If an analyst leans strongly in one direction, he may despise talk of intra-psychic "objects" as being artificial distortions of the real, live human being. ("Life is green; theory gray, etc.") Existentialist psychologists voice that complaint. Much of the animus against "ego psychology" arises from those who prefer process. (They do not realize that the "ego psychologists," too, were engaged in restoring the organismic process significance of the Freudian parts [see Friedman 1989].) Since people ordinarily recognize mental "objects" only in a casual, untheorized, taken-for-granted way ("He has no shame"), extremely detailed, conscientious efforts to explicitly work out the relationship between parts and process, aspects and flow may look like obsessional scholasticism. Any effort to abstract "standard," constant parts from the unique flow of life is sometimes condemned as arrogant prejudice, disrespectful of individuality, and a grandiose pretense of expertise in the face of untamable novelty. (See Friedman [2002] on abstraction and [1999] on realists and nominalists.)

In turn, those who match their theory more poetically to the flood of life are sometimes deemed gullible and sentimental. We hear the complaint that a process theory cannot be considered psychoanalysis because it is not "conflict psychology." Of course, that poses the question, but what it expresses is the fact that conflict is a way of isolating elements. Psychoanalysis defines elements by opposing them to each other. Without conflict, we might have only an impoverished description of a patient's general anguish. If parts are ruled out as artificial inventions of a prejudiced observer, it is hard to carve clinical phenomena into shapes.[6]

It is a problem for all kinds of thinking

The history of this problem suggests that truth straddles the fence, and we must be able to think both ways. And there is nothing special to psychoanalytic thinking about the problem of lifting something unchanging out of the flow of time. (For a discussion of abstraction, see Friedman 2002.) One recognizes the antiquity of the problem. The river of Heraclitus that you can't step into twice is just the most familiar image of it. The entire history of philosophy can be seen as a study of this problem. Lifting something out of the flow of time is just what thinking does, and science does it with a vengeance (Meyerson, 1930). What is special to the study of the mind is a certain desperation. In other domains, thing-making can use spatial location to orient definitions. Physical things transition in time, but they reassuringly stay within spatial envelopes. Things of the mind are different. Internal mental things do not occupy a given space at a given time, and so we cannot quite settle on them as things, even though we nominalize them as things when we talk about them (Bergson, 2007). And we tend to picture them in spatial terms even though we don't take the picture literally. The only way Freud could dissect the mind was to lay it out on a spatial table. He never lost sight of the metaphoric nature of his maneuver, but Loewald (1960) was pilloried for ever-so-gently reminding analysts that the structural theory was a spatialized metaphor for something of a different sort. It must surely be one of the attractions that neuroscience holds for psychoanalysts that it provides spatial equivalents for mental things.

It would be an error to dismiss arguments about these difficulties as quibbling about language or indulging the narcissism of small differences. Taken to extremes, the polarity of concreteness *vs.* abstraction moves people to contrasting views of life and, perforce, professional practice. I have hinted at this above, but anyone who cares to tangle with the same issue writ large in philosophy or intellectual history may glimpse what is at stake in the balance between discrete thought and continuous experience by revisiting the 1928 face-off between Martin Heidegger and Ernst Cassirer in Davos, Switzerland (M. Friedman 2000; Gordon 2010).

The moral of the story

As in most philosophical issues, the *Zeitgeist* (fashion) rules. But there is some room for individual choice. Analysts will, for characterological reasons, lean to one side or the other of these philosophical problems. The polarities cannot be avoided in practice any more than they can be settled in philosophy. There is something here to discomfort everyone.

The power of Freud's theory is that it lives awkwardly with both sides of the controversy, but no more awkwardly than necessary. One might say that Freud's theory of the mind is the paradigm of a theory that accepts the disharmony of the continuous and the discrete (Ricoeur 1970; Friedman 1988). It is, therefore, positioned to orient a practitioner who must deal with both worlds at once.

Notes

1 *Papers on Technique* does not pull together scattered contributions bearing on the subject; it is a consecutive series of installments written between 1911 and 1915 that chart in real time the progressive discovery of the ingredients of psychoanalytic treatment. The series of papers, supplemented by six other technique papers, was ultimately published along with metapsychology papers as a book, *Zur Technik der Psychoanalyse und zur Metapsychologie* (Freud, 1924). Although the tone of the *Papers* is didactic and deceptively settled, each one of the series is just the report of that moment—one stage of an ongoing investigation that takes its leave from suggestion, catharsis, and dream interpretation, and journeys onward to psychoanalysis proper. Although Freud uses an exploratory question-and-answer style that elsewhere serves as a teaching device for expounding already achieved conclusions, in *Papers* this is not a rhetorical artifice, and its progression reveals it as Freud's conversation with himself. The book is best understood by reading the individual papers consecutively as though they were a

file of undoctored laboratory notes, recording the attitudes and behaviors that were found to turn on or turn off the new psychoanalytic phenomenon. The overall discovery required a progressive working out of puzzles and challenges presented by patients' behaviors. Most of the discoveries were learned from untoward consequences of analyst actions that would thenceforth be regarded as errors. Freud conveyed this experimental data in the form of warnings of the sort "If you do such-and-such, you will experience the following difficulties." The ways Freud works out the dilemmas constitute psychoanalytic technique. The "mistakes" are mostly natural behaviors of any therapist. That fact reveals the unique character of psychoanalysis and explains a peculiarity of *Papers* that has misled many commentators: It is assumed that, no matter what it's called, a list of warnings about mistakes cannot be a primary text on technique. But this *is* the primary text on technique, and it does proceed very largely—though not exclusively—by saying what not to do, and then providing a way of thinking that makes that discipline feel reasonable. As Freud works out the reasonableness of the odd interaction, the nature of the analytic interaction and the analytic process gradually comes into view. His solutions are conveyed in reproducible images, pithy phrases, and colorful metaphors for analysts to use as reminders of how to evoke an analytic process and avoid scuttling it. (Unfortunately, these terms and metaphors are often more memorable than their original meanings.) Two of the hallmarks of psychoanalytic technique are apparent here: its inhibition of natural response, and its paradoxical ideals. Freud published this progressive series of papers together as a book, the unmodified early solutions sitting side-by-side with later revisions, leaving the impression that an analyst must replace his social responses with several difficult and contradictory attitudes, and Freud sometimes says as much (see Friedman, 1991a, 2008, 2009). It is sometimes necessary to look behind Freud's rhetoric. If instead of being read as a record of Freud's own mistakes, *Papers on Technique* is read as random corrections of miscellaneous howlers perpetrated by stupid or unethical students, reining them in with rigid rules to match their dull wit (as Freud did indeed sometimes suggest), a unique insight into the discovery and rationale of psychoanalytic treatment will be lost. To counteract this, educators should make use of Ellman's astute, paragraph-by-paragraph commentary to *Papers* (1991), which is ingeniously accompanied by a point-for-point comparison with some contemporary theorists. Ellman's reading is very close to my own, though he retains a bit more of what generations have layered over the original meaning of working through.

2 Strachey's misunderstanding of Freud's message goes beyond a single word. In this paragraph, Freud first says that the analyst apprises the patient of the resistance. Freud's verb is *mitteilt*. Further down, Freud writes that the analyst should realize that it isn't sufficient to name the resistance (the verb is *benennen*). In other words, the analyst has *apprised* the patient of the resistance by *naming* it. Then, in effect, Freud wants to say in the second edition that this activity of the analyst (*mitteilen* by *benennen*, or apprising by naming), while alerting the patient to the resistance, leaves the resistance still unknown, or unfamiliar (the adjective is *unbekannt*). The patient will yet need the actual experience of the drive that feeds the resistance, and only then, presumably, will he have become acquainted with it.

Instead of following the logic of this passage, Strachey first promotes *mitteilt* to *acquainted*, and then ignores the further specification that it is mere naming. That specification should have sent him back to retranslate *mitteilt*, but he lets it stand as *acquainted*, which, then, renders senseless Freud's substitution of *unknown* for *known* a few lines below. In short, it is Strachey's own mistake that forces him to "correct" Freud. In contrast, Riviere, in her translation (Freud, 1924), gets it exactly right.

3 Some people associate "acquaint" mainly with the word "acquaintance," as in "He's not really a friend—just an acquaintance." But, as the *Oxford English Dictionary* indicates, being acquainted specifies empirical knowledge, not superficiality.

4 Actually, this distinction precisely reflects one of the changes undergone by the concept of resistance in the course of these papers. Originally "resistance" designated a phenomenon that the analyst did know by (bitter) acquaintance. He could feel it in his muscles (so to speak) as it pulled against him when he tried to drag traumatic memories out of repression. Had Freud retained that original sense of resistance from pre-psychoanalytic treatment, Schafer's criticism of the term (1992) would be well founded: "resistance" would simply reflect Freud's countertransference. But Schafer's criticism is not valid against the radically changed concept in the mature psychoanalysis established by Freud in 1914. Indeed, Freud's new meaning is exactly opposite to the one Schafer criticized, since it is designed to bolster the analyst's *patience* while he lets the analysand be the one who feels the struggle. It is a testimonial to the strength of the age-old misunderstanding that even a fair and empathic reader like Schafer finds the "pressuring sense" of the term in his close reading of this paper, and can allow only one point at which a "slight but significant revision of wording. . . [is] the beginning of his transition to the modern understanding of the idea" (p. 225). It is not a slight revision of wording; it is the sense of the whole paper—indeed of the whole book. Schafer's "modern meaning" is the express meaning for which the term *working through* was devised.

5 Freud seems to have been straining his eyes to spot an organic, shape-shifting power within the seemingly ideational or intellectual new treatment he had discovered. I have the impression that he could not mollify his own skepticism until he identified an engine within the new treatment equivalent to the old blast of hypnotic catharsis so obviously commensurate with its claimed effect. He knew that discovery was his main interest, not treatment, and it would be all too easy for him to gloss over the question of healing. At the end of this paper, almost as an aside to himself, Freud adds (with a sigh?) that he has at last found that sort of force in the concept of "working through" (p. 156). How far he would have been from being able to check off the missing explosive factor if "working through" merely meant patiently wearing down a resistance by repeated interpretations. In passing, one may observe that Freud's biologism is not confined to a hypothetical and presumably discredited energy hypothesis, but extends to the commonsense experience of push and torment and the stubborn strength of motivation. "Working through" is better thought of as "suffering through" than as diligent repetition.

6 Brenner attempted to circumvent that difficulty by allowing all psychic phenomena to be simultaneously flexible and formed: "compromise formation" (see Friedman, 2011). But if this formula were carried to its logical conclusion and all determinate parts, all structures and levels of awareness, were erased, the mind would be a featureless continuum. About such a mind all we could say is that everything about it expresses everything else about it. (In reality, most process theories smuggle defined entities back into the mind in the form of enduring dramas called fantasies.)

References

Bergson, H. (2007). *Matter and Memory*, transl. N.M. Paul & W.S. Palmer. New York: Cosimo.

Bion, W. (1962). The psycho-analytic study of thinking. *International Journal of Psychoanalysis*, 43: 306–310.

Breuer, J. & Freud, S. (1893–1895). *Studies on Hysteria. S.E.*, 2. London: Hogarth Press.

Bruner, J. (1990). *Acts of Meaning*. Cambridge: Harvard University Press.

Bucci, W. (2002). From subsymbolic to symbolic and back: Therapeutic impact of the referential process. In R. Lasky (Ed.), *Symbolization and Desymbolization: Essays in Honor of Norbert Freedman* (pp. 50–74). New York: Other Press.

Ellman, S.T. (1991). *Freud's Technique Papers: A Contemporary Perspective*. Northvale, NJ: Aronson.

Faimberg, H. (1996). Listening to listening. *International Journal of Psychoanalysis, 77*: 667–677.

Fonagy, P., Gergeley, G., Jurist, L., & Target, M. (2002). *Affect Regulation, Mentalization, and the Development of the Self*. New York: Other Press.

Freud, S. (1911–1915). Papers on technique. *S.E., 12*: 91–171. London: Hogarth Press.

Freud, S. (1914g). Remembering, repeating and working-through. *S.E., 12*:147–156. London: Hogarth Press.

Freud, S. (1918). Erinnern, Wiederholen und Durcharbeiten. In *Sammlung kleiner Schriften zur Neurosenlehre* 4:441–452. Leipzig & Vienna: H. Heller.

Freud, S. (1922). Erinnern, Wiederholen und Durcharbeiten. In *Sammlung kleiner Schriften zur Neurosenlehre* 4:441–452 (2nd edn). Vienna: Internationaler Psychoanalytischer Verlag.

Freud, S. (1924). Erinnern, Wiederholen und Durcharbeiten. In *Zur Technik der Psychoanalyse und zur Metapsycholgie* (pp. 109–119). Vienna: Internationaler Psychoanalytischer Verlag.

Freud, S. (1924). Further recommendations in the technique of psychoanalysis: Recollection, repetition and working through, J. Riviere (transl. and ed.). *Collected Papers*, 2: 366–376. London: Hogarth Press.

Freud, S. (1925). Erinnern, Wiederholen und Durcharbeiten. *Gesammelte Schriften*, 6:109–119. Vienna: Internationaler Psychoanalytischer Verlag.

Freud, S. (1937c). Analysis terminable and interminable. *S.E., 23*: 216–253. London: Hogarth Press.

Friedman, L. (1982). Sublimation. In: S.L. Gilman (Ed.), *Introducing Psychoanalytic Theory* (pp. 68–76). New York: Bruner/Mazel.

Friedman, L. (1988). *The Anatomy of Psychotherapy*. Hillsdale, NJ: Analytic Press.

Friedman, L. (1989). Hartmann's *Ego Psychology and the Problem of Adaptation. Psychoanalytic Quarterly, 58*: 526–550.

Friedman, L. (1991a). A reading of Freud's *Papers on Technique. Psychoanalytic Quarterly, 60*: 564–595.

Friedman, L. (1991b). On the therapeutic action of Loewald's theory. In G.I. Fogel (Ed.), *The Work of Hans Loewald: An Introduction and Commentary* (pp. 91–104)/Northvale, NJ: Aronson.

Friedman, L. (1999). Why is reality a troubling concept? *Journal of the American Psychoanalytic Association, 47*: 401–425.

Friedman, L. (2002). Symbolizing as abstraction: Its role in psychoanalytic treatment. In R. Lasky (Ed.), *Symbolization and Desymbolization: Essays in Honor of Norbert Freedman* (pp. 204–230). New York: Other Press.

Friedman, L. (2007). Who needs theory of therapeutic action? *Psychoanalytic Quarterly, 76*(Suppl.): 1635–1662.

Friedman, L. (2008). A renaissance for Freud's *Papers on Technique. Psychoanalytic Quarterly, 77*: 1031–1044.

Friedman, L. (2009). Freud's technique: More from experience than theory. *Psychoanalytic Quarterly, 78*: 913–924.

Friedman, L. (2011). Charles Brenner: A practitioner's theorist. *Journal of the American Psychoanalytic Association, 59*: 679–700.

Friedman, M. (2000). *A Parting of the Ways: Carnap, Cassirer, and Heidegger.* Chicago, IL: Open Court.

Gendlin, E.T. (1962). *Experiencing and the Creation of Meaning: A Philosophical and Psychological Approach to the Subjective.* New York: Macmillan.

Gill, M.M. (1963). *Topography and Systems in Psychoanalytic Theory.* Psychological Issues Monograph 10. New York: International Universities Press.

Glover, E. (1931). The therapeutic effect of inexact interpretation: A contribution to the theory of suggestion. *International Journal of Psychoanalysis, 12*: 397–411.

Gordon, P.E. (2010). *Continental Divide: Heidegger, Cassirer, Davos.* Cambridge, MA: Harvard University Press.

Hartmann, H. (1951). Technical implications of ego psychology. In *Essays on Ego Psychology: Selected Problems in Psychoanalytic Theory* (pp. 142–154). New York: International Universities Press, 1964.

Kohut, H. (1971). *The Analysis of the Self: A Systematic Approach to the Psychoanalytic Treatment of Narcissistic Personality Disorder.* New York: International Universities Press.

Kris, E. (1975). On preconscious mental processes. In L.M. Newman (Ed.), *Selected Papers of Ernst Kris* (pp. 217–236). New Haven, CT: Yale University Press.

Loewald, H.W. (1960). On the therapeutic action of psychoanalysis. *International Journal of Psychoanalysis, 41*: 16–33.

Mead, G.H. (1934). *Mind, Self, and Society from the Standpoint of a Social Behaviorist,* C.W. Morris (Ed.). Chicago, IL: University of Chicago Press.

Merleau-Ponty, M. (1989). *The Phenomenology of Perception,* C. Smith (, transl.). London: Routledge.

Meyerson, E. (1930). *Identity and Reality,* K. Loewenberg (transl.). London: Allen & Unwin, 1930.

Rapaport, D. (1960). *The Structure of Psychoanalytic Theory: A Systematizing Attempt.* Psychological Issues Monograph 6. New York: International Universities Press.

Ricouer, P. (1970). *Freud and Philosophy: An Essay on Interpretation,* D. Savage transl.). New Haven: Yale University Press.

Russell, B. (1940). *An Inquiry into Meaning and Truth.* London: Allen & Unwin.

Schafer, R. (1992). Resistance: The wrong story? In *Retelling a Life: Narration and Dialogue in Psychoanalysis* (pp. 219–247). New York: Basic Books.

Schlesinger, H.J. (2013). *The Texture of Treatment: On the Matter of Psychoanalytic Technique.* Hillsdale, NJ: Analytic Press.

Schur, M. (1966). *The Id and the Regulatory Principles of Functioning.* New York: International Universities Press.

Stern, D.B. (1997). *Unformulated Experience: From Dissociation to Imagination in Psychoanalysis.* Hillsdale, NJ: Analytic Press.

Stern, D.N. (2010). *Forms of Vitality: Exploring Dynamic Experience in Psychology, the Arts, Psychotherapy, and Development.* Oxford: Oxford University Press.

Waelder, R. (1976). The principle of multiple function: Observations on overdetermination. In S. Guttman (Ed.), *Psychoanalysis: Observation, Theory, Application. Selected Papers of Robert Waelder* (pp. 68–83). New York: International Universities Press.

6   The Cunning of the Deed

Laurence Kahn

"Remembering, Repeating and Working-Through" is a pivotal text. A pivot between the first and second Freudian topographic models, contemporary with the treatment of the Wolf Man, it is stretched between "The Dynamics of Transference" (1912b) and *Beyond the Pleasure Principle* (1920g). It also inherits the renewed views of "On Narcissism: An Introduction" (Freud, 1914c) regarding the mechanism of repression and the formation of resistance. One could almost consider this text as a milestone, born at a time when Freud sensed the great upheaval that would take place after "Mourning and Melancholia" (1917e)—i.e. as he was measuring the probable extent of the negative therapeutic reaction, and attempting to unravel the entanglements resulting from the action of hatred and the irruption of acting-in during treatment.

However, while the term "repetition compulsion" makes its appearance for the first time in this text, repetition is not yet the basic binding activity and the preparatory function that, in *Beyond the Pleasure Principle*, possibly gives the psychic apparatus the capacity to deal with excessive amounts of excitation and to establish the domination of the pleasure principle (Freud, 1920g, p. 62). Besides, the primary purpose of this paper is not metapsychological. It is meant to be technical. It responds in some way to the concern that Freud expressed to Pfister in June 1910: not only is the transference "our cross," but "the unyielding stubbornness of the illness"[1], the one that made him renounce suggestion, cannot be entirely eliminated by psychoanalysis, but only limited. The transference, which "feeds on what is left of it," is its manifestation. However, this phenomenon is quite difficult to handle: "The rules often break down, one must adjust to the singularity of the patient and not try to totally renounce his personal note."[2] Does this mean that "Remembering, Repeating and Working-Through", following on from "Recommendations to Physicians Practising Analysis" (1912e), is like a set of rules, or at least guidelines, a sort of manual for navigating by sight, allowing one to spot the stumbling blocks? In fact, the first title of this text was "*Weitere Ratschläge zur Technik der Psychoanalyse (II): Erinnern, Wiederholen und Durcharbeiten*" ("Further Advice on the Technique of Psychoanalysis (II): Remembering, Repeating and Working-Through"). In other words, these were new recommendations on how to "tame" the will of the disease.

DOI: 10.4324/9781003458340-6

The difficulty is indeed always the same: "to pass the bridle of the transference to the wild drives" is to try to neutralize this *Gegenwille*; this will to "go against," described as early as 1892 in "A Case of Successful Treatment by Hypnotism" (Freud, 1892). Let us recall that, strictly speaking, in this pre-analytic text the "contrast representation" does not prefigure the repressed representation. This uncontrollable product of a will that leads to generating precisely that which one is fighting against—such as Emmy's tongue-lashing—results from the clash between the projects and the inhibited in principle, scenarios of their failure, the latter rushing into the vacancy of anxious expectation. These scenarios are indeed "stored up and enjoy an unsuspected existence in a sort of shadow kingdom, till they emerge like bad spirits and take control of the body, which is as a rule under the orders of the predominant ego-consciousness" p. 127). Thus motility ends up serving the counter-will.

This model of an act performed by a body that escapes the control of censorship remains one of the strong figures of the overflow of the therapeutic territory. Two decades after renouncing hypnosis, and after taking countless theoretical steps, the same savagery of drives had still to be curbed, but this time by putting its strength to good use: it would be allowed to operate on condition that it did not overstep the limits of the field of action allocated to it by the analytic situation: that is to say, the transference. Like the dream scene (dubbed, just as the transference, a *Tummelplatz*— a playground), the drives' energy will have almost total freedom in this "place to frolic," whereby they should give access to the hidden part of the pathogenic impulses. Thus, just as dream analysis was the royal road to the unconscious, transference and its interpretation would be the royal road to the most opaque zones of the analysand's psychic life. The lock placed at the pole directing outward motor action makes of this delimited space a place where repressed impulses can be satisfied in a tempered way, even if their content is extremely virulent.

Distortion is another legacy from *The Interpretation of Dreams* and a major entry point to the theory of the psychic act. Just as "Dreaming has taken the place of action" (Freud, 1900a, p. 124) so that the forbidden contents are disguised, so Freud ascribes the power and complexity of the transferential phenomenon to the work of distortion. A point made in "The Dynamics of Transference," where he emphasizes that

[t]he longer an analytic treatment lasts and the more clearly the patient realizes that distortions of the pathogenic material cannot by themselves offer any protection against its being uncovered, the more consistently does he make use of the one sort of distortion which obviously affords him the greatest advantages – distortion through transference.

(Freud, 1912b, p. 104.)

The traces of this conception of transferential disguise are deep in "Remembering, Repeating and Working-Through". Not only does the transference never give access to the infantile arrangement itself, since the person of the analyst is only a "cover" used by the actualization of desire; as in screen-memories, the cover distorts in order to accomplish the intentionality of the unconscious formations, the initial substratum of the ground remaining unknown.[3] Also, necessarily subjected to the antagonistic games of fulfillment and prohibition, of pleasure and disappointment, transference juxtaposes with resistance. This explains why, as in the case of the dream, only the attention paid to the "psychic surface," that is to say, to all that emerges and is propelled towards consciousness as disguised offshoots, will make it possible to cross the barrier of resistance against becoming aware of the libidinal scenario.

*

So be it, but this works only as long as the transference remains wisely within the limits allotted by the "talking cure." In other words, as long as the "transference on the person" does not supplant the "transference on the spoken word";[4] as long as the zone of reflexivity linked to the cathexis of discourse and words is not eclipsed by the cathexis of the link to the object-analyst. This is especially so if such cathexis is destined to ward off narcissistic distress due to the failure of the primary links, the consequence being the impossibility of coping with the wave of excitation aroused by their transferential revival.

Yet, sometimes the transference is a sleepwalker, so that instead of remaining "a mild and unpronounced positive transference" (Freud 1912b, p. 151), suddenly its excess, whether of love or hate, crosses a threshold. Instead of soberly using speech in the service of recollection, transference triggers an action in the world. This for Freud is not a new discovery: since Dora's interruption of treatment the file on transferential action has never been closed. With Dora, not only did Freud understand that the intrapsychic structure of this action is not made of the same dough as the symptomatic act, but he also learned the hard way that the said action begins by operating on the analyst's "unconscious feelings"[5] before it leads to a proper act. This is how Dora fulfilled, even seduced, Freud by offering him with "eagerness" a part of the pathogenic material, even though she was "preparing the rupture with another part of this same material."[6] She has gratified him so well that he misses the first warning signs, which are nevertheless present in the repetition of the dream of the fire. But Freud's attention is captured by the hallucinatory vivacity of her recollections, which masks the joint revival of incendiary love and of revenge. Until the moment when Dora inflicts on Freud, in action (*sie agierte*), the same slap she once gave to Mr. K.

From this episode the first chapter of our method was born: "repetition" in transferential action during the treatment defeats the "reproduction" of memories and fantasies[7]—the vividness of the recollections can itself be in the service of resistance (and it will appear that the same is true of dreams that accumulate from session to session, whose unconscious aim is in fact to forbid any elaboration under the guise of oneiric richness). Hence the second chapter of our method, which advocates slowing down: "Where one manages to include the transference in the analysis at an early stage, the latter unfolds more slowly and becomes less clear, but it is better protected against sudden and invincible resistance."[8] This gives rise to a third chapter, perhaps less immediately visible, concerning the proper use of countertransference and its interpretative force. For what did Freud say to Dora when, fifteen months later, she returned affected by a facial neuralgia? "I don't know what kind of help she wanted to ask me for, but I promised to forgive her for depriving me of the satisfaction of freeing her more radically from her suffering."[9] After analyzing his disappointment and, no doubt, the hostile feelings provoked by the annihilation of his therapeutic and theoretical hopes, Freud is able to give Dora a transference interpretation nourished by this countertransferential experience. He then ties the transference of Dora's hatred for Mr. K onto himself with the punishment that she inflicts on herself in return, a neuralgia in the form of a slap—this at the moment when the resentment is re-actualized in the midst of the exciting news of Freud's professorship. In order to free Dora from her painful self-punishment, there is, therefore, no way other than the promise to forgive her for having satisfied her hatred by destroying the treatment. Let us note that Freud is, thus, led to interpret the action of a superego that he has not yet begun to absolutely theorize.

The echo of Dora's "*sie agierte*" is powerful in "Remembering, Repeating and Working-Through" as Freud specifies that when the transference becomes hostile, recollection immediately gives way to action and as he envisages the modalities of such action. Just as the sensory presentation in the dream had put him on the path of the mechanism of dream "realization"—the hallucinatory presence wins the dreamer's credence by replacing the optative of the wish—so, here too, presence allows for the realization of the transferential act in the present tense of the interpersonal relationship. As Jean-Luc Donnet (2009, p. 211) writes, with "Remembering, Repeating and Working-Through" Freud makes "of the *Agieren*—i.e. the enacted repetition of transference—a kind of new royal road", upon which, of course, falls the shadow of the repetition compulsion and its "unwished-for exactitude", but which draws its remarkable productivity in the treatment from its position at the interface of the intrapsychic conflict and the relation between the two protagonists in the analytic situation. With the notion of action by means of speech, the Freudian conception is, thus, enriched with "the most *radical* actualization of a transference that confuses past and present" (*ibid.*).

Such actualization does not spare the analyst's intrapsychic movements. If his "unconscious sensitivity" is engaged in the interpsychic relation, it is because, besides the affective and semantic contents expressed in the discourse addressed to him, the analyst is indeed unknowingly touched by expressive forms that colonize the field of enunciation beyond the explicit semiological markers. In other words, he is at grips with the perlocutionary activity of discourse, in the form of that part of doing which operates through the intermediary of speech, managing to bypass the conscious sphere of representations. It is even the embedding of this action of words within the "piece of activity"[10] that is the drive that makes speech the formidable servant of the "weapons of the past". Hostage to this clandestine activity is the countertransference.

It is understandable, then, why in "Remembering, Repeating and Working-Through" Freud speaks at such length of the old method of hypnosis. In this nostalgic description of the good old days, where recollection was all the more ideal as resistance was ignored, where chronology was all the more intact since the attention of the protagonists was centered on the symptom and the temporal circumstances of its formation, the "reproduction" that was sought in order to obtain abreaction occurred in a controlled manner. Moreover, the patient never seemed to confuse the ancient situation with the present one. Thus, one could count on the "conscious activity" to unroll the psychic processes at the origin of the pathology to their end. In this sense, the "reproduction" benefited from the ignorance of the cunning censorship and of the unconscious. It also benefited from the extreme simplicity of the model explaining the transposition of unconscious processes into conscious ones. But most of all, it benefited from the remarkable illusion attached to the power of hypnosis. It is precisely this power of action of the analyst that was belied by facts. The recollections obtained were only "mnemonic fictions." Invoking the unconscious fantasy became mandatory. But suggestion remained the Achilles' heel of psychoanalysis.

Now, suggestion means action on the part of the analyst. Suggestion also points at the the analyst's power, depending on the use he makes of the idealization of which he is the object, something Freud has in mind when writing "Narcissism. An Introduction" (1914c). Finally, suggestion means depriving the patient of the major action of becoming conscious: the moment when the invisible censorship is commuted into a decision, analysis "replacing [the] repression by [a] judgment of condemnation" (Freud, 1909b, p. 145, footnote; Freud, 1923e, p. 145). Obtaining the surrender of the will through the exercise of a seduction that draws its authority from that once exerted by powerful childhood figures (Freud, 1921c, pp. 115, 127), the influencing analyst short-circuits the slow work of working-through and, in so doing, leaves the narcissistic sources of resistance intact.

Moreover, if the time before seemed "so smooth," it is also because the analyst was unaware that he himself was subjected to the occult effect of the patient's words, not always having the possibility of detecting and promptly giving form to this subterranean movement. Attentive to the affects explicitly expressed by his patient, misled by the manifest experience, he does not see that it is he who is subjugated by the patient's action and his use of speech.

*

A patient once said to me: "If I had been a boy, would I be so sure that my daughter is my mother?" This woman was fighting toe to toe against madness, against the start in life that had made her the child of a mad mother who terrorized her daughters into submission. She owed her survival to flight and to the obstinacy of her denial: this story was not hers. But when she gave birth to a daughter, she was overcome by the certainty that she would destroy her as her mother had destroyed her sisters. And her spontaneous gestures as a mother, dominated by this belief, became, one by one, impossible gestures; as for the calculated gestures—she calculated a lot—they were just as impossible, because they all went in the same direction, restarting her story all over again. Punishment, expiation: her guilt for having survived by abandoning the others found in every detail of her daily life the motive for the punishment that would have relieved her, had she not transformed this life into a hell. During the first two years of her analysis, four times a week, she began each session with a list of the disasters that were on the horizon at the time, and ended it with the threat to interrupt her treatment.

"If I had been a boy ..." she says to me, and I hear inwardly: "If the mother I have in me had been the mother of a boy, would she burden me as much?" And I also hear: "If I were the father of my daughter instead of the mother, would I burden her as much?" "No, it wouldn't have made any difference," this woman continues, "because my daughter is really my mother. When I see her, I see my mother, pretentious, rude, too much make-up." So, nothing changes. Yet the question, in its very form, represents a change, an unprecedented mobility, the harbinger that bisexual positions might be acknowledged. The question appears to me as an unexpected continuation of an interpretation communicated shortly before, about the masculine features of her favorite sister. But most importantly, it is perhaps my own guilt at not being able to interrupt the infernal cycle of violence and excitation in which she engages me, that draws me into a cloud of thoughts: nothing will ever change ... I won't be able to do it. ... Later, maybe change will come; later ... when I grow up, something will change and it will happen. But it won't happen, I know it ... And what about me, if I had been a boy?

I don't know how the excitement, the punishment, and the girlishness added up. I only know that, faced with the most painful prophecies, I was able to wait for the sequel, that is, the double bottom of the prophecy, to emerge. But when this woman told me in detail the horrors she proffered to her daughter, she was almost certain to get an interpretation, because I could not help trying to make her "understand" ... The *transferential acting* consisted in the way that she had of making me speak. And always in the same way, so that I would protect the child that she had been from the mother that she was today. It is in this knot, so openly and so wildly homosexual, that appeared to me little by little the loving and violent provocation, secretly addressed to a father able to take us out of our feminine *tête-à-tête*. *And what about me, if I had been a boy* ... Of the sudden departure of this father, very little had been said until this day.

In line with that example, let us simply recall the conclusion of "The Dynamics of the Transference": the drive impulses "want" and do; and if the transferential *Agierenwollen*, which unceasingly demands to be actualized, that is, to do things, is still our best tool, it is because "it is impossible to destroy anyone *in absentia* or *in effigie*" (Freud, 1912b, p. 108). "Remembering, Repeating and Working-Through" literally seizes the bouncing ball, definitively opening the fourth chapter of our method: not only is it not possible to kill an enemy who is absent or not close enough, but, what is more, the analyst merely has at his disposal the palpation of psychic surfaces, both the patient's and his own, to discern the unconscious movements at work underneath.

We can only smile, therefore, when Freud affirms in "Remembering, Repeating and Working-Through" that the final goal of the treatment remains "unchanged." From the moment that the heart of the treatment is conceived in terms of action, whole areas of theory and practice are redirected, beginning with the theory of the birth of psychic agencies, which will also soon be profoundly modified. This movement is initiated by the description of the mechanism of repression proposed in "Narcissism. An Introduction",[11] which makes the organ of censorship, the ego ideal, an agent formed from a series of identificatory actions. Subsequently, it will become increasingly clear that the formation of the agencies proceeds from actions that determine their division and function.

We must therefore salute Strachey for his decision to translate *Instanz* to *agency*: we are indeed in a model where the act founds the different institutions of the psychic person, without the agent being the subject. But what about the translation of *agieren* to *acting out*? Why not keep the "to act" that, for example, renders *Agierenwollen* very well in the expression "*seeking to act*"?[12]

*

This question affected a good part of the subsequent analytic literature. Witness to this is the distinction made by Jean Laplanche and J.-B. Pontalis in *Vocabulaire de la psychanalyse* (1967/1973) between "*mise en acte*" ("putting into action"), whose German equivalent given at the head of the chapter is *agieren*, and "acting out", whose register would be different, "even opposed to the field of transference", insofar as recourse to acting out can be seen "as an attempt to break the analytic relation" (1973, p. 5). To what extent, moreover, does this distinction emanate, even partially, from an earlier work by Piera Aulagnier and J.-B. Pontalis? In their text "Reflections on action and enactment in their relation to the analytic transference" (1963), the diffusion of which has remained rather limited, these authors question the nature of the action designated by the verb *agieren* in "Remembering, Repeating and Working-Through". Is it a question of "acting out" or of "transference"? Although the question seems to be addressed mainly to ego-psychologists—"psychoanalysts often tend to qualify as acting out everything emanating from their patient that escapes their grasp," they write referring to Phyllis Greenacre,[13] its source is actually from Lacan's contemporary reflection on anxiety, the object of that year's seminar. Namely, in his session of January 23, 1963, Lacan (1963, pp. 144–146) posits that "everything that is acting out is the opposite of 'taking action' (*passage à l'acte*)." Rereading Freud's text "On the Psychogenesis of a Case of Female Homosexuality" (Freud, 1920a), he continues: "If the suicide attempt [of the young girl] is a taking action (*passage à l'acte*), the whole adventure with the lady of doubtful reputation who is brought to the function of supreme object is an acting out", where "acting out" maintains a necessary relationship with the object *a* and the problematic of castration. Yet, this poses a problem in the eyes of Aulagnier and Pontalis, "the term '*passage à l'acte*' [being] usually, in the French psychoanalytical milieu, considered as translating the term 'acting out'" (Aulagnier and Pontalis, 1963, p. 13). Hence their proposal: to name the girl's suicide attempt "acting out" while the homosexual passion will be called "enacted transference" (*transfert agi*).

By introducing this notion of "enacted transference", the authors aim at two things: to revisit the problem of translation in the *Standard Edition*, which rendered "*sondern er agiere es*" by "but [he/she] acts it out" (Freud, 1914g, p. 150), and, in doing so, to re-specify the divergence between repression with the return of the repressed in the form of an act, and foreclosure (*forclusion*) where what is "rejected," in the absence of any symbolization, reappears outside in a forcing of the real. At stake, therefore, are the psychic mechanisms at play in neurosis and in psychosis, respectively.

Thus, if Lacan considers the enamoration of the young homosexual girl as an acting out, it is because, according to him, not only does this love take its source in the powerful attachment of this girl to her father, the disappointment inflicted by the birth of a young brother, and the phallic problematic of resentment and revenge, but it is above all because the girl's amorous conduct is displayed for all to see—"the acting out [being] essentially something, in the subject's conduct, that shows itself." And what is shown in the scandalous publicity of this relationship, "is that she would have wanted a child from the father" (Lacan, 1963, p. 145). Having failed in the realization of her desire, the girl, who behaves like a lover, realizes it in another way, posing herself in what she does not have, the phallus, and giving it to show that she has it. This demonstrative feature of the acting out, this address, are, in Lacan's eyes, consubstantially linked to a wild, undomesticated transference (1963, p. 148) which at once veils and unveils the scene of the fantasy.

On the other hand, Lacan sees in the fall from the bridge a "taking action" (*passage à l'acte*) because the suicidal gesture, which occurs immediately after the young girl, in the company of the beloved lady, has met the father and his furious gaze, this gesture therefore literally takes the neurotic configuration in reverse. The young girl is brutally confronted with the law which is presented in the terrible gaze of the father—a look which devastates her, all specular support being thus refused to her. The fantasy is shattered and, with it, the scene in which the subject found her identificatory consistency by showing herself in the guise of the lady's "servant knight." Through the effect of the father's annihilating gaze, she is suddenly "rejected, thrown out of the scene" (Lacan, 1963, pp. 129–133), her "taking action" (*passage à l'acte*) corresponding to the desperate attempt to reconstitute in the real the incestuous scene that has lost its symbolic marking: *niederkommen* (falling from the bridge) means both falling and "giving birth." For Lacan, the *"passage à l'acte"* is considered as that which, subtracted from the symbolic, "reappears in the real", and does so "erratically, that is to say, in relations of resistance without transference" (Lacan, 1966, p. 388).

Aulagnier and Pontalis, therefore, contest the fact that Lacan can oppose acting out and *"passage à l'acte"* (taking action). Not only is *"passage à l'acte"* in principle the French translation of "acting out," but, moreover, its strong psychiatric connotation is very embarrassing. This is why they keep the English term "acting out" to designate the act of the suicidal gesture, and they introduce the notion of "enacted transference" to qualify the homosexual love relationship. In their view, this relationship, though being an action, can, in fact, be reinserted into the transferential discourse of the subject—the other being at the center of the address in the "enacted transference." Conversely, the *acting out* is not addressed to the other. It is situated beyond what the subject can or cannot say. Appearing as absurd, "as a fragment of an 'Other Scene' projected onto that of the world," the acting out testifies to the fact that the ego is totally offside, which triggers a feeling of stupor.

Granted, for Aulagnier and Pontalis the challenge is to describe, in metapsychological terms and based on detailed clinical examples, the relations between these two forms of action and castration, its symbolic marks and anxiety.[14] Nevertheless, the debate with Lacan reveals first of all the impact of translation. We can see this when we open the English translation of the *Vocabulaire de la psychanalyse* (Laplanche and Pontalis, 1967). Indeed, in its English version (*The Language of Psycho-Analysis*, 1973), on the one hand, the item *acting out* is presented as the equivalent of the German *agieren*, whereas in the French original, as has already been mentioned, *agieren* was referred to the item *"mise en acte"*. On the other hand, the notion of *"mise-en-scène"* (so noted in *The Language of Psycho-Analysis*) appears in the item *phantasy*, under the aspect of the scene of fantasy.[15]

What can we learn from this game of the four corners? Without doubt, Aulagnier and Pontalis were already extremely sensitive to the fate of the notion of acting out in the treatment, in particular in Greenacre (1950), for whom a low tolerance to frustration, associated with serious childhood trauma, would determine a very early disturbance in the relation between speech and action, a disturbance noticeable in the poor investment of speech in the analytic situation.

Indeed, five years later, at the 25th International Congress of the IPA, one could clearly see what had gradually come to occupy the field of *acting out* in the Anglo-Saxon world, just as the notion of *enactment* was emerging as a possible solution. Anna Freud (1968) shows, in particular, how the treatment of character neuroses with delinquent behavior, as well as of pre-psychotic, psychotic and paranoid states, and of patients suffering from addiction, had modified the psychoanalytical value of the notion of "act." As transference interpretation became an indispensable technical means, "re-living in the transference" was taken for granted. As a result, the term "acting out" referred less and less to repetition in the transference and was reserved for "the re-enactment of the past outside the analysis." In her opinion, this change in usage was regrettable "because, on the one hand, it obscures the initially clear distinction between recollection and repetition and, on the other hand, it conceals the differences between the various forms of 'acting out'." In her view, there is a close link between "the qualitative and quantitative properties of the 'forgotten past'" and the modalities of its return during the analytic experience. Sometimes, this revival takes the form of a simple memory, or it occurs in the form of re-experiencing, re-living, re-enacting, or it returns in various forms of controlled or uncontrolled repetition. Let us add that Julien Rouart (1968)—author of one of the two reports to the 28th Congress of Psychoanalysts of Romance Languages, entitled "Acting (*Agir*) and the analytic process," and contributor in the same IPA Congress as Anna Freud—insists on the fact that *acting out* cannot be assimilated to the impulsivity of the *"passage à l'acte"*, underlining, in turn, the strong psychiatric connotation of the term.

We know how subsequently successful the term *enactment* has been.[16] In the wake of *re-enactment*, used early on by Glover in his "Lectures on technique in psycho-analysis" (Glover, 1927), enactment gradually took on the analytical value of fantasy and its action in a "staging" akin to a dramatic play. Hans Loewald (1975), for instance, sees in the repetition of re-enactment the possibility of reorganizing and reinterpreting the original action according to the parameters of the transferential experience, thus giving full value to the transformative dimension of a dramatic play. The term *enactment* consequently had the immense merit, in Anglo-Saxon literature, of taking the transferential *Agieren* out of the impasse of *acting out*, which, as it came closer to the psychiatric description of the *"passage à l'acte"*, saw its possible ties with symbolization and working-through unravel.

This is certainly what Aulagnier and Pontalis were aiming at when they proposed to use "enacted transference" (*transfert agi*) in cases where the analyst remains the prop of an imaginary transference—even if the latter is "provoked" in the realm—and to reserve the term "acting out" for the cases where the patient tries to find an answer in the real by projecting there the word of the analyst stepping in after the imaginary territory has been shattered.

*

At this point of the debate, what could be more interesting than to return to Freud's text "On the Psychogenesis of a Case of Female Homosexuality"? We can see that, according to him, the girl's suicide attempt must be understood as altogether fulfilling her desire to have a child by the father and her self-punishment. Indeed, if her disappointment has pushed her into homosexuality, her taking action (*passage à l'acte*) simultaneously realizes the victory of desire, since she now "falls" by her father's fault. At no moment, therefore, does Freud distinguish between two forms of action, not even as he describes how, during the treatment, he encounters, under the aspect of defiance, the repetition of the revenge against the father. A resistance, he writes, analogous to that of "a *grande dame* being taken over a museum and glancing through her lorgnon at objects to which she was completely indifferent" (Freud, 1920a, p. 163.) Having thus "transferred" onto Freud her general resentment against men, the young woman's hatred manifests itself in a calm, "stormless" fashion, by rendering vain all the efforts of the analyst.

Neither does Freud distinguish between two modalities of the *Agieren* when he explains this subtly deceptive accomplishment that leads the young woman to "[long] for a man's love and for children" (p. 165). Dreams that are "easily translated"—and, no doubt, this is where the "slight impression" alerting Freud comes from—and which go against the grain of the patient's conscious aims: to get married in order to escape her father's tyranny and to live her real inclinations without hindrance by muzzling her husband. However, these "hypocritical" dreams are indeed part of the *Agieren* in the treatment: here, the psychic act of dreaming repeats the actions by which the young woman deceived her father and, indeed, the dreaming ceases when Freud interprets their unconscious intentionality. In addition to the fact that they were intended to mislead him, these transference dreams also contained a part of seduction aiming to arouse his interest in order to better deceive him later. The two intentions were thus combined: to deceive the father and to please the father—the pleasing being rooted in the infantile desire, and the deceiving coming both from the repression of pleasing and the accomplishment of revenge.

As far as *Agieren* is concerned, the lesson from Dora has, thus, been perfectly learned. What, indeed causes Freud's "slight impression"? The *"leise,"*, with its musical connotation, suggests that the first perception of the patient's *Agieren*, or, rather, the very first clue, took the form of a sensory experience. Is this not what Freud had missed with Dora? And is this not what "Remembering, Repeating and Working-Through" develops, making use of a wide range of vocabulary relating to the act (*Tat, Tätigkeit, Agieren, Wirkung, Wirkungbereich, Aktion, motorisch*), just as the palpation of the patient's psychic surface becomes the tool for perceiving the conflict between the forces of resistance and the reflexive current which should lead to insight?

As one can imagine, the importance given to the senses in the identification of the effects of action will sooner or later seriously confound the differentiation between real and unreal, which is what the "feeling of effective reality"[17] experienced by the Wolf Man suggests, when the question arises of the real or fantasized character of the primitive scene brought back by his dream. Thus, far from making the boundaries between present and past firmer (Freud, 1915a), far from clarifying the gaps between real, unreal, and genuine (Freud, 1914c, p. 167), "Remembering, Repeating and Working-Through" takes us along a path that will soon lead to "The 'Uncanny'".

(translated by Dominique Scarfone)

Notes

1 See Freud & Pfister (1909–1939) Letter 22F, 5 June 1910): "das eigenwillig Unbändigte der Krankheit".

2 "Da lassen die Regeln oft im Stiche, mann wird sich nach der Eigenart des Kranken richten müssen und auch seine persönnliche Note nicht ganz aufgeben wollen."The full English rendition reads: "The transference is indeed a cross. The unyielding stubbornness of the illness, because of which we abandoned indirect suggestion and direct hypnotic suggestion, cannot be entirely eliminated by analysis, but can only be diminished, and its relics make their appearance in the transference. These are generally conspicuous enough, and the rules often let one down, but one must be guided by the patient's character and not entirely give up one's personal note" (Freud, 1954).

3 "The falsified memory is the first of which we are aware; the material of the memory-traces from which it was forged remains unknown to us in its original form" (Freud, 1899a, p. 322.)

4 These opposed terms were introduced by A. Green in "Le langage dans la psychanalyse," in *Langages*, Les Belles Lettres, 1984 (cf., *The Fabric of Affect in the Psychoanalytic Discourse*, postscript, 1999, p. 297: transference on to the speech, transference on to the object) ; see also Jean-Luc Donnet, *La situation analysante*, Paris, PUF, 2005 (*The Analyzing Situation*: transference on to the speech, p. 10).

5 Das unbewußte Fühlen (Freud, 1910a, p. 108. English Translation: Freud, 1910d, p. 144).

6 Freud (1905e) p. 118 "Owing to the readiness with which Dora put one part of the pathogenic material at my disposal during the treatment, I neglected the precaution of looking out for the first signs of transference, which was being prepared in connection with another part of the same material – a part of which I was in ignorance."

7 "In this way the transference took me unawares, and, because of the unknown quantity in me which reminded Dora of Herr K., she took her revenge on me as she wanted to take her revenge on him, and deserted me as she believed herself to have been deceived and deserted by him. Thus she acted out an essential part

of her recollections and phantasies instead of reproducing it in the treatment" (Freud, 1905e, p. 119).

8 *Ibid.*
9 *Ibid.*, p. 122.
10 "No doubt 'in the beginning was the deed' and the word came later; in some circumstances it meant an advance in civilization when deeds were softened into words. But originally the word was magic – a magical act; and it has retained much of its ancient power" (Freud, 1926e, p. 188; Freud, 1915c, p. 122).
11 "the formation of an ideal would be the conditioning factor of repression" (Freud, 1914c, p. 94).
12 Freud, 1912b, p. 108: This struggle between the doctor and the patient, between intellect and instinctual life, between understanding and seeking to act, is played out almost exclusively in the phenomena of transference.
13 *Ibid.*, p. 8; see also Greenacre, 1950.
14 In the lesson of March 20, 1963, Piera Aulagnier is roundly chided by Lacan (1963, pp. 217–219), Pontalis not being mentioned no doubt because of the contemporary process that will lead to the foundation of the Association Psychanalytique de France.
15 *Mise-en-scène"* is the translation retained by J. Derrida (2000, p. 41), after Lacan, for *Darstellung* and the term used by J.- F. Lyotard (1977) to distinguish the primary messages that do not speak and their transcriptions in stagings, about "A Child is Being Beaten"; see also Lacan, 1964, p. 72, as well as the *Seminar X* (Lacan, 1963) on anxiety about the relation between the fantasy and the "seeing."
16 On the further evolution of enactment, see W. Bohleber *et al.*, 2013.
17 *Wirklichkeitsgefühl*, is in "Remembering, Repeating and Working-Through" and repeated in *From the History of an Infantile Neurosis* as "sense of reality" (Freud, 1918b, p. 33).

References

Aulagnier, P. and Pontalis, J.-B. (1963). Réflexions sur l'action et l'agir dans leur relation au transfert analytique. In *Provinciales de Société Française de Psychanalyse*. Paris: Jacques Dupont.

Bohleber, W., Fonagy, P., Jimenez, J.P., Scarfone, D., Varvin, S., & Zysman, S. (2013). Towards a Better Use of Psychoanalytic Concepts: A Model Illustrated Using the Concept of Enactment. *International Journal of Psychoanalysis*, 94(3): 501–530.

Derrida, J. (2000). *États d'âme de la psychanalyse*. Paris: Galilée,

Donnet, J.-L. (2005). *La situation analysante*. Paris: PUP. English translation: *The Analyzing Situation* (2018). New York: Routledge.

Donnet, J.-L. (2009). Entre l'agir et la parole. In *L'humour et la honte*. Paris: PUP.

Freud, A. (1968). Acting Out. *International Journal of Psychoanalysis*, 49: 165–170.

Freud, S. (1892). A Case of Successful Treatment by Hypnotism: With Some Remarks on the Origin of Hysterical Symptoms through 'Counter-Will'. *S.E.*, 1: 115–128. London: Hogarth Press.

Freud, S. (1899a). Screen Memories. *S.E.*, 3: 299–322. London: Hogarth Press.

Freud, S. (1900a). *The Interpretation of Dreams*. *S.E.*, 4–5. London: Hogarth Press.

Freud, S. (1905e). *Fragment of an Analysis of a Case of Hysteria*. *S.E.*, 7: 3–122. London: Hogarth Press.

Freud, S. (1909b). *Analysis of a Phobia in a Five-Year-Old Boy*. *S.E.*, 10: 1–150. London: Hogarth Press.

Freud, S. (1910d). The Future Prospects of Psycho-Analytic Therapy. *S.E.*, *11*:139–152. London: Hogarth Press.

Freud, S. (1910d). Die zukünftigen Chancen der psychoanalytischen Therapie, *Gesammelte Werke*, *8*: 104–115.

Freud, S. (1912b). The Dynamics of Transference. *S.E.*, *12*: 97–108. London: Hogarth Press.

Freud, S. (1914c). On Narcissism: An Introduction. *S.E.*, *14*: 67–102. London: Hogarth Press.

Freud, S. (1914g). Remembering, Repeating and Working-Through, *S.E.*, *12*: 145–156. London: Hogarth Press.

Freud, S. (1915a). Observations on Transference Love, *S.E.*, *12*: 157–171. London: Hogarth Press.

Freud, S. (1915c). Instincts and their Vicissitudes, *S.E.*, *14*: 109–140. London: Hogarth Press.

Freud, S. (1918b). *From the History of an Infantile Neurosis*. *S.E.*, *17*: 11–24. London: Hogarth Press.

Freud, S. (1920g). *Beyond the Pleasure Principle*, *S.E.*, *18*: 1–64. London: Hogarth Press.

Freud, S. (1920a). The Psychogenesis of a Case of Homosexuality in a Woman, *S.E.*, *18*: 145–172. London: Hogarth Press.

Freud, S. (1921c). *Group Psychology and the Analysis of the Ego*. *S.E.*, *18*: 65–144. London: Hogarth Press.

Freud, S. (1923e). The Infantile Genital Organization. *S.E.*, *19*: 139–146. London: Hogarth Press.

Freud, S. (1926e). *The Question of Lay Analysis*, *S.E.*, *20*: 177–258. London: Hogarth Press.

Freud, S. (1954). *Psychoanalysis and Faith: The Letters of Sigmund Freud and Oskar Pfister*. London: Imago.

Freud, S. & Pfister, O. (2014). *Briefwechsel 1909–1939* (I. Noth (Ed.). Zürich: Theologischer Verlag.

Glover, E. (1927). Lectures on Technique in Psycho-analysis. *International Journal of Psycho-Analysis*, *8*: 486–520.

Green, A. (1984). Le langage dans la psychanalyse. In *Langages*. Paris: Les Belles Lettres.

Green, A. (1999). *The Fabric of Affect in the Psychoanalytic Discourse*. London: Routledge.

Greenacre, P. (1950). General Problems of Acting Out. *Psychoanalytic Quarterly*, *19*: 455–467.

Lacan, J. (1963). *Le Séminaire livre X, L'angoisse*, Paris: éd. du Seuil, 2004.

Lacan, J. (1964). *Le Séminaire XI. Les quatre concepts fondamentaux de la psychanalyse*. Paris, Éditions du Seuil, 1970.

Lacan, J. (1966). *Écrits*, Paris: Seuil, Le champ freudien.

Laplanche, J. & Pontalis, J.-B. (1967). *Vocabulaire de la psychanalyse*, Paris: PUP. English translation: *The Language of Psycho-Analysis* (1973), Donald Nicholson-Smith (transl.). London: Hogarth Press.

Loewald, H.W. (1975). Psychoanalysis as an Art and the Fantasy Character of the Psychoanalytic Situation. *Journal of the American Psychoanalytic Association*, *23*: 277–299.

Lyotard, J.F. (1977). The Unconscious as Mise-en-scène. In M. Benamou & C Caramello (Eds), *Performance in Post-Modern Culture* (pp. 87–98). Madison, WI: Coda Press.

Rouart, J. (1968). 'Agir' et processus analytique. *Revue Française de Psychanalyse*, *32*: 891–988. English translation: "Acting" Out and the Psychoanalytical Process. *International Journal of Psychoanalysis*, *49*: 185–187.

7 Again, and Again, and Again

Towards sovereign experience[1]

Avgi Saketopoulou

Breathless excitement

Two years ago, I was ravished by Jeremy O. Harris's theatrical work, *Slave Play* (2018).

Describing my experience this way may sound melodramatic. But my language is intentional, meant to do more than amplify how much I liked this play, or felt changed by it—although both are true. What took me over was far wilder and infinitely more bizarre: it felt utterly exigent. The first time I saw this play I felt my whole being called to attention, rousing my senses in a way that no work of art ever has. From thereon I was overcome with a new desire: to experience the play again, and again, and again. All I knew was that I wanted more. The experience was like a possession, as if being taken over by a strange force. I became preoccupied with reading and re-reading the script, and with thinking and re-thinking[2] the dominant themes. Week after week I attended Sunday discussions organized by the play's production team. I went enthusiastically and enjoyed them immensely. But I was also quite chagrined to realize that I couldn't *not* go. Even as other obligations pressed for my time, I nonetheless found myself heading out for these Sunday salons, eager and yet helpless to resist.

I was fascinated but also scared by this play, and by my own reactions to it. In retrospect, I was drawn to it like one who, standing over a cliff, looks down and, feeling an inexplicable pull, steps back. Only I didn't take a step back. For a year and a half, I watched the play again, and again, and again. I watched it alone, and I watched it with others. I went at planned times, and I went impulsively because I couldn't bear the separation. One repetition after another, I started observing small differences in how the actors enunciated their lines, how their bodies' affective charge shifted across performances, how different audiences laughed (or didn't) at certain lines. I followed the playwright around New York City to hear him discuss his play. Friends forwarded me announcements about his talks and alerted me to his radio interviews and podcasts, enabling my preoccupation.

Becoming so infatuated with a work of art is not an experience I had had before. It was dazzlingly intense—I felt fiercely alive and throbbingly

DOI: 10.4324/9781003458340-7

present. And it was also dizzyingly burdensome; I found the "demands" of my interest confusing, exhausting, and, at times, even terrifying. Still, I followed the play the way one follows around a lover before one's first heartbreak, before, that is, one learns to hold some things back. This particular response was, of course, specific to me and I have given much thought to what kept me so engaged, though I should say that I am far from being the only person whose involvement with this play grew unusually intense.[3]

My dramatic experience with *Slave Play* continues to intrigue me. It has led to much introspection, although the particular dynamics that drove my compulsion are beyond the scope of this essay. When the play's run was ending, I attended the closing performance to bid the play farewell. Leaving the theatre that night, I was bereft. I have been feeling torn from it ever since.

Strangely and despite its compulsively iterative and, at times, torturous quality, this irresistible press did not impair me. During this period, I developed a strange meditative curiosity about this thrillingly vexing experience, yet I was able to continue to work clinically, to teach and supervise, to run my study groups, and to publish work. Unsurprisingly, my relationship to this play left its imprint on my writing and teaching: for example, the script now appears in my syllabi on courses on psychosexuality. I am not mentioning this productivity to extoll the play's fruitful impact on me (as you will see, I am moving in a very different direction than simply professing the play's "utility"), but more so because I have been genuinely surprised that my taxing need to experience the play again and again did not compromise me.

So, while it would not be inaccurate to say that the play spurred a creative process for me (this chapter, I hope, speaks to that), and that it absolutely changed me (I will say a bit about that, too), these were far less important than what, to me, was infinitely more salient: while I was under the play's spell, *I had an experience.* Not an experience *of* something but what I can only, and inexactly, describe as pure experience. There were moments when I was singularly focused, acutely present, and, despite the general disorienting state I described, I felt overflowing with life. In this chapter, which, methodologically, follows on the tradition of "autotheory,"[4] I try to bring what I have thus learned to bear on our metapsychology.

Re-presenting slavery

On appearance, *Slave Play* is about the ghastly history of slavery in the United States Antebellum South and its continued afterlife in the present. Thanks to the playwright's brilliance, the theatergoers stand to come into contact with their ongoing investment in racism. I am purposefully using the term "investment" rather than, say, "participation," because *Slave Play* is after something more drastic than merely representing the horrors of slavery or pushing white audience members to see how they continue to benefit from it.

Slave Play opens in a Southern plantation, startling its audience with three interracial psychosexual encounters that include nudity and simulated sex. The White and White-passing partners subject their Black partners to different varieties of erotically tinged, racially offensive humiliations. The depictions are rousing in the many senses of the term, an effect dexterously achieved by the playwright's use of humor, which lowers the audience's defenses (almost daring its audience not to laugh at things many will also be horrified to find amusing), and the director's calculated decision to deny the theatergoer any respite from the first Act's intensities (the play purposefully runs with no intermission).

In the second Act we find out that the first Act's erotic debasements were staged and, in fact, requested by the Black partners as part of an unorthodox couples' treatment aiming to restore the Black partner's dissipating sexual desire. The second Act works to bind the excitements and excitations roused by the first Act. Filled with theory and terminology that "explains" to the characters, and to the audience, what occurred in the preceding Act, the second Act is an economic downshift moving the audience from a less bound state to a more bound one.

After having pacified the first Act's excitatory effects, the third Act delivers the most forceful blow. The White husband, who, in the first Act, had only reluctantly participated in the racialized sexual debasement requested by his wife, seems finally to be on board. More readily adopting his role as plantation overseer, he demeans her like a slave, using racially charged epithets. It is not clear if this more full-throated role-play issues from a lifting of his previously inhibited desires, or whether it is spurred by her distress, voiced in Act Two, about his earlier, lukewarm participation. What ensues materializes as a question mark: is his participation *real* (is he now "getting off" on her racialized abjection?) or is it *make-believe* (is he play-acting, doing it just for her?). As for her, it is similarly unclear if she is getting what she (thought she) wanted, or if she is finding herself in a messed-up replay of her historical past (the character's ancestors were slaves). The play comes to its abrupt end immediately following a scene of not not-rape. We are left in doubt as to whether the husband, under the play-acting guise, raped his wife, or whether he has dutifully, and perhaps all too convincingly, followed her instructions to take her against her protests. The curtain closes with a puddle of tears at the site of enigma, with the audience not quite knowing how to decipher what has just happened. Deliberately refusing to tell us what to make of this mess (Feldman, 2019), the playwright leaves us unsettled and confused about what we have just watched, and about what he, and the play itself, want from us.

What J.O. Harris ingenuously manages to do is to re-present[5] racism's enduring arrangements, hitting the audience with a force that does not just alert the theater-goers to their racism, including its erotic charge (Holland, 2012), but rouses it. This re-presentation of white America's ancestral crime is not just as a revivified representation of a past memory; it *blisters through the present.* Now *in vivo*, slavery and its erotic life have been brought into presence—not history, done and over with, or something to be remembered, but thunderously now. The disturbance this causes is amplified by Harris's refusal to tell the viewer what to do with or about this live wire. The play's argument, if one can be attributed to it, is that the history of slavery has not yet been inserted into psychic time and that, in that sense, for most white and for some black people, it remains what Scarfone has called, the *unpast* (2015). It has remained unpast because slavery has not yet fully become instituted as an event of the *psychic* past, but is alive, throbbing in the present (e.g., the continued toleration of anti-blackness and the murder of black people). The question of how one may engage a past of such proportions to establish a personal relationship to it is one of the big questions of the play. This is where repetition steps in: the repetition of the sexual indignities of slavery that are re-presented *in* the play, the rogue desires that the re-representation of these sexual indignities rouse in audience members, and the related repetition of those who, like me, became preoccupied with *Slave Play.*

The driving force of repetition

Bruce Reis describes as *creative* those repetitions that do not repeat as fixation, but which instead carry, "a yield of pleasure" (2020 p. 104). Unlike repetitions that incessantly restage trauma or those driven by daemonic force, as Freud described repetition compulsion (1920, p. 36), creative repetitions open up paths to the possibilities of *new* experience. Critical to this distinction for Reis is their insertion in a scene of transferential address (2009, see also Scarfone, 2011). Drawing on Aulagnier (1975), Reis posits that creative repetitions hinge on the analyst's capacity to experience pleasure. To illustrate, he shares exquisite and sensitively handled clinical process where his unexpected tide of enjoyment regarding a patient's material became central to the patient's creative repetition. Reis's important contributions join a developing body of analytic theorizing that has been contesting the notion that repetition is always destructive or ruinous, and that has persuasively argued that repetition works to usher in novel experience.

To further our thinking about repetition, I want to apply some pressure on this particular elucidation of creative repetition.

First, from a Laplanchean perspective (1995) the pleasurable and the daemonic do not belong to different and *desexualized* registers but are ontologically co-implicated and definitionally sexual (in the enlarged, Freudian sense of the word). This makes a distinction between varieties of repetition that hinges on pleasure *versus* suffering harder to uphold. If the demonic and the pleasurable conjointly constitute the sexual drive, we cannot justify, on the level of metapsychology, the positing of a watertight frontier between creative and compulsive repetition. "Destruction and creation" Blanchot writes, "when they bear upon the essential … are hardly distinguishable (2011, p. 146). So, although some repetitions may appear distinctively demonic and others may look more benign, making the latter more likely to be "enjoyed" by the analyst, pleasure *and* suffering co-exist in repetition. (This, as I have discussed, was certainly the case for me with *Slave Play*.)

One could object that even as both enjoyment and suffering may be at work, one aspect eventually prevails, suggesting that different kinds of repetition may be creative or destructive. Surely the fact that some repetitions *appear* joyful while others *appear* anguishing may tempt us to pronounce the former creative and to denounce the latter as destructive. But I would argue that such appearances mark not repetition itself, but its outcomes they judge, that is, something that can only be judged in the *après-coup*. However, if a clear distinction between creative and destructive repetitions may only be posited retroactively, repetition as a force can go either way, depending on the interplay, each time, of binding forces (sexual life drive/ being) and unbinding forces (sexual drive of death/non-being). For example, I very much enjoyed *Slave Play*. But to say only that something creative came out of my enjoyment of a play that so graphically re-presents the sexual atrocities of slavery and that stirs its audience with intemperate displays of sexual abjection would be to leave out the darker, rawer elements that drew me, and so many others, to it.[6] It would clean up our experience of the play.

Secondly, the notion of creative repetition may be insufficient as a framework for understanding experiences like the one I had with *Slave Play*, where creative outcomes may well be present and, yet, be the much lesser yield. I don't want to minimize that yield: I was singularly changed by the experience of this play, having come to an appreciably deeper understanding of my own racialization. And I have become invested in racial justice in entirely new ways. These were invaluable gains. But to say that this reshuffling of myself is what I got out of my experience would miss the point. No. What mattered to me most during the period of my infatuation was the *experience itself*: even as I was unable to articulate it to myself at the time, and even as I still stumble for words to explain it, having that experience again and again is something I fiercely, and at some cost to myself, protected.

A view of repetition that takes both creative and daemonic forces into consideration has helped me understand not only the compelling force of my preoccupation, but also to account for why it is so hard to put into words.

Repetition progressively wears down the binding of psychic energy that has been effected by symbolization/translation. It does so by delivering smaller-than-fully-traumatic, yet persistent traumatisms that work at the limit of our consent (I gave myself over to the play thus permitting it to "work on" me: so while I went willingly to the Sunday discussions, I also felt helpless to resist). I use the word "traumatism", as opposed to "trauma," to mark the distinction between a flooding of the ego *versus* pain (physical but also psychic), which Freud described as "the protective shield having been broken through in a *limited* area" (1920g, p. 30, emphasis added). Traumatisms that repeat operate like a persistent micro-dosing of pain that, with enough build-up, can incite a crisis in the organized ego. Such a crisis can dissipate the ego's boundaries to bring about a state of "overwhelm" (Saketopoulou, 2019). In the overwhelm state, the connective tissue between translations (in Freudian language, the psychic coating) and the enigmatic core (in Freudian language, the Thing) dissolve, leaving one as close as is possible to the raw presence of the drive. However, because the surge of energy that produces the ego's shattering is unbearable, the ego will then spontaneously move to reorganize itself, bearing new translations and fresh self-configurations. I have written elsewhere about these ideas (Saketopoulou, 2014, 2019, 2020), explaining how the ego's dissolution is a risky perch atop from which generative turbulences or destructive outcomes are equally likely to proceed. Overwhelm is risky territory.

My experience with *Slave Play* has helped me probe deeper into what happens in this area of "contact" with the drive that arises after the ego has been shattered (Bersani, 1986) and *before* the ego quickly reassembles itself, or new repressions set in. (I put "contact" in quotes to mark my insistence that one is never really in direct, unmediated contact with the drive.) This contact zone, I propose, is the domain of pure experience as opposed to an experience of something. Here, standing in the openness of being, one may undergo a very fleeting divestment from the burdens of subjectivity, to bathe in what Bataille called *sovereign experience* (1976), a precious and transitory burst of intense liveliness. "[A]ttention passes then from 'projects' … to this inner presence," Bataille writes, delivering a "startled jump of our entire being [that] detest[s] the servility of discourse" (*ibid.*, p. 113).

Sovereign experience is a most private and personal space, although here words fail me. When I say "personal," I do not mean it from the perspective of an "I" who speaks for itself or from the standpoint of an organized ego. In fact, the experiential domain I am describing is arguably the very opposite of a notion of "lived experience" in the sense of first-hand accounts and impressions of living as a member of a particular group. Rather, it is experience that is disaggregated from identitarian projects, from the competing interpellations of the social, and from the demands of the political realm. Because it is resolutely outside relationality, a space where we don't rely on the other to recognize our existence, we can, instead, luxuriate in the pure experience of being. This is as intimate an experience as one can undergo with oneself: a space where existence is not affirmed through the other's recognition, but is singularly felt, available to us as if in heightened form. Because sovereign experience is transiently stripped of the workings of power, discourse, and self-narrativization, it can be felt as a boundless sense of freedom.

To prevent any misunderstandings of the loaded term "sovereignty," I want to clarify that I am not referring to a process by which one attains a durable sense of self-possession vacated of personal history, historical events, or social forces. Neither am I unaware of the complex political line-ages around indigeneity, tribal land claims, and anticolonial movements that trail the term "sovereignty." My use is also not meant to codify an autonomous self as fantasized by, and promised to us by, neoliberalism, of a self, that is, that wills choices and selects experience as if from a buffet of consumerist options. Rather, I rely on the term in the way it has been used by Bataille, who was interested in wresting space for an experience of being that confronts non-being, an immeasurably brief emancipation from the pummeling effects of political projects. Sovereign experience is, thus, not about the acquisition of a sturdy sense of self-possession or institutional power (as when used in political theory). It is, to the contrary, conditioned by the very risk overwhelm poses to the sovereign/organized ego (Saketo-poulou, 2019). It arises in the confrontation of being with non-being, where one puts everything at risk (Blanchot, 2011), contesting the ego and brush-ing up against the limit of what is possible (Bataille, 1957).

It must be obvious by now that sovereign experience is not necessarily pleasant or satisfying, but that it can also be anguishing. Sovereign experi-ence is not something we can produce on demand or by strenuous effort, and, when it comes, it is short-lived, a spike of non-duration, if you will. It flashes into existence and then quickly recedes, with new bindings (and the subjectivities they breed) taking over.[7] This description is consistent with a psychoanalytic estimation of what it might be like to find oneself in the proximity of an uncoated drive and, again, we have to think of it as a "proximity," because the drive can only be approached asymptotically/obliquely (Laplanche, 1984). What does it mean, though, for experience to "flash" before us? It is not about a previously obscured "truth" becoming il-luminated or something enigmatic coming into clear focus. Whatever feels new, creative, or even clarifying (e.g., my substantially fresh appreciation of my racialization and of race relations) issues from what the ego crafts *as a way of patching up the hole opened up* through overwhelm. These patches are certainly meaningful; for instance, to return to *Slave Play*, new transla-tions *vis-à-vis* whiteness and white supremacy are urgently needed. And, certainly, a deeper appreciation of the grasp of history and race relations is no small advancement. But to say that my own expansion as a white subject is the creative return of my obsessional repetition is, to my mind, to settle for too little when it comes to what repetition has to offer us. My different appreciation of my whiteness did amount to a shift in my subjectivity, but it was preceded by something much more inchoate: having undergone sov-ereign experience. Here, we may be helped by Foucault who offered that experience does not follow on subjecthood but, rather, that "experience … results in a subject, or rather, in subjects" (1984, p. 253).

But let me linger a moment longer on what I intend to convey here by using the word "flash" to describe, as much as I can, the texture of un-dergoing sovereign experience. In saying that sovereign experience flashes before us I am speaking of time that comes to a passing, yet heightened, standstill. This is an intensified sense of "now" where time does not flow, where a hyper-pixelated "now" is all there is. The temporality of sovereign experience is a temporality akin to Scarfone's notion of *actual time*, "a very specific kind of present, not [an] eternal but [an] atemporal [one]" (2015, p. 77). This ("the atemporal") is how, we will recall, Freud (1915e) described the temporality of the unconscious. Scarfone insists on the distinction between time that is eternal, where one may be caught in an inescapable, ongoing loop, *versus* time that is atemporal, time that does not pass. This distinction is consequential for our thinking about repetition because it suggests that a significant difference may exist between stalled and still time, that is, time that is "stuck" and time that, in its stillness, may become co-extensive with experience. Stilled time is like a pronounced now with no unfolding of time, a sense of being fully claimed by the present. From that angle, sovereign experience is a temporary stilling that, in breaking up the flow of chronological time, immerses us in a paradoxically elongated sense of presence where the fullness of life may be experienced at its full intensity.

Because it arises in the crevasses of the ego's dissolution, where our very being is at stake, repetition stands to bring us into contact with the extravagance of life.[8] And it is this very fact that furnishes repetition with its daemonic character: that it can bring us into a confrontation with the hollow that opens up when the ego comes undone. This is a somewhat different type of daemonic force than the one Freud posited when he proposed a desexualized death drive (1920g), where death is not the organismic end of life, but the *petite morte* of the ego. This is a death of much different stakes indeed: on the one hand, it does not necessarily destroy life, but may be the preamble to new forms of selfhood. But, on the other hand, its stakes are, in some sense, even higher, as an encounter with one's ego death is one for which one is acutely and singularly present (as opposed to the body's decay that occurs when we are no longer there to experience it).

That there is something fugitive in that transitory opening does not render it unimportant. On the contrary, it highlights its significance. As I mentioned earlier, these high-energy psychic states are quickly transduced to new translations (or repression), and while one hopes that these new translations will work better than the ones that have been broken down by repetition's daemonic force, this is by no means guaranteed. *Neither is it the goal of repetition.* A "better translation" (e.g., my new relationship to my whiteness) is not the telos, but a fortuitous epiphenomenon, a side effect, if you will, that can be attributed to the ego's expeditious work, which is to restore itself to a more intact, enclosed state. New translations that are crafted in the wake of sovereign experience are also valuable in another respect. After sovereign experience has flashed through and disappeared, these new translations will be the sole lingering trace that an experience of sovereignty has been endured. Some rudimentary memory of one having undergone sovereign experience will, thus, be faintly inscribed into the fresh translation. Not every new translation carries such a trace, since not all new translating is undergirded by sovereign experience. But when it does, these new translations may be especially prized possessions, having been conditioned from a unique sense of freedom and personal innovation. And, for the same reason, they can then also come to be held with special vigor and vehemence, presenting fortified resistances to further de-translation.

The "it" that repeats has to appear: The actual and the enigmatic

In 2000, the well-known art historian T.J. Clark found himself entranced by two works by Poussin, which he began visiting again, and again, and again. Uncertain, yet curious as to what was unfolding, he recorded his daily reflections. "[A]stonishing things happen" he wrote,

> if one gives oneself over to the process of seeing again and again: aspect after aspect of the picture seems to surface, what is salient and what incidental alter bewilderingly from day to day ... the depiction breaks up, crystallizes, fragments again, persists like an afterimage ... slowly the question arises: What is it, fundamentally, that I am returning to in this particular case?
>
> (2006, p. 5)

This query (what is "it" that we return to in repetition) is one I incessantly asked myself as I visited and re-visited *Slave Play*. For Freud, as we know, what repeats is the repressed, returning as symptom or compulsion. To answer the question of what repeats, then, we have to delve deeper first into what is the "it" that is repressed. In its most widely utilized meaning, repression refers to an inscribed mnemic event that becomes encrypted in the unconscious having acquired a psychic coating through the workings of primary process. From within this submerged vault, the repressed then emits offshoots in disguised form (symptoms, etc.—a second coating of sorts) (Scarfone, 2015) that announce their presence. This makes the repressed recoverable (or, perhaps, better said, re-covered), assuming one can skillfully strip back these successive psychic coatings. Put simply, "where id was, there shall ego be."

But in Laplanchean metapsychology, things are somewhat different: repression is the inescapable fate that awaits that some of the sexual surplus (enigma) that remains after the surcharged messages the adult addresses to the child are translated/symbolized. This original enigmatic dimension, related to the other's effraction into us, is traumatic yet inevitable [Laplanche called this process the *Fundamental Anthropological Situation* (FAS) to mark its universality (1987)]. An enigmatic load always escapes translation; that residue becomes repressed, forming the unconscious. Now operating as an "internal foreign body" (Laplanche, 1979, p. 207), it presses from within for further translation/symbolization.

These different meanings of the term "repression" should make it clear that, in the Laplanchean sense, repetition must mean something different than just marking the return of a painful or unacceptable inscription. The "it" that repeats, from this angle, is not an obscured memory but the trauma of enigma itself. How, though, we would be justified to ask, can that trauma repeat when enigma is itself a hollow, devoid of content? It repeats, I would say, as experience, or, to be (slightly) more precise, as a contentless experience that puts us *in the presence* of the unknown. Repetition, in this sense, does something else entirely than to re-present *something*: it re-presents, in the sense of presenting again (Scarfone, 2015) not some originary content *but an originary experience*. What is this originary experience that it presents again? I would say it is our original wound, which is, as well, the site of our becoming: the FAS. This may be one way to understand Laplanche's notion of how certain processes (e.g., the psychoanalytic process) reopen us to the FAS.

We would still need to ask, though, what it means for something to repeat as experience. Or, rather, how would we sense its recurrence?[9] We sense it, I propose, by its propulsive force where it has "the effect of presence …" (Scarfone, 2015, p. 117), "convey[ing] something more and something other than the semantic order" (p. 118). We live it as quantity, marked by the "again and again," and the "more and more" (Saketopoulou, 2019, p. 786) of experience. But, you might ask, in saying this haven't I just relocated the problem of "what" repeats to this mysterious "again"? In other words, what does the "again" refer to if there is no particular event that repeats? For it to become felt, the force of this "again" has to appear phenomenally. How? It would appear by borrowing some rudimentary representational form to assume a proto-psychic coating of sorts. I say "borrow" to highlight that this involves a lending of a good-enough form in which that force can be vestigially bound. What might serve a such a form? Would anything do? No. A sort of goodness of fit, Scarfone suggests (2015), has to exist for a form to be chosen for this work. What does fit mean, though, when the originary is not filled-in, but, rather, hollowed-out?

For Laplanche, this "fit" is a matter of an energetic match (1980): the arsonist he mentions as an example is drawn to fire because of its economic correspondence to the internal excitation which he both savors and suffers. Why is economy so pivotal in the matter of "fit"? Because the only thing we "know" about enigma has to do with its energetic overflow, that it is traumatic precisely because it could not be translated to begin with. We begin to see, thus, that not all forms lend themselves to being used as psychic coating; those that are more energetically charged are more likely candidates for this kind of work, more apposite than others. While what is charged varies across different individuals, there do exist some common denominators: the body's excitability makes bodily experiences more likely to serve such functions, making sexual repetitions and those that are more enfleshed[10] especially available forms to psychically coat enigma. Things of the past that have wounded us, in the sense of a historical trauma (the trauma of personal history, or of History with a capital H) are also especially likely to draw us closer to experience, offering a "stickier" kind of coating (Ahmed, 2004), because they are energetically charged in ways that may more readily link up with the excitation of enigma.[11] In *Slave Play* these materialize at the intersection of some of the most raw and the most brutal forms the sexual drive can take: sexual violation and the exploitation of the other.

In closing

Reflecting on the time I was preoccupied with *Slave Play*, I might say in hindsight that, for reasons both personal and impersonal, I was caught in the force of the art work's *re-presentation*. I did not just watch the play, I related to it as if it were personally addressed to me, not out of some sense of grandiosity, but because, in lowering my guard and giving myself over to it again, and again, and again, I was summoned by it. Thus, I entered an experience that was no doubt aesthetic and that also yielded some self-knowledge for which I am grateful. But this was not what most commanded me during the period of my possession. By making myself subject to the play and to its force, a force that traveled on the carrier wave of sexuality, traumatic history, and the excitable body, the play claimed me, producing temporal bursts where I felt entirely alone with myself, a privacy I have rarely before experienced. Such effects cannot be produced on demand; they require of us as human beings to risk experience at the limit of the bearable, to become, we might say, more traumatophilic, rather than, as psychoanalysis has often done, to seek to understand, heal, or resolve trauma. It requires us, that is, to take risks.

Notes

1 My deep appreciation to Samantha Hill and Ann Pellegrini whose readings and comments on earlier drafts of this essay have appreciably helped my thinking. Much gratitude also to Brent Zachery for his curation of *Slave Play*'s Sunday discussions.
2 Each time we engage in the activity of thinking we think the object of contemplation anew. In this sense, it is not just memory, as Loewald (1971) offered, but also thinking itself that is ensconced in repetition. One might say that we re-think the object of contemplation, which means that even in repetition the thinking is never quite the same.
3 *Slave Play* has by now earned a record number of twelve Tony nominations. It received rave reviews as well as unusually lacerating critique, including petitions to shut it down. More than its reception though, it is the impassioned way in which theatergoers loved or hated it that I am alluding to. At the Sunday salons, I met several others who had also attended the play multiple times and were now, like me, regularly attending the Sunday discussions.

4 Auto-theory, a term introduced by Paul Preciado (2013) but is most often credited to Nelson's 2016 *The Argonauts*. It is a genre-bending form of theory-building that conjoins self-observation with critical reflection (Wiegman, 2020) with no established parallel in psychoanalysis—though new work is emerging on that front (Colombo, 2021). As analysts, we justifiably treat self-observation cautiously: observing oneself is not a straightforward or uncomplicated enterprise. In this essay, I try to be mindful of this problem as, I hope, will become obvious. I also choose this method to mark, and resist, the unspoken psychoanalytic convention of circumventing the problems of "autobiographical writing that exceeds the boundaries of the personal" (Wiegman, 2020, p. 2), by repackaging the analyst's personal experience as clinical or supervisory material [e.g. Kohut (1979)].

5 I am using the term re-present here per Scarfone (2011) to mark that something is presented again rather than represented. I return to these ideas shortly.

6 It is, in fact, this very vexed enjoyment that the play artfully provokes that made some black theater-goers distrust not only the play but also the playwright himself, calling for the play's cancellation. Were white people, the concern was, enjoying it too readily and in "the wrong way" by uninhibitedly identifying with the figure of the plantation master (A. Harris, 2019)?

7 New repressions, of course, are also possible.

8 This is one way to understand analytically what Bataille refers to (and what he takes issue with in Hegel) when he posits that a confrontation with non-being is at the center of life. It is tempting, but space does not permit me to follow, here, the exciting links with Scarfone's proposition that the actual is both impediment and an inflection point for what's possible (2015). Further, I want to mark the connections between the notion that a confrontation with non-being (a dissolved, shattered ego) is at the center of life, with Zaltzman's important work on the anarchic drive (1979)—another point I can't go into in depth presently.

9 The more precise one tries to be with such elusive concepts, the more slippery they get. As an approximation, permit me this exercise: imagine closing your eyes while holding in each of your hands the same pole of a magnet. Imagine now trying to bring your hands together. At some point you will start feeling a repulsive force. If you try to bring your hands together at somewhat of an angle to avoid the pushback, you will almost sense the force moving around a shape of sorts, almost as if the contours of the magnetic field are tangibly there. You open your eyes and see nothing. No content, just force.

10 This quick reference to "flesh" marks an important link to Spillers' and Musser's work on flesh that I cannot pursue here due to space constraints.

11 Trauma may deliver us to a relationship with ourselves, rather than becoming the discursive material onto which one stakes one's subjectivity.

References

Ahmed, S. (2004). Affective Economies. *Social Text*, 22(2): 117–139.

Aulagnier, P. (1975). *The Violence of Interpretation: From Pictogram to Statement*. London: Routledge.

Bataille, G. (1957). *Erotism: Death and Sexuality*. San Francisco: City Lights.

Bataille, G. (1976). *The Accursed Share: An Essay on General Economy, Volume II, volume III* (R. Hurley, Trans.). New York: Zone Books.

Bersani, L. (1986). *The Freudian Body: Psychoanalysis and Art*. New York: Columbia University Press.

Blanchot, M. (2011). *The Infinite Conversation: Theory and History of Literature* (Vol. 82) (S. Hanson, Trans.). University of Minnesota Press. (Original work published 1969.)

Clark, T.J. (2008). *The Sight of Death: An Experiment in Art Writing*. New Haven, CT: Yale University Press.

Colombo, D. (2021). Autotheory: Reading Maggie Nelson's *The Argonauts* and Rachel Cusk's *Outline* as case studies in analytic framing. Ticho Lecture, APsaA, American Psychoanalytic Association Winter Meeting, New York, February 12.

Feldman, A. (2019). Interview with Slave Play Author Jeremy O. Harris: Jeremy O. Harris Brings His Shocking and Thrilling New Drama *Slave Play* to Broadway. Accessed June 26, 2020 from https://www.timeout.com/newyork/theater/jeremy-o-harris-interview-slave-play-broadway

Foucault, M. (1989[1984]) The Return of Morality, in L. D. Kritzman (Ed.), *Michel Foucault: Politics, Philosophy, Culture. Interviews and Other Writings 1977–84* (pp. 242–254). New York: Routledge

Freud, S. (1915e). The Unconscious. *S.E.*, *14*: 159–215. London: Hogarth Press.

Freud, S. (1919). 'A Child is Being Beaten'. *S.E.*, *17*: 175–204. London: Hogarth Press.

Freud, S. (1920g). *Beyond the Pleasure Principle*. *S.E.*, *18*: 1–64. London: Hogarth Press.

Harris, A. (2019). What It's Like to See 'Slave Play' as a Black Person. Accessed June 29, 2020 from https://www.nytimes.com/2019/10/07/opinion/slave-play-broadway.html

Harris, J.O. (2018). *Slave Play*. New York: New York Theatre Workshop.

Holland, S.P. (2012). *The Erotic Life of Racism*. Durham, NC: Duke University Press.

Kohut, H. (1979). The Two Analyses of Mr. Z. *International Journal of Psychoanalysis*, *60*: 3–27.

Laplanche, J. (1979). A Metapsychology Put to the Test of Anxiety. In *The Unfinished Copernican Revolution: Selected Works, 1967–1992* (pp. 197–216). New York: Unconscious in Translation Press.

Laplanche, J. (1980). *Problématiques III: Sublimation*. Paris: PUF.

Laplanche, J. (1984). The Drive and its Source-object: Its Fate in the Transference. In *The Unfinished Copernican Revolution: Selected Works, 1967–1992* (pp. 293–212). New York: Unconscious in Translation Press.

Laplanche, J. (1987). *New Foundations for Psychoanalysis* (J. House, Trans.). New York: Unconscious in Translation.

Laplanche, J. (1995). The So-called Death Drive: A Sexual Drive. In *The Temptations of Biology* (pp. 159–182). New York: The Unconscious in Translation.

Loewald, H.W. (1971). Some Considerations on Repetition and Repetition Compulsion. *International Journal of Psychoanalysis*, *52*: 59–66.

Nelson, M. (2016). *The Argonauts*. San Francisco, CA: Graywolf Press.

Preciado, Paul B. (2013). *Testo-junkie: Sex, Drugs, and Biopolitics in the Pharmacopornographic Era*. New York: The Feminist Press.

Reis, B. (2020). *Creative Repetition and Intersubjectivity*. New York: Routledge.

Saketopoulou, A. (2014). To Suffer Pleasure: The Shattering of the Ego as the Psychic Labor of Perverse Sexuality. *Studies in Gender and Sexuality*, *15*(4): 254–268.

Saketopoulou, A. (2019). The Draw to Overwhelm: Risk, Limit Consent and the Retranslation of Enigma. *Journal of the American Psychoanalytic Association*, *67*(1): 133–167.

Saketopoulou, A. (2020). Sexuality Beyond Consent; Overwhelm and Traumatisms that Incite. *Psychoanalytic Quarterly*, *89*(4): 771–811.

Scarfone, D. (2011). Repetition: Between Presence and Meaning. *Canadian Journal of Psychoanalysis*, *19*(1): 70–86.

Scarfone, D. (2015). *The Unpast*. New York: The Unconscious in Translation.

Wiegman, R. (2020). Introduction: Autotheory Theory. *Arizona Quarterly, A Journal of American Literature, Culture, and Theory*, 76(1): 1–14.

Zaltzman, N. (1979). Η Αναρχική Ενόρμηση (La Pulsion Anarchiste). Αθήνα: Βιβλιοπωλείον της Εστίας (translation from French by Γιώργος Καράμπελας, 2019). [[PLACE, PUBLISHER]].

8 Remembering, Repeating and Working-Through as a Step in Freud's Ongoing Struggle with the "What", "Why", and "How" of Analytic Knowing in the Curative Process

Rachel B. Blass

The background: Freud's struggle with the development of his ideas on the analytic process

In previous papers (most recently, Blass, 2016) I have argued that throughout his life Freud struggled to articulate some very basic aspects of the analytic aim and process, which he knew of and adhered to through insightful experience. While he clearly considered analysis to be a process of coming to know repressed and denied unconscious truths, of "know[ing] yourself", of "look[ing] into your own depth" (Freud, 1917a, pp. 142–143) what this knowing specifically means and how and why it takes place was much more difficult for him to conceptualize and communicate. That is, Freud readily affirmed that our symptoms and psychic disorders are problematic and distorted expressions of denial and of that which has been denied and so naturally, knowing instead of denying, facing psychic reality, cures. But what does facing reality actually mean? Here, matters became complex and clouded. It is not, Freud emphasizes throughout his analytic writing, simply a matter of owning up to facts, affirming ideas; conscious knowledge does not prevent unconscious denial. We can understand that we are anxious because of denied oedipal wishes, and we may be convinced that such wishes exist because of their appearance in the transference, and still those wishes may maintain their unconscious anxiety-arousing influence. And taking this a step further, if we are to fathom another kind of knowledge of psychic truth which is more directly unconscious, should we, indeed, think of it as knowledge of a factual kind, only now in the unconscious? That is, is cure a matter of knowing in the sense of having ideas, unconsciously, of facts about one's psychic life, for example, the fact of the existence of oedipal wishes? The careful study of his writings over the years (clinical and theoretical alike) suggests that Freud was struggling to describe some other kind of knowledge of truth—not merely affirming ideas about the facts of psychic reality; rather, some kind of lived integrative process of knowing.

DOI: 10.4324/9781003458340-8

Strachey, for one, seems to be speaking of this when, in his effort to shed light on what Freud means by making something conscious analytically, refers to "bringing together" conscious knowledge (conveyed in the interpretation) with an unconscious "objectionable trend." So, we have "trends" rather than facts, and an act of "bringing together" of the trends rather than thinking or having ideas about the facts. But Strachey himself acknowledged that he was not sure what putting it this way could mean exactly (Strachey, 1934, p. 129). The fact that Freud was alive at the time and could be asked, apparently didn't make things easier. Freud himself, a few years after Strachey's paper, in one of his final texts, continues to acknowledge an ongoing ambiguity. He speaks of the analytic process as one whereby the unconscious instinct "is brought completely into the harmony of the ego, becomes accessible to all the influences of the other trends in the ego and no longer seeks to go its independent way to satisfaction." And he adds, "If we are asked by what methods and means this result is achieved, it is not easy to find an answer" (Freud, 1937c, p. 224).

It should be stressed here that Freud's introduction of the notion of the transference and the centrality he gives it within the analytic process from quite early on does not, in itself, provide an answer. The fact that the patient lives out things in the transference does not explain how coming to know about what is being lived out changes anything. The analyst can inform the patient that he has oedipal wishes, as apparent in the transference, and the patient may agree that this indeed seems to be the case; he may feel conviction of this having recognized it in the transference. But how does this change those wishes? Freud leaves unanswered the most basic analytic question of how coming to know denied truth cures remains not completely resolved.

But it is not only the "what" and "how" of analytic knowing that are not easy to describe; it may be seen that this is the case also for the "why" of it. It is not hard to understand that one would wish to be rid of mental disorder and unpleasant symptoms and seek treatment to that end. But given the vested interest in not knowing, given that unconsciously the person has "chosen" to deny despite the unpleasant consequences, the question arises as to what impels the person to change within analysis; what makes him desire to know or willing to do so. At times Freud seems to suggest that, in fact, nothing does. The patient remains just as opposed to knowing truth, but now the analyst is forcing this upon him in a kind of analytic battle. As Freud famously writes at the very end of "The Dynamics of Transference", the patient in the transference

> seeks to put his passions into action without taking any account of the real situation" and what ensues is a "struggle between the doctor and the patient, between intellect and instinctual life, between understanding and seeking to act … For when all is said and done, it is impossible to destroy anyone in *absentia* or *effigie*.
>
> (Freud, 1912b, p. 108)

And yet, this view of the analyst as merely imposing his thinking on the patient does not sit well with other aspects of Freud's thinking, such as his ideas on the importance of respect for the patient's individuality (Freud, 1919a), but more importantly with his notion, not always openly espoused, that the person is in part driven by an inherent desire to know truth—epistemophilia, an instinct for research, or *Wissbegeirde*, as he put it at different points (Blass, 2006). It would seem that Freud did not feel that he had a firm enough framework within which to formally present this desire and so the patient's motives for seeking truth in the analytic situation often remain somewhat obscure.

As I have argued in earlier papers, Freud's ongoing struggle with these ideas may be best understood in the light of the gradual evolution of his thinking and the fact that some of his early theoretical conceptualizations and models, and some firmly established preconceptions, were limiting him. Most notable in this regard are the following: Freud's early trauma theories in which the filling in of missing memories of actual events play an important role; his view of the individual as basically self-serving, egoistic, guided by the desire for gratification and self-preservation; and the complex relationship between drive and thought that emerges as he gradually shifts from a view of the origin of pathology being in external trauma to one of it being in internal conflict (Blass, 1992). I have, furthermore, maintained that these limitations are overcome through Klein's development of Freud's insights.

Two steps are central here: (1) *The introduction of the Kleinian notion of unconscious phantasy*: this notion allows for a more integrative view of the person, in which drive and thought are more intimately tied and this combined entity or state constitutes the mind of the person. What this means is that instead of regarding the mind as a container of ideas (to which varying degrees of energy may be attached) and the person as one who is influenced by drives (which take the form of wishes about which he may think) the notion of phantasy offers a further-developed conception of driven ideas. In the Kleinian notion of phantasy, these driven ideas are primarily expressions or manifestations of our internal object relationships, of the meanings we ascribed to our experiences and become the very building blocks of our minds (Blass, 2017). From this Kleinian perspective the psychic truths that become known in analysis are unconscious phantasies and to know them is not to think *about* the facts of one's dynamics, in the sense of having an idea about them, but, rather, is to live, or to have revived, that dynamic in one's mind. As knowledge and lived dynamics are here intertwined, Freud's insight that knowledge of truth cures becomes more understandable.[1]

(2) *Klein's full integration of Freud's dual instinct theory.* It is this theory that provides a more complex understanding of motivation in which an inherent desire to know truth, to see reality as it is, can be grounded. The life instincts, Eros, are presented as a force or principle that moves the person beyond the egoism of the pleasure principle and impels him towards true

encounter with the other (Blass, 2006, 2019, 2020). This encounter includes the live state of knowing psychic truth, of meeting reality, that Freud posited at the center of the analytic process.

It is important to recognize the nature of Freud's struggle in this context because it opens us to a deeper understanding of the complexity of his thinking about knowledge and the analytic process. Without this recognition, Freud may be seen as a kind of cognitive therapist, who believed that informing the patient of their way of thinking and acting can in itself change it; that after conscious understanding the patient will and can choose to be different. I would suggest that some of the modifications of analytic practice that developed following Freud, including shifts towards more active, supportive, and corrective approaches, resulted from viewing Freud in this limited way—if this is what Freud has to offer then clearly something more mutative was needed.

"Remembering, Repeating and Working-through" may be seen to be a significant step in Freud's efforts to articulate the "what," "why," and "how" of analytic knowledge in the curative process of analysis. In what follows, I will try to bring this out and, in so doing, offer a new appreciation of the role and value of the text.

Reading "Remembering, Repeating and Working-Through"

Remembering—The "what"

Freud begins the paper by recounting some of the evolution of his ideas on the analytic process from the start of his clinical practice until the time of this paper (1915). He refers to the first phase as that of "Breuer's catharsis," in which hypnosis is applied to facilitate recollection and reproduction of the mental processes, the thoughts and feelings involved at the moment of the formation of the symptom, in order to abreact them. In the second phase, free association takes the place of hypnosis. The resistance to memory of the "forgotten" mental processes was now dealt with by interpretation and overcoming resistance by making it known to the patient gradually took the place of abreaction. In the third phase, the one Freud espoused at the time of the writing of the paper, the analyst "gives up the attempt to bring a particular moment or problem into focus" and "contents himself with studying whatever is present for the time being on the surface of the patient's mind." Freud concludes: "The aim of these different techniques has, of course, remained the same. Descriptively speaking, it is to fill in gaps in memory; dynamically speaking, it is to overcome resistances due to repression." Here, Freud apparently regards abreaction as a kind of overcoming of resistance. But Freud's emphasis of similar aims belies the significant developments that actually took place. Not only is abreaction as a process of discharge different from overcoming of resistance to one's thoughts, but also it would seem that with the shift away from the moment of symptom formation, an actual moment that could be returned to, and the facts of the mind going on in it consciously recalled, the meaning of filling in gaps in memory shifted too.

Freud knew this. He immediately goes on to "interpolate a few remarks" that bring out this change in his understanding, albeit without, at this point, actually acknowledging it as such (in fact, in the first edition of the text, these remarks—three paragraphs—were printed in a smaller type). First, he tells us that what is remembered in the analytic process was not really forgotten. Patients will admit that they have always known the supposedly "forgotten" memory. It is more a matter of shutting it off. Moreover, screen memories, retain *"all* of what is essential from childhood."￼ Secondly, and I would think more importantly, what is to be recalled is not always an event, an impression or an experience. Rather, Freud notes that there is another "group of psychical processes" that cannot truly be forgotten—nor could they be remembered for that matter. This other group includes "phantasies, processes of reference, emotional impulses, thought-connections," which, he explains, are "purely internal acts" and are to be "contrasted with impressions and experiences ... [and] considered separately." He goes on to explain that "In these processes it particularly often happens that something is 'remembered' which could never have been 'forgotten' because it was never at any time noticed—was never conscious." Freud's next statement makes even clearer that memory and filling in gaps in memory is not the analytic concern:

> As regards the course taken by psychical events it seems to make no difference whatever whether such a 'thought-connection' was conscious and then forgotten or whether it never managed to become conscious at all. The conviction which the patient obtains in the course of his analysis is quite independent of this kind of memory.

Here, when Freud speaks of obtaining conviction, he is not adopting a kind of post-modern perspective that brackets the truth of convictions, but rather, is concerned with coming to a deep, "convinced" experience of truth. And accordingly, he is suggesting here that what is important to the analytic process and its aim is coming to know the truth of the psychical events, the phantasies and thought-connections, in this deep experiential way—not memory *per se.*

Freud continues to argue against his own claim that the aim of analysis remains filling gaps in memory by now pointing to (a) how, in the case of obsessional neurosis, what appears as "forgetting" is actually "dissolving thought-connections, failing to draw the right conclusions and isolating memories." And (b) how there are childhood experiences that were not understood at the time of their occurrence and so, while impacting the child's mind, were not actually known to him and, thus, he cannot actually have memory of them. In analysis, he can come to know them, but this knowledge, Freud notes, is not memory; rather, the patient first comes to know what was in the mind in some un-understandable, infantile, form.

These "interpolated remarks" lead Freud to a more explicit acknowledgement of the change that took place in the evolution of the technique. After first noting that the present technique leaves nothing of the "delightfully smooth course of events" that took place when hypnosis was applied, he openly affirms that, in fact, now, under the new technique, "the patient does not *remember* anything of what he has forgotten and repressed," rather, Freud stresses, he "*acts* it out." Freud continues: "He reproduces it not as a memory but as an action; he *repeats* it, without, of course, knowing that he is repeating it." Freud presents some examples of how one lives out, in the present with the analyst, unwanted psychical reality. These examples are not of definite contents, thoughts, and feelings at certain moments, but, rather, basic mental attitudes, underlying trends at work in the patient's mind, and libidinal impulses that shape the way he thinks and perceives the world. Specifically, Freud refers to defiance of authority, a desperate sense of inevitable failure, feelings of shame in engaging with the analyst, of having nothing to say and awaiting input on the part of the analyst, which Freud understands as manifestations, expression in action, in the transference, of basic early stances—in regard to parental authority, to the failure of infantile "sexual research," sexual activity, and homosexual wishes.

At the time of writing this paper Freud has already introduced and elaborated his notion of transference. But the way in which he focuses here on the tie of what is repeated in the transference to the notion of memory brings to the fore his struggle to articulate a more complex notion of the thought processes going on in psychic reality that would explain especially the "what" of knowing within the analytic process.

At one point Freud, in effect, puts this question directly on the table and tries to answer it. He writes:

> We have learnt that the patient repeats instead of remembering, and repeats under the conditions of resistance. *We may now ask what it is that he in fact repeats or acts out.* The answer is that he repeats everything that has already made its way from the sources of the repressed into his manifest <u>personality</u>—his inhibitions and unserviceable attitudes and his pathological character-traits.
>
> (Freud, 1914g, p. 151, my italics)

In sum, the "what" of analytic knowing now moves beyond specific memory of events and associated feelings and thoughts in terms of both content and form. It is not a matter of remembering ideas and feelings, but states of being, and these states were never best or first expressed as ideas or feelings. From another perspective, it may be said that Freud is trying to say (albeit with some difficulty) that the reproductions of transference are not later, more distanced, versions of memories—the memories being what truly needs to be known in analysis. Rather, paradoxically perhaps, the re-production is also the original; it is a "conjur[ed] up piece of real life", and it is this piece of "real life" that needs to be known in analysis. It is some kind of encounter with it—not a recollection—that is curative.

It is in his notion of compulsion to repeat that the "why" of analytic knowing comes more clearly into focus.

Compulsion to repeat—The "why"

The concept of "compulsion to repeat" first appears in Freud's writings in "Remembering, Repeating and Working-Through". Referring to the fact that so-called memories find expression in action Freud states: "As long as the patient is in the treatment he cannot escape from this compulsion to repeat; and in the end we understand that this is his way of remembering." But what is this compulsion to repeat? Why is the person subject to it? What is this force pushing him to remember that which he wishes not to?

To consider these questions it is important to first take note of what may be seen to be Freud's contradictory description of repetition. While, as we see here, he regards it as a "way of remembering," he also (as he does in other parts of his technical writings) <u>contrasts</u> it with remembering, speaking of it as taking the place of "the impulse to remember"—a mysterious term, which, interestingly, Freud uses only in this paper. "The greater the resistance", Freud tells us, the more extensively will acting out (repetition) *replace* remembering" (my italics). The contradiction suggests that Freud has two notions of remembering. There is what he refers to as "the ideal remembering of what has been forgotten", a clear kind of conscious recollection, associated with his hypnotic method and the complete overcoming of resistance. And there is memory that takes place under the sway of resistance—this is repetition. Freud is ambiguous in regard to the latter—at times acknowledging it as a form of remembering and at other times emphasizing its opposition to remembering—at these times seemingly limiting the notion of remembering only to its "ideal" form of clear, conscious recollection. The shifts to this limited view are especially notable because, in this text, Freud's presentation of what it is that has to be remembered is, as noted just previously, closer to something lived through repetition than consciously recollected.

This ambiguity points to the complexity not only of Freud's notion of remembering, but also of his conception of the motives for doing so. In effect, Freud is suggesting here that there is in the person a force pushing towards memory, an *impulse* to remember, which at times finds expression as a compulsion to repeat. Depending on which notion of remembering Freud has in mind at the moment, the compulsion is regarded as either in the service of the impulse to remember or in opposition to it, joining forces with the resistance. But Freud never openly discusses the impulse to remember, only the compulsion to repeat. It would seem as though he was more comfortable discussing the person's opposition to knowing than his desire to know. And the compulsion to repeat, regarded in part as an oppositional force, could, thus, provide a good cover under which he could begin to explore the notion of a desire to know.

In other contexts, I have discussed the complex factors underlying Freud's difficulty with justifying the person's desire to know (e.g., Blass, 2006), but, without going into the long and complex details, one can readily see that it does not sit well with Freud's general view of human motivation. Depending on the model applied, this general view has centered on wish-fulfillment, gratification, discharge of tension, self-preservation or pleasure seeking. Indeed, Freud also emphasizes that the person has a need to see reality, but only to maximize the attainment of the other aims. In this context, it is easy to see why repression takes place (it's the natural opposition to the pain or unpleasure of knowledge), but difficult to account for an inherent desire to know and, later, to remember.

Within "Remembering, Repeating and Working-Through" Freud goes beyond his regular framework of motivation, and does indeed, albeit somewhat covertly, posit a force pushing towards knowledge, towards memory, but he cannot at this point actually back it up. He allows for a compulsion to repeat as an inner inescapable force impelling the person towards some form of remembering, and yet is quick to shift to the repressive view of it. In turn the patient's move towards remembering is viewed either as a result of an intellectual understanding on the part of the patient that knowledge would have a curative effect, which is ultimately in his best interest and/ or something instigated and driven by the analyst, who is the one actually concerned with remembering.

These ideas are not directly discussed and emerge here mainly in the context of Freud's reflections on the dangers of repetition in analysis. For example, in this context, Freud speaks of the courageous, open, and tolerant attitude the patient must come to adopt in relation to his illness, through awareness (in part encouraged by the analyst) of the benefits of mental health. He writes that the patient

> must find the courage to direct his attention to the phenomena of his illness. His illness itself must no longer seem to him contemptible, but must become an enemy worthy of his mettle, a piece of his personality, which has solid ground for its existence and out of which things of value for his future life have to be derived. The way is thus paved from the beginning for a reconciliation with the repressed material which is coming to expression in his symptoms, while at the same time place is found for a certain tolerance for the state of being ill. If this new attitude towards the illness intensifies the conflicts and brings to the fore symptoms which till then had been indistinct, one can easily console the patient by pointing out that these are only necessary and temporary aggravations and that one cannot overcome an enemy who is absent or not within range.

The notion of the desire for knowledge residing in the analyst may be seen in the picture Freud paints of the analysis being a kind of field of battle between the analyst and patient (reminiscent of the conclusion of Freud's "Dynamics of Transference"). The analyst, Freud writes,

> is prepared for a perpetual struggle with his patient to keep in the psychical sphere all the impulses which the patient would like to direct into the motor sphere; and he celebrates it as a triumph for the treatment if he can bring it about that something that the patient wishes to discharge in action is disposed of through the work of remembering.

Freud goes on to explain that what facilitates this analytic triumph is positive transference.

But the intellectual understanding of the benefits of remembering or the pressure to do so on the part of the analyst does not capture Freud's idea (embedded in his notion of a compulsion to repeat) of there being an inherent impulse to remember. And these intellectual and external forces seem far too meagre to counter the unconscious inner forces that feed the repression.

The fact that something here is missing points once again to the transitional nature of this text. It is only when Freud begins to seriously revise his thinking on motivation six years later in his *Beyond the Pleasure Principle* (1920g), that the idea that there is a force within the person moving towards self-knowledge finds at least *some* theoretical grounding. In that text, Freud argues that a closer look at human behavior, both in the clinical situation and outside it, makes clear that the person is not, as he had previously thought, driven by pleasure–seeking alone. He repeatedly engages in activities that can produce no pleasure, allow no satisfaction and cannot be reframed as providing covert pleasure and satisfaction. In this context Freud presented his famous examples of trauma dreams and of children's play (the 'fort da' play) in which clearly unpleasurable states are repeatedly returned to. However, Freud is quick to offer alternative explanations that might still account for these within a pleasure centered model. Ultimately, it was the transference, and especially the return within it to narcissistic injuries of childhood, that were never pleasurable and could never be so that convinced Freud. Indeed, he concluded, there must be another internal force, a compulsion to repeat, that runs counter to the pleasure principle.

As Freud develops his ideas in *Beyond the Pleasure Principle*, the fact that he is continuing from where he left off in "Remembering, Repeating and Working-Through" is very notable. He first returns to his view of the analyst and patient opposing each other's aims in the analytic situation. He writes:

> There is no doubt that the resistance of the conscious and unconscious ego operates under the sway of the pleasure principle: it seeks to avoid the unpleasure which would be produced by the liberation

of the repressed. *Our* efforts, on the other hand, are directed towards procuring the toleration of that unpleasure by an appeal to the reality principle.

The analyst is the one who seeks knowledge; the patient, dominated by the pleasure principle, seeks to repress it, but may be persuaded by the analyst that this is not good for him. But then Freud takes a decisive step forward from "Remembering, Repeating and Working Through" and directly confronts the question that he refrained from asking in that earlier text. He asks: "But how is the compulsion to repeat—the manifestation of the power of the repressed—related to the pleasure principle?" And his answer is that there is no escape from positing that it is a force that runs counter to the pleasure principle. In other words, he openly declares that it does not merely serve repression. Freud draws this conclusion only very reluctantly. In a recent paper, I explained (Blass, 2020, p. 59):

> Freud does not merely present the pros and cons of assuming this concept, with the pros winning the day. Rather he acknowledges the compulsion to repeat painful experience in a way that contradicts the pleasure principle and then explains that it is only seemingly so, and then again acknowledges it and then again explains it away. Moreover, when Freud finally goes with the assumption of the existence of a compulsion to repeat he speaks of this as an act of "courage" on his part (1920, p. 22), and at the very end of his book he reminds us that this act may not be sufficiently grounded, that he may have "overestimated" the significance of "the facts of the compulsion to repeat" out of "deep-rooted internal prejudices, into whose hands our speculation unwittingly plays", especially "where ultimate things, the great problems of science and life, are concerned".

The ultimate things at stake here, as I went on to argue, was the conception of human motivation, a momentous move towards a view of the person as non-egoistic, non-self-serving, which contradicted the grounds of much of Freud's earlier thinking. And what takes its place is a view of the person as seeking life and truth *per se*, regardless of benefits to the self. This new conception is less explicitly discussed by Freud, but may be discerned if one carefully traces his thinking in the final chapters of the *Beyond the Pleasure Principle*, chapters in which he tries to understand what underlies the compulsion to repeat, what its end is, *why* repeat. His answer is that we repeat in order to bind, which, I suggest, in effect means, to make excessive stimulation going on in the mind part of ourselves, thinkable. But when Freud goes on to propose that this effort to think is actually a preliminary step to pleasurable discharge and, thus, only a temporary respite from the pleasure principle, he offers another solution to what lies beyond. What lies beyond the pleasure principle, beyond the satisfaction of the wishes and needs of the self, is life. Pleasure lowers tension and is, thus, associated with a pull towards death, which is opposed, Freud now proposes, by the life instincts, by Eros. As I concluded in my study of Freud's *Beyond the Pleasure Principle* (and counter to some commonly accepted readings of the text), the compulsion to repeat

> draws us to experience that which is painful, to think painful reality. This is important. But like the self-preservative instincts, it is ultimately self-serving and the knowledge it provides is geared towards one's own interests. In contrast, Eros extends beyond the self; it reflects a basic desire to encounter reality, all reality. We want to know not only to fulfil wishes and reduce pain (in accordance with the pleasure and reality principles) or to get a grip on traumatic events around us (through repetition compulsion), but, rather, because of our basic pull to live, to encounter reality, including our own inner reality, truthfully.
>
> (Blass, 2020, p. 1196)

These ideas were fully taken up by Melanie Klein and significantly developed by her. Klein, free of Freud's ideational history and early commitments, could present the desire to be an integrated person, to know oneself, and to recognize reality, however painful and guilt-arousing that may be, as inherent to human nature, as integral to the life instincts, and as the reason why, in analysis, the patient would want to know rather than repress. In "Remembering, Repeating and Working-Through", Freud, through the introduction of a compulsion to repeat has taken some difficult steps in this direction.

Working Through—The "how"

Towards the end of his paper Freud facetiously comments that "but for the title of this paper" he would have ended the paper without discussing the topic of "working through". The question he, apparently, wishes to avoid is *how* remembering, knowing the repressed, cures. Clearly, informing the patient of his resistances does not make them go away, Freud affirms; "giving the resistance a name could not result in its immediate cessation." Freud immediately offers an alternative in the form of "working through" but is brief on the meaning and grounding of this terms. He writes:

> One must allow the patient time to become more conversant with this resistance with which he has now become acquainted, to *work through* it, to overcome it, by continuing, in defiance of it, the analytic work according to the fundamental rule of analysis. Only when the resistance is at its height can the analyst, working in common with his patient, discover the repressed instinctual impulses which are feeding

the resistance; and it is this kind of experience which convinces the patient of the existence and power of such impulses.

On the one hand, Freud seems here to be saying that working through is simply a matter of keeping to business as usual, continuing "analytic work according to the fundamental rule", plodding on—time will help. On the other hand, Freud also offers some vague hints as to why time would help; why sticking to something which, in itself, is unhelpful helps. He speaks here of becoming conversant with the resistance, of the analyst and patient working in common towards discovery of instinctual impulses, and that this involves an experience that allows for conviction. Right before the section on working through Freud writes something similar:

> The main instrument, however, for curbing the patient's compulsion to repeat and for turning it into a motive for remembering lies in the handling of the transference. We render the compulsion harmless, and indeed useful, by giving it the right to assert itself in a definite field. We admit it into the transference as a playground in which it is allowed to expand in almost complete freedom and in which it is expected to display to us everything in the way of pathogenic instincts that is hidden in the patient's mind. ... The transference ... is a piece of real experience.

As the transference becomes alive and real in the analytic situation, it not only provides knowledge of the underlying psychic situation but somehow transforms it. Freud does not go into the details of this and seems to not have worked them out. In fact, his ambiguity is so great that Strachey decides that at one point Freud must have meant the opposite of what he wrote and translates accordingly. This occurs around the comment with which Freud introduces the notion of "working through", which is that patients must "become more conversant with this resistance with which he has now become acquainted, to *work through* it." But this sentence, Strachey tells us, is an accurate translation only of the first edition in German. In all subsequent editions, an accurate translation would be: "to become more conversant with the resistance that is unknown to him." Strachey decided to stay with the first edition text in this context because, as he explains, the later editions "make less good sense." However, I would suggest here that what makes less sense perhaps better captures an intuition regarding the analytic process that Freud was struggling to articulate with limited success. Something happens as the transference is kept alive and regarded as real and present which allows the patient to become conversant with that which is *unknown*, which is not yet a thought or memory *per se*, a dialogue within one's internal world.

While providing little details about this transformative process of working through, Freud concludes the paper by stating that, while difficult both for analyst and patient, "it is a part of the work which effects the greatest changes in the patient and which distinguishes analytic treatment from any kind of treatment by suggestion."

Freud later develops his thinking on working through in *Inhibitions, Symptoms and Anxiety*, the only other text in which he specifically refers to this term. There, he first distinguishes between two kinds of resistance (a bit later broadening this to five kinds). There is resistance of the ego, which can be overcome by "bring[ing] forward logical arguments against it; [and] promis[ing] the ego rewards and advantages if it will give up its resistance." And there is resistance of the unconscious (later referred to as resistance of the id), which, "after the ego resistance has been removed," requires "working through" in order to overcome "the power of the compulsion to repeat" (1926d, p. 153). Similarly, he comes back to this issue (without mentioning "working through") again towards the end of "Analysis Terminable and Interminable" (1937c). But little becomes clearer in terms of the process itself. Freud is apparently aware that the analytic process involves something more deeply unconscious, a conversation with what indeed is "unknown", which he can flag as "working through" but cannot conceptualize in a developed way.

This idea, too, is later developed in Klein's writings (Blass, 2011, 2016), which emphasize how the analytic setting provides a space, a kind of "playground" in which "the whole gamut of love and hatred, anxiety, grief and guilt in relation to the primary objects ... [can be] experienced again and again" (Klein, 1950, p. 79) and through the interpretation of the transference "the negative as well as the positive" (p. 80), a process of integration takes place:

> the earliest frightening figures undergo an essential alternation in the patient's mind—one might say that they basically improve. Good objects—as distinct from idealized ones—can be securely established in the mind only if the strong split between persecutory and ideal figures has diminished, if aggressive and libidinal impulses have come closer together and hatred has become mitigated by love. Such advance in the capacity to synthesize is proof that the splitting processes, which, in my view, originate in earliest infancy, have diminished and that integration of the ego in depth has come about.

In other words, Klein clarifies (or, at least, takes very significant steps towards clarifying) how through this working through and interpretation in the here and now of the repetition that it involves, the patient does not come to know *about* his dynamics, but rather the repressed unconscious world becomes more known to itself; loved and hated objects, learn of and become "conversant" with each other and, in this process, the mind is essentially altered.

Conclusion

While it is well known that basic to traditional psychoanalysis is the tenet that coming to know one's truth in analysis is curative, in Freud's writing this basic tenet is not so readily grounded as one may think. For the idea that knowledge can meaningfully change the forces operative in the person to make sense requires having a conceptual framework that includes notions of knowing that are not intellectual *per se*, of dynamic forces that are regarded as primarily mental states, and of the person as desiring truth at the expense of egoistic aims. I have argued here that, in "Remembering, Repeating and Working-Through," one may see Freud struggling with his insights regarding the curative value of truth. These, it should be noted, are conveyed in the content of what he writes, but also come alive in his very act of writing this text. It is in the writing itself that we find Freud trying to work through ideas that do not make good sense to him, which he cannot yet articulate, and yet cannot let go of, and feels compelled to repeatedly return to, despite overt reluctance and displeasure. This lived struggle leads Freud closer to the development of the conceptual framework needed to ground his ideas on the curative nature of analytic knowledge, but it is, I have maintained, in Melanie Klein's work, that Freud's efforts are taken forward in a significant way.

This understanding of "Remembering, Repeating and Working-Through" brings out the close tie between Klein and Freud and highlights the richness and complexity of traditional analytic thinking. It also reminds us of the difficulty of adhering to the analytic task of providing meaningful and mutative understanding and of the great value in so doing.

Author's note

An earlier version of this paper was published in *International Journal of Psychoanalysis*, 104(3): 436–451.

Note

1 As I have stressed elsewhere, for Freud too, internal object relationships are central (Blass, 2001, 2016), but Klein advanced his thinking about them and, especially, their relationship to thought and knowledge.

References

Blass, R.B. (1992). Did Dora have an Oedipus Complex? A reexamination of the theoretical context of Freud's "fragment of an analysis". *Psychoanalytic Study of the Child, 47*: 159–187.

Blass, R.B. (2001). The teaching of the Oedipus Complex: On making Freud meaningful to university students by unveiling his essential ideas on the human condition. *International Journal of Psychoanalysis, 82*(6): 1105–1121.

Blass, R.B. (2006). A psychoanalytic understanding of the desire for knowledge as reflected in Freud's Leonardo da Vinci and a memory of his childhood. *International Journal of Psychoanalysis, 87*(5): 1259–1276.

Blass, R.B. (2011). On the immediacy of unconscious truth: Understanding Betty Joseph's 'here and now' through comparison with alternative views of it outside of and within Kleinian thinking. *International Journal of Psychoanalysis, 92*(5): 1137–1157.

Blass, R.B. (2016). The quest for truth as the foundation of psychoanalytic practice: A traditional Freudian–Kleinian perspective. *Psychoanalytic Quarterly, 85*(2): 305–337.

Blass, R.B. (2017). Reflections on Klein's radical notion of phantasy and its implications for analytic practice. *International Journal of Psychoanalysis, 98*(3): 841–859.

Blass, R.B. (2019). Freud's view of death and repetition as grounds of a Kleinian approach to narcissism: Implications for clinical practice. *International Journal of Psychoanalysis, 100*(6): 1286–1305.

Blass, R.B. (2020). The role of repetition in narcissism and self-sacrifice: A Freudian Kleinian reflection on the person's foundational love of the other. *International Journal of Psychoanalysis, 101*(6): 1188–1202.

Freud, S. (1912b). The Dynamics of Transference. *S.E., 12*: 97–108. London: Hogarth Press.

Freud, S. (1914g). Remembering, Repeating and Working-Through. *S.E., 12*: 147–156. London: Hogarth Press.

Freud, S. (1917a). A Difficulty in the Path of Psycho-Analysis. *S.E., 17*: 135–144. London: Hogarth Press.

Freud, S. (1919a). Lines of Advance in Psycho-Analytic Therapy. *S.E., 17*: 157–168. London: Hogarth Press.

Freud, S. (1920g). *Beyond the Pleasure Principle. S.E., 18*: 1–64. London: Hogarth Press.

Freud, S. (1926). *Inhibitions, Symptoms and Anxiety. S.E., 20*: 75–176. London: Hogarth Press.

Freud, S. (1937c). Analysis Terminable and Interminable. *S.E., 23*: 209–254. London: Hogarth Press.

Klein, M. (1950). On the criteria for the termination of a psycho-Analysis. In *Envy and Gratitude and Other Works 1946–1963* (pp. 43–47). London: Hogarth, 1975.

Strachey, J. (1934). The nature of the therapeutic action of psychoanalysis. *International Journal of Psychoanalysis, 15*: 127–159.

9 To be Worked Through, or the Untimeliness of *Durcharbeiten*

Riccardo Galiani

Preliminary remarks

As I prepared for my contribution to this collective reflection on "Remembering, Repeating and Working-through", and once I had finished reading (in 2020) the few recent articles explicitly dedicated to this specific Freudian work, I realized I had been magnetized by writings dealing essentially with repetition and its eponym, compulsion. The same thing happened with reading non-psychoanalytic literature. At first, I attributed this attraction to the familiar link between transference and repetition, but although I was rather at home with such "explanation," it still felt awkward and, as such, "suspicious," and possibly symptomatic. Be that as it may, the results of my preliminary inroads into the psychoanalytic literature showed that the attention devoted to "Remembering, Repeating and Working-through" is dominated and, in many cases, burdened, by the question of repetition.[1]

Partly in reaction to that discovery, I started turning my interest to the following question: how can one assess the weight of the *triad* promoted by Freud in the very title of his 1914 article, especially considering the value of what was brought in by the clinical discoveries that led to the turning point of 1920?

The circumstances are such that, a century after Freud was forced to cope with the pervasive trauma of war, my own elaboration was happening at a time when psychoanalytic practice was again challenged by the need to work *with and in* a state of emergency (due to the pandemic)–a condition marked by the need for a rapid response to requests for intervention. Hence, while the importance of remembering and the power of repetition remain unchanged, the function of the third element in the Freudian title seems in danger of being forfeited. And yet, working-through is often identified, following Freud's own indications, as another *shibboleth* of psychoanalysis (Semi, 2006). Freud indeed assigns a defining role to the working-through of the resistances when (with rhetorics in no way naive) he begins the conclusion of his paper by saying that it is working-through "which effects the greatest changes in the patient and which distinguishes analytic treatment from any kind of treatment by suggestion" (Freud, 1914g, pp. 154–155).

DOI: 10.4324/9781003458340-9

The "motive" of the present study thus became ever more clearly concerned with the role of *durcharbeiten* and what it can possibly have to say about today's analytical practice. This also implies asking whether its link with repetition should still be taken for granted, or if we should rather think of a *durcharbeiten* beyond and before, or this side of, repetition.

1. Repetition

In support of this motive, let us first be reminded that what, in the *Standard Edition* and elsewhere, stands under the term "repetition" refers to a variety of experiences not always accompanied by compulsion and sometimes not even "repetitive." This polysemy gives rise to a difficulty similar to that encountered in some translations of the book *Gjentagelsen*, by Søren Kierkegaard (1843). Indeed, in spite of the word used in the title, the book essentially refers to an experience other than repetition. *Gjentagelsen* defines first a "second beginning," a restart, the new beginning being that of Søren's and Regine's relationship, that is, not its mere repetition, but its renewal. While the term "repetition" evokes either similarity in the reproduction of a word or gesture, or the sclerosis of habit, implying "more of the same," Kierkegaard's *Gjentagelsen*, on the contrary, is a new life, that of the new reconciled creature ("reconciliation is resumption *sensu eminentori*," writes Kierkegaard). This new creature is still "I", still the same, and yet always "other", in every moment (Viallaneix, 1990, p. 57). In this perspective, repetition appears as a sort of "failing" of the human aptitude for reprise (in the musical sense), for a "second time" or for the dimension of the "*nach*" (in the Freudian sense).

In summarizing the psychoanalytic implications of this question, Balsamo (2007, p. 957) recalls that its centrality was well highlighted by Lacan. As we know, Lacan considered repetition one of the four fundamental concepts of psychoanalysis (Lacan, 1973). He observed that to repeat (*wiederholen*) and to reproduce (*reproduzieren*) are not the same thing, for while the (symptomatic) reproduction appears as a reproduction of the same (e.g., as in the reproduction of a painting), repetition is inherent to a symbolic dimension that, being always active, introduces a difference with respect to the original. Deleuze (1968, pp. 39–40; English translation, 1994, p. 24), theorized two levels of repetition: one "horizontal," as repetition of the same, represented by automatism, by the blocking of concepts and representation, the other "vertical," that of symbolic determination, specified by displacements and transformations.

Hence, repetition is not a univocal concept and compulsion itself and, far from clarifying its mode of action, requires in turn some "interpretative proposals" in trying to account for this lack of univocality (Pozzi, 1987, p. 141). It could be said that the capacity to take different forms is in the nature of the urge to repeat. This urge is a blind and impersonal force, compulsively aimed at de-subjectalization, but it is also a force whose compulsive nature, manifest through the phenomena of transference, tends to bring the subject back to a time that is "non-existent except in actualization," a time "in which he had never been", as De Renzis (2009, p. 48) recalls, using the words of Giorgio Caproni.[2] Thus, the interaction between the three verbs in Freud's title (remembering, repeating, working-through), before giving way to the predominance of the second term, opens up this potential variety of repetition.

2.

"Remembering, Repeating and Working-through" is a writing in which Freud, after decisively "settling the scores" with Jung, feels he can express more clearly, in an almost definitive form, his views on analytical practice (see letter to Karl Abraham of 29 July, 1914; Sedat, 2019). Perhaps that is why, by including the intrapsychic dynamics of the patient in the midst of what was meant to be a "technical paper," Freud can now look at the phenomenon of repetition in a way that reveals its paradoxically transformative potential: the capacity to act on the (compulsive) binding aspects of repetition itself. In fact, the clinical examples proposed by Freud highlight transmutations occurring within the session, that is, a passage from the act to its potentiality, from there to the act of enunciation, and from the latter to its flowing back on the subject (Bouchard, 2000).

The potentialities of repetition—in part still without compulsion but already hinting at what is revolutionary when clinical work is linked to repetition (Garella, 2007)—correspond to the salient aspects of a process defined by Freud using the wide semantic field of the preposition *durch* and the verb *arbeiten*.

As a whole, the title of the paper, with its substantivized verbs that designate acts, draws an "exemplary form of trilogical conjunction" (Assoun, 2009). While the first two terms designate familiar notions, the novelty of the paper rests on the third element: *durcharbeiten*. A verb that brings to our attention the characteristics of an elaboration (*arbeiten*) exerted through (*durch*), the resistances, and which uses repetition (at least at its beginning) as a substitute for the unavailable memory. Thus, in a warning directed at both young analysts and seasoned practitioners, the introduction of a "time for working-through" (Bouchard, 2000) first signals the insufficiency of recollection and then the relative ineffectiveness of interpretation. What will later be called "resistance of the unconscious" (Freud, 1926d, p. 160) in fact inaugurates a new awareness: that analysis is not a "positive" therapeutic work, in that it lacks the pre-defined points of reference of a strategy. Defined as "the most complete characterization of the patient's role in analysis" (Sedler, 1983, p. 75) and complemented with the heightened role of the analyst's patience and capacity to wait, now deemed an essential therapeutic stance, the introduction of *durcharbeiten* highlights the special kind of work required for the unfolding of a proper analytic process.[3]

3.

In the few lines explicitly dedicated at the end of the writing to *durcharbeiten*, Freud makes us grasp this peculiarity by underlining a step-by-step logic, in which the duration of the treatment is incompressible and evolves at its own pace, with no real pause between the sessions (Bouchard, 2000, p. 1081), and, above all, finding its roots in the theory of the *après-coup* (*Nachträglichkeit*). What emerges is a "tool" with little appeal on the market of quick therapeutic efficacy; a "dis-appeal" that Freud, however, will even accentuate at the end of his life. Returning to *durcharbeiten*—without naming it—in the *Outline of Psychoanalysis*, he describes it as a work requiring an incessant effort paid back with an uncertain outcome (Freud, 1940a[1938], pp. 178–182). In the wake of Sedat, we could say that the introduction of working-through in 1914 announced the end of the direction of treatment: "To rise to the occasion and to stay free of any theoretical hold, the analyst must be level with the patient" (Sedat, 2011, p. 64, my translation). Placing himself at the level of the patient, yet without underestimating the necessary dissymmetry (Fédida, 1973), the analyst encounters various modalities of working-through as well as their dependence "on the kind of psychoanalytic work required by different transference situations and different modes of mental functioning" (Roussillon, 2010, pp. 1405–1406). These different modes involve different degrees of "ego strength" and different time frames for becoming "conversant with the resistance" (Freud, 1914g, p. 155) and with pathogenic defense (Sedler, 1983, p. 81).

To be conversant with resistance and defenses one must be able to imagine a suitable interlocutor, open to dialogue yet not too easily influenced; an average strong ego, in short. Today, this kind of statement could make one lean towards the shelving of working-through, since most of contemporary patients enter the analytic room without being able to formulate a request for analysis, but rather with the hope of finding the proper conditions for building the strength they do not feel they possess.

Although it is possible to recognize the "signs" of working-through even in analysands "at the limits of the analyzable" (Montagnier, 2000), yet, even in the latter, the same insistence implied by the repetition of the drive motions is what summons a form of working-through, be it a process already present or one that needs to be facilitated. Working-through is necessary because the drive insists.[4]

"Working-through" would then be the name for both a psychic process *and* a direction to follow in the continuous search for a central feature, if only to come to terms with another trait of psychoanalytic practice that has become increasingly dominant, which is the duration of treatment.

Brenner (1987, p. 92) was not far from the truth when he stated that the introduction of working-through in 1914 and Freud's attempts in subsequent years to define it more precisely were already

> attempting to answer the question: 'Why does analysis take so long? Why doesn't a patient get well as soon as the analyst has understood correctly the nature and origins of the patient's unconscious wishes and correctly interpreted them to the patient?'

In view of which Brenner concluded: "Working-through is not a regrettable delay in the process of analytic cure. It *is* analysis" (p. 103).

With its unique stride, *durch*/through qualifies psychoanalysis by being the only work on resistance that, operating on that singular form of repetition that is transference, can produce a psychic change in the patient. It is perhaps also for this reason that, in a passage from "The direction of the treatment and the principles in its power", Lacan (1958) translates *Durcharbeitung* with "transference work" (in Fink's English rendition, p. 526). It is, indeed, in transference that "repeating becomes a reason to remember" (Assoun, 1994, p. 350): to remember and to experience the memory, but differently from an alleged reconstruction of the past: "everything/is *still* as/I have *never* left it".

What, then, is the analyst's stance in support of such activity of the patient? Is it necessarily another form of activity? No, not necessarily. For example, one could also think of a complementary experience, which takes place when the analyst does not interpret and does not speak; we could say then, with Guarnieri, that "the analyst's 'free floating attention' in the session represents the best the condition for working-through to take place" (2013, p. 31, translation slightly modified). Or, with Rolland (2006), we could go so far as to formulate a real "elaborative" or "working-through" form of listening, letting working-through help us identify some conditions for a properly analytic listening, that is, a listening that "creates the transferential address" (Scarfone, 2020, p. 377).

4.

At the present stage of my own experience, I agree with those who maintain that listening becomes analytical when, over time, with the continuous working and reworking of the residues of their own analysis, and of all the other analyses they took part in, analysts "de-semanticize," "de-signify," ever more constantly and ever less intentionally, what they hear. This "anasemic" stance, which I mention in reference to N. Abraham (1968), Fédida (1984), but also Russo (2009), is not some analytic "skill", but a mode of functioning, or even better, an *experience*, which is progressively allowed to take over our listening, thus creating a sort of counterweight to the effects of the "universal marker of the unconscious", that is, *Entstellung*, distortion (Hock, 2020, p. 425).

We could say, about listening, what Fédida said of a thought: that it is psychoanalytic when "it is [itself] the gap in the spoken words, or when it is the existence of spoken words in the gap separating them from their being pronounced" (Fédida, 1984, p. 118). As we can see, whatever activity there is in this listening, it is the one exerted by words, in their turning up, with their own knowledge of things beyond the things said: "The words that are about to emerge know things about us that we don't know about them."[5]

Considering this activity of words, and in order to represent the analyst's condition, we must move towards an anticipatory disposition, similar to that capacity that Winnicott (1960) hoped the analyst would be gifted with for attaining an adequate interpretation: "the analyst is prepared to wait a long time to be in a position to do exactly this kind of work" (p. 37). This *preparedness to wait a long time to be in a given position* is equivalent to a readiness to be, so to speak, "worked-through" by what, being misunderstood, acts from within the words that are heard, be it in the patient's speech or in one's own inner discourse. Such an experience is probably more usefully thought of in terms of "passivity".

I am tempted to also read in this key Laurence Kahn's (2012) suggestion regarding the action performed in terms of *palpation* of the "psychic surfaces" that we deal with in the session. Writes Kahn:

> the action of the analyst is in truth carried out with respect to the very configuration of the relation: not in terms of the 'handling' of the transference, but precisely because of its 'palpable' character. Or, more to the point, *because* of the influence of palpation on the psychic formation itself. For what kind of palpation are we talking of? It is for sure the palpation of the 'psychic surface' of the patient, which must be known at all times in order to determine which complexes and resistances are elicited. But how to conceive of this palpation except as the analyst's use of his own unconscious as an instrument of perception, since the patient's action – not what he says, but what he does by saying it – operates by 'influencing the analyst's unconscious sensitivity'?
>
> (pp. 158–159)[6]

But what else is "the analyst's use of his own unconscious" if not a readiness to be "used", influenced, modified, unbeknown to him, by the action of this perceptual tool? Being both "allo-" and "auto-", this "palpation" helps us conceive of what it means for the analyst to be "worked-through" by a form created by the libidinal investments within his unconscious. A form that acts on the analyst's unconscious through what, in the pronounced words, was listened to and "heard", that is, through the affective signals carried by the voice, its tones, its intonations (2012, pp. 107–109; Kahn, 2016).

I believe the readiness to let oneself be "worked-through" by a form supports what Scarfone (2004) called the "negative rule of working-through," that is, "the ethical duty of the analyst … to not know where this is all going to lead" (p. 116). In agreement with the advice to heed more closely a neglected analogy (Mahon, 2004), one could say that rather than hoping for the patient's active effort towards change, even outside of the session (e.g., "the patient must be willing to do some of the analytic work outside of the hour"; Greenson, in Schmale, 1966, p. 177), the negative rule of working-through aims at creating the conditions for experiencing working as a "playing."

Beyond what this reference to playing may suggest, this attitude, this readiness of the analyst to let himself be modified was repeatedly designated by Scarfone (1994, 2019) with the term *passibility*, borrowed from Lyotard (1988). The analyst's passibility creates the prerequisites for a similar disposition in the patient, who, in turn, will be better able to tolerate in himself mutative processes, starting from those resulting from the analytical situation, and among them working-through.

5.

The link that I am trying to evince between working-through and overcoming the analyst-centered conception of our work is a tight and long-lasting one; this impression was supported when I consulted the series of papers that Lawrence Friedman devoted to Freud's technical writings.[7] After more than a century, then, it appears that in this link lie the reasons why the concept of working-through was unwelcome by Freud's fellow analysts (Friedman, 2014, p. 23). Their defensive attitude was elicited by the ghosts that the idea of working-through had awakened by overshadowing the conception of an analyst as a "wise" interpreter, engaged in a positive role and an active performance. Such "Copernican" relativization of the analyst's position (Laplanche, 1992) brings with it the confirmation of the need for a second, third, fourth … moment, at any rate, for a time operating always "after" the time of the hand-to-hand encounter between the patient's ego and the offshoots of the timeless unconscious. Quoting Freud again:

> One *must* allow the patient time to become more conversant with this resistance with which he has now become acquainted, to *work through* it, to overcome it, by continuing, in defiance of it, the analytic work according to the fundamental rule of analysis.
>
> (Freud, 1914g, p. 155; italics added to "must")

The topicality of working-through lies precisely in this emphasis on the time needed for the patient to converse with the resistances ever more identified as the resistances of the unconscious. In this sense, the paper revealing the role of working-through to the psychoanalytic community is also remarkable for its decisive role in redefining the analytical space. A space requiring less of an active presence—that is, of the person of the analyst— and a greater readiness to listen and be open to something whose anachronistic nature can possibly endow the present with memory (Fédida, 1985). In other words, a listening that is open to the dimension of experience defined by Nietzsche (1874) as *Unzeitgemässe* (untimely) and that Deleuze and Guattari (1991) portray as "… blocs of childhood that are the becoming-child of the present …" (p. 168).[8] In its own way, psychoanalysis—a discipline which, being itself untimely, is concerned with the untimely— contributes to relocating these blocs with working-through, carrying them over to the field of transferential dynamics.

If working-through belongs to "Freud's legacy to the psychoanalysis of the future" (Riolo, 2008), it is precisely because it emphasizes the analytic method's "specific operational sense." Accordingly, we can conceive of this specificity as "a system of transformation, whereby unconscious somatopsychic processes (whether repressed or non-repressed) become representable" (*ibid.*, p. 9). A system that does not, however, alter the characteristics proper to the consistency of psychic reality and comes to terms with latency and *après-coup*. Thus, while remaining a "system," it can also be thought of (following Jean-Luc Donnet, 2005, p. 115) as an "opaque crossing."

For Donnet there is, in fact, an even more specific link between working-through and the future: not only does it connote the latency time implied by *après-coup*, as described in "Remembering, Repeating and Working-Through," but it also refers to a "psychic vagrancy, […] a necessary wandering, […] to openness towards the unknown, in short to indeterminacy. By binding and dissolving the past and the present, working-through makes possible the projection into the future" (p. 113). A working-through, Donnet goes on, that all the same showed its insufficiency when confronted with the appearance of the "dark side" of repetitive *agieren*, which, in 1914, gave the lived experience of/in the transference its irreplaceable value. Only in its original sense of working-through the resistances, can the movement of working-through acquire a therapeutic function. A movement going from present to past; from the timelessness of the unconscious in action to the chronological construction that creates meaning.

Donnet's view converges nicely with a precise remark by Friedman:

[T]he term *working-through* is expressly coined to refer to an action on a *resistance*, because the 'through' depicts a rough trip under assault from a countervailing barrage. One can work *on* many things but, as the term is used here, there is nothing one can work *through* other than a resistance. The term is invented to give that activity both a name and a picture. It is worth asking why the plain meaning of this passage is regularly ignored in favor of any and all associations that an analyst may have to the English words, 'working' and 'through'.

(Friedman, 2014, p. 17)

This activity *of the patient* (p. 20) must be prepared, however, through reciprocal elaborative cross-references, in which what reaches the patient is not so much the analyst's ability to understand and/or interpret, but, rather, the link between this ability and the analyst's capacity to let himself be modified by his own unconscious. An unconscious that has "perceived" the offshoots of the patient's unconscious, which I would say is the equivalent of the working-through of his own resistances (Lacan, 1978, p. 267). Only to the extent that it arises from this *common ground of possibility* can the working-through of the resistances consolidate the patient's disposition to tolerate in himself, and thus progressively integrate, "the radically singular experience of his own psychic reality" (Donnet, 2005).

When I considered them in this perspective, Ekstein's (1965) observations on "the philosophy of ending" (p. 58) took a strong relevance, and all the more so those of Sedat (2019) on the relationship between working-through and the progression of analytic treatment:

> Working-through allows to do away with the terminable/interminable issue in analysis. It could indeed be argued that analysis does have an end, which is the end of the addiction to the other, to others, for the patient to the analyst, and for the analyst to the patient.
>
> (p. 39)[9]

Far from being a relic of classical treatment, with its relativization of the analyst's activity as investigator/interpreter, "Remembering, repeating and working-through" introduces what today, following Scarfone, we can consider as the resources of the "passivity" of both patient and analyst in the analytic situation. To be in analysis is to be "worked-through."

The topicality of working-through, then, resides in its untimeliness: a situation marked by an elaboration that is repeatedly experienced, "endured" by both analyst and analysand, and which, as it were, makes *patients* of them both, with respect to the scansion of the time for comprehending (Lacan, 1975, p. 314), or, rather, to the scansion of a rhythm always necessarily lagging behind the representations of consciousness (here again I come across what Francesco Napolitano mentioned to me about his research project). Moreover, by working inside and through this temporality, transference "libidinizes" repetition, as was once said with some good reasons (Lagache, 1951).

"Libidinizing" repetition is a claim that only analytical practice can make, founded as it is on a method that ceaselessly tries to remain in tune with the "*nach*" or posterior, two-step scansion, specific to human psychic life, traversed since its inception by the infantile sexual. The time of analysis, then, can only coincide with that of working-through: a "reverberation time" (Birksted-Breen, 2009, 2012), delayed time, repeated time, endured time, capable of preparing constructions that will later become fully recognizable. The "passive" untimeliness of working-through is the untimeliness of psychoanalysis itself.

Notes

1 In a lexicological analysis carried out on the results of a previous research on the psychoanalytic literature dedicated to transference (in Galiani & Napolitano, 2016), the frequency ratio of the term "repetition" to that of "working-through" (and their various translations) was about 100 to 1.

2 Ritorno ("Return"), 1971: "Sono tornato là / dove non ero mai stato. / Nulla, da come non fu, è mutato. / Sul tavolo (sull'incerato / a quadretti) ammezzato / ho ritrovato il bicchiere / mai riempito. Tutto / è ancora rimasto quale / mai l'avevo lasciato"; in G. Caproni, *L'opera in versi*, 1982 ["I returned there / Where I had never been. / Nothing, from how it was not, has changed. / On the table (the checkered / cloth), half-filled / I found the glass / never filled. Everything / is still as / I have never left it." In *The Wall of the Earth* (1964–1975), English translation by P. Verdicchio; Guernica Editions, Toronto, 1992; p. 374].

3 Prior to 1914, Freud used the substantive *Durcharbeitung* in *Studien über Hysterie* (*Studies on Hysteria*) in relation to remembering (see, for instance, Bouchard, 2000; Amigorena - Rosenberg, 2008).

4 For Montagnier (2000, pp. 1108–1109) the signs that point at working-through with an analysand "at the limit" are: the appearing of screen-memories; the presence of dreams and phantasies; the passage from fragmented representations, affects and thoughts, to the capacity for transformation in which the present has a future that also speaks of the past; the achievement of a point of integration of the narcissistic drive motions.

5 "Les mots qui vont surgir savent de nous des choses que nous ignorons d'eux": René Char, Ma feuille vineuse, in *Chants de la Balandrane*, 1975–1977.

6 "L'action de l'analyste s'exerce en vérité dans la configuration même de la relation : non pas sous l'aspect du « maniement » du transfert, mais justement du fait de son caractère « palpable ». Ou, plus exactement, du fait de l'influence de la palpation sur la formation psychique elle-même. Car de quelle palpation s'agit-il ? De celle de la « surface psychique » du patient certes, qu'il importe de connaître à tout moment, afin de déterminer quels complexes et quelles résistances sont mobilisés. Mais comment concevoir cette palpation en dehors de l'usage par l'analyste de son propre inconscient comme instrument de perception, puisque l'action du patient – non pas ce qu'il dit, mais ce qu'il fait en disant – opère par « influence sur la sensibilité inconsciente » de l'analyste ?"

7 I owe the appreciation of Friedman's work (1991, 2014) to Francesco Napolitano who, for his part, is starting a research into the roots of working-through in Freud's *Project*, a research involving a closer look at the two representations (one conscious, the other repressed) resulting from interpretation. These are subjected to attempts at connection thanks to a working-through that gives way—always in a delayed manner—to the opening of new paths for thinking (Napolitano, 2020).

8 "...blocs d'enfance qui sont des devenirs enfant du présent". It is not for me to say how complex is the issue of translating, in different languages, the adjective "*unzeitgemässe*" and the term *Unzeitgemässheit* derived from it. As far as the English language is concerned, to the more well-established translation "untimely" (e.g., Large, 1994) has been added that of *unfashionable*, in an edition (Standford, 1999) that is said to follow almost to the letter the work of Giorgio Colli and Mazzino Montinari, the curators of the German edition of Nietzsche's works, who, in the Italian translation, opt for "inattuale" (untimely) and "inattualità" (untimeliness).

9 "La perlaboration permet de sortir de la problématique analyse finie / analyse infinie. On peut en effet soutenir que l'analyse a bien une fin, qui est la fin de l'addiction à l'autre, aux autres, pour l'analysant à son analyste, et aussi pour l'analyste à son analysant."

References

Abraham, N. (1968). The Shell and the Kernel: The Scope and Originality of Freudian Psychoanalysis. In N. Abraham and M. Torok, *The Shell and the Kernel: Renewals of Psychoanalysis*. Chicago, IL: University of Chicago Press, 1994.

Amigorena-Rosenberg, N. (2008). Perlaboration. In C. Le Guen (Ed.), *Dictionnaire freudien*. Paris: PUF.

Assoun, P.L. (1994). *La passion de répétition. Genèse et figures de la compulsion dans la métapsychologie freudienne*. RFP, 2.

Assoun, P.L. (2009). *Dictionnaire des œuvres psychanalytiques* (pp. 1173–1175). Paris: PUF.

Balsamo, M. (2007). Ripetizione, coazione a ripetere, destino. In F. Barale, M. Bertani, V. Gallese, S. Mistura, A. Zamperini (Eds), *Psiche. Dizionario storico di psicologia, psichiatria, psicoanalisi, neuroscienze*. Turin: Einaudi.

Birksted-Breen D. (2009), Reverberation time, dreaming and the capacity to dream. In *The International Journal of Psychoanalysis, 90*: 35–51.

Birksted-Breen, D. (2012). Taking time: The tempo of psychoanalysis. *International Journal of Psychoanalysis, 93*: 819–835.

Bouchard, C. (2000). Processus analytique et insaisissable perlaboration. *Revue Française de Psychanalyse, 4*: 1077–1092.

Brenner, C. (1987). Working-Through: 1914–1984. *Psychoanalytic Quarterly, 56*: 88–108.

Caproni, G. (1982). *L'opera in versi*. Milan: Meridiani Mondadori.

Deleuze, G. (1968). *Différence et Répétition*. Paris: PUF [English translation: *Difference and Repetition*. New York: Columbia University Press, 1994].

Deleuze, G. & Guattari, F. (1991). *Qu'est-ce que la philosophie?* Paris: Les Editions de Minuit.

De Renzis, G. (2009). Ripetizione e violenza. In A. Garella, R. Musella (Eds), *Violenza e simbolizzazione*. Bari-Roma: labiblioteca.

Donnet, J.L. (2005). Le silence de la perlaboration. In *La situation analysante*. Paris: PUF [English translation: *The Analyzing Situation*. London: Karnac Books, 2009; Routledge, 2018].

Ekstein, R. (1965). Working-through and Termination of Analysis. *Journal of the American Psychoanalytic Association, 13*(1): 57–78.

Fédida, P. (1973). D'une essentielle dissymétrie dans la psychanalyse. In *Nouvelle Revue de Psychanalyse, 3* [Italian translation in P. Fédida, *Aprire la parola. Scritti 1968–2002*. Rome: Borla, 2012].

Fédida, P. (1984). Technique psychanalytique et métapsychologie. In P. Fédida, *Ouvrir la parole (textes choisis par R. Galiani)*. Paris: MJW Fédition, 2014.

Fédida, P. (1985). Passé anachronique et présent réminiscent. Epos et puissance mémoriale du langage. *L'Ecrits du temps*, n. 10 [Italian translation: in P. Fédida, *Aprire la parola*.].

Freud, S. (1895). *Project for a Scientific Psychology*. S.E., 1: 283–397. London: Hogarth Press.

Freud, S. (1914g). Remembering, Repeating and Working-Through. S.E., 12: 145–156. London: Hogarth Press.

Freud, S. (1926d). *Inhibitions, Symptoms and Anxiety*. S.E., 20: 77–174. London: Hogarth Press.

Freud, S. (1940a[1938]). *An Outline of Psycho-Analysis*. S.E., 23: 141–207. London: Hogarth Press.

Friedman, L. (1991). A Reading of Freud's Papers on Technique. *Psychoanalytic Quarterly*, LX: 564–595.

Friedman, L. (2014). The Discrete and the Continuous in Freud's "Remembering, Repeating and Working-Through". *Journal of the American Psychoanalytic Association*, 62: 11–34

Galiani, R. & Napolitano, S. (Eds) (2016). *Il problema del transfert. 1895–2015*. Rome: Alpes Italia.

Garella, A. (2007). Coazione a ripetere. *Rivista di psicoanalisi*, LIII(2): 447–480.

Greenson, R.R. (1965). The Problem of Working-through. In *Drives, Affects, Behavior, Vol. 2* (pp. 277–314). New York: International Universities Press.

Guarnieri, R. (2013). *Durcharbeitung*. The Time of *perlaboration* (or Working-through). *The Italian Psychoanalytic Annual*: 27–38.

Hock, U. (2020). Sortir des impasses du pluralisme: la notion de *Entstellung*. In O. Bombarde, F. Neau, & C. Matha (Eds), *Quelques motifs de la psychanalyse. Á partir des travaux de Laurence Kahn*. Paris: Les Belles Lettres.

Kahn, L. (2012). *L'écoute de l'analyste. De l'acte à la forme*. Paris: PUF.

Kahn, L. (2016). L'action de la forme. In L. Danon Boileau, & J.Y. Tamet (Eds), *Des psychanalystes en séance. Glossaire clinique de psychanalyse contemporaine*. Paris: Gallimard.

Kierkegaard, S. (1843). *La ripresa. Tentativo di psicologia sperimentale di Constantin Constantius* [Italian translation, S.E., Milan 2013].

Lacan J. (1958). The Direction of the Treatment and the Principles of its Power. In *Ecrits*, English translation. New York: Norton, 2006.

Lacan, J. (1973). *Le Séminaire. Livre XI. Les quatre concepts fondamentaux de la psychanalyse*, 1964, Seuil, Paris [*The Seminar. Book XI. The Four Fundamental Concepts of Psychoanalysis*. London: Hogarth Press and the Institute of Psycho-Analysis, 1977].

Lacan, J. (1975), *Le Séminaire. Livre I. Les écrits techniques de Freud, 1953–4*. Paris: Seuil [*The Seminar. Book I. Freud's Papers on Technique. 1953–4*. Cambridge: Cambridge University Press, 1987].

Lacan, J. (1978). *Le Séminaire. Livre II. Le moi dans la théorie de Freud et dans la technique de la psychanalyse, 1954–55*. Paris: Seuil [*The Seminar. Book II. The Ego in Freud's Theory and in the Technique of Psychoanalysis, 1954–55*, Cambridge University Press, Cambridge, 1988]

Lagache, D. (1951). Le problème du transfert. *Revue Française de Psychanalyse*, XVI(1–2), Janvier-juin 1952.

Laplanche, J. (1992). The Unfinished Copernican Revolution. In *Essays on Otherness*. London: Routledge, 1999.

Large, D. (1994). On "Untimeliness": Temporal Structures in Nietzsche or "The Day after Tomorrow Belongs to Me". *Journal of Nietzsche Studies*, 8.

Lyotard, J.F. (1988). *L'inhumain. Causeries sur le temps*. Paris: Galilée.

Mahon, E.J. (2004). Playing and Working-through: A Neglected Analogy. *Psychoanalytic Quarterly*, LXXIII: 379–413.

Montagnier, M.T. (2000). Aux limites de l'analysable, la perlaboration. *Revue Française de Psychanalyse*, 4: 1093–1113.

Nietzsche, F. (1874). *Unfashionable Observations: Volume 2*. Stanford, CA: Stanford University Press, 1998.

Napolitano, F. (2020). Personal communication.

Pozzi, O. (1987). Coazione e ripetizione. In A. Muratori (Ed.), *Il "continuo" e il "discreto" in psicoanalisi*. Rome: Borla.

Riolo, F. (2008). Remembering, Repeating and Working-through: Freud's Legacy to the Psychoanalysis of the Future. *The Italian Psychoanalytic Annual.*

Rolland, J.-C. (2006). *Avant d'être celui qui parle.* Paris: Gallimard.

Roussillon, R. (2010). Working-through and its various models. *International Journal of Psychoanalysis, 91:* 1405–1417.

Russo, L. (2009). *Destini dell'identità.* Borla, Rome.

Scarfone, D. (1994). Le féminin comme «passible». In *Revue québécoise de psychologie, 15*(1): 27–67.

Scarfone, D. (2004). À quoi œuvre l'analyse? *Libres cahiers pour la psychanalyse, 9*(1): 109–123.

Scarfone, D. (2019). The feminine, the analyst and the child theorist. *International Journal of Psychoanalysis, 100*(3): 567–575.

Scarfone, D. (2020). Trace et transduction. In O. Bombarde, F. Neau, & C. Matha (Eds), *Quelques motifs de la psychanalyse. À partir des travaux de Laurence Kahn.* Paris: Les Belles Lettres.

Schmale, H.T. (1966). Working-through [Panel Report]. *Journal of the American Psychoanalytic Association, 14:* 172–182.

Sedat, J. (2011). Le déclin de l'interprétation: de l'analyste interprète à l'émergence de la perlaboration. *Figures de la psychanalyse, 21:* 51–67.

Sedat, J. (2019). La perlaboration (Durcharbeitung). *Figures de la psychanalyse, 37:* 27–40.

Sedler, M.J. (1983). Freud's Concept of Working-Through. *Psychoanalytic Quarterly, LII:* 73–98.

Semi, A.A. (2006). Uno sguardo sugli scritti di tecnica di Freud. *Rivista di Psicoanalisi, LII*(4): 1107–1115.

Viallaneix, N. (1990). Introduction. In S. Kierkegaard (1843), *La reprise.* Paris. GF Flammarion.

Winnicott, D.W.W. (1960). The Theory of the Parent–Infant Relationship. In *The Theory of the Parent–Infant Relationship.* London: Hogarth Press and the Institute of Psycho-Analysis, 1965.

10 Working-Through and Memory

Some theoretical and clinical remarks

Roberta Guarnieri

The rereading of a Freudian text seems to me to be, already in and of itself, a proposal brimful of consequences: texts which are continually subjected to re-reading and reinterpretation are defined as "classics," a term applicable above all to literature and to philosophy. In the field of psychoanalysis too, a corpus of classic works has formed, of which Freud's work is the generative center.

Freud's essay, "Remembering, Repeating, and Working-Through" (1914g) is positioned at about midpoint of the collected writings and, according to Paul-Laurent Assoun's persuasive definition, has the characteristics of a "hinge text": it takes stock of the essential aspects of clinical practice, as it had been conceived up to that date, and opens up new perspectives, beginning with the practical difficulties encountered by analysts.

In their short chapter for the present volume, Udo Hock and Dominique Scarfone have provided a very helpful and lucid account of why Freud's essay cannot be described as purely technical: although it takes technical problems as its starting point, it brings general values into play, opening up aesthetic, ethical, and ontological perspectives.

Freud is very explicit, both in "Remembering, Repeating and Working-Through, but also in the closely related *Beyond the Pleasure Principle* (1920g), about what we know to be his theoretical way of proceeding: no previous acquisitions are rejected but must be re-thought in the light of new hypotheses. Freud was the first to return to those passages that had permitted analytic discoveries so that he could give them fresh consideration, whether they emerged from "remembering in the old way," or from the contribution of therapies inspired by suggestion, or even from the complex subsequent development described in *Beyond the Pleasure Principle*: the identification of the logic of the pleasure principle. This new and startling discovery of the "compulsion to repeat" arose from clinical observation and threw into question everything that had hitherto been understood about psychic functioning. "And now we can observe that in drawing attention to the compulsion to repeat we have acquired no new fact, but only a more comprehensive view" (Freud, 1914g, p. 151).

It is in this sense that the observations of P.-L. Assoun are particularly useful: in his view, tireless "reiteration" presupposes that the function

DOI: 10.4324/9781003458340-10

of repetition is to therefore ensure a "hold" on the thing that has to be thought. It is vital not to lose sight of the fact that the "hypothesis of the unconscious" is as necessary as it is "volatile"—to the extent that one is "distracted" virtually at all times. All Freudian writing is destined to complement this effect of "recall." And it is precisely for this reason that "what seems to be a repetition is never completely so" (Assoun, 1997, p. 722).

In the present chapter, I have chosen to explore some clinical issues concerning memory, remembering, and elaboration, defined by Freud as *working-through (Durcharbeitung/perlaboration)*, which arise during the course of analysis. Other aspects, in particular ethical and ontological aspects will obviously come into play, even if they are not the object of my re-reading.

Freud was always careful about proffering technical "advice," having invented a method that, in its simplicity, has such significant therapeutic and cognitive value that the so-called analytical "technique," wholly inscribed within the method itself, should never prevail over the method. These aspects have been recently developed by Riolo (2017), giving a specific attention to the so called "setting variations."

Freud's discovery, of which he gives an account in this paper, concerns, as we know, the impasses created in the analytical work and lamented by the analysts of the time because of having to deal with acting-out (*agieren*) rather than the act of remembering, as well as denials regarding the efficacy of the treatment and its therapeutic results. Just as significant, in my opinion, is the importance attributed by Freud to *working-through* as a third element: without consideration of this aspect, it would be impossible to understand how the patient is able to transform *agieren* into something that is "[reproduced] in the psychical field."

In fact, *agieren* has occupied a central place in clinical thinking in recent decades. One of the most important contributions has been that of Jean-Luc Donnet, with his precise attention to Freud's writings and continuous reference to his own clinical and self-analytical practice. He has defined *agieren* as the "new royal road" of analysis (2009). In works dedicated to this theme, he has brought about a broadening of our perspective by capturing the quality of experiences characterized by patients' actings out, within the use of the word itself: the "acted word (speech)." His attention to the question of working-through has also been present: his paper, "The silence of working-through", has provided inspiration for many analysts in their writings and shows how much both these aspects are interrelated.

*

Analytical work is played out, I believe, around the question of how to modify the past. The fact that, during the analysis, the past manifests itself as a present marked by the forced and unconscious repetition of events that belong to a past that has never actually become such only makes the question even more complex: a point on which Freud expressed himself very clearly and in a "modern" way. It is the *working-through*, with its long, slow, and silent activity that allows the modification of a past that has not become a past, and that makes this transformation possible.

Freud's postulation of the existence and necessity of this third, elaborative time, which unlike the emergence of memories or the presence of acts, is difficult to detect on a phenomenal level, seems to me very significant: these three elements: remembering, repeating, and *working-through*—the dynamic and procedural quality of which is denoted by being expressed as three verbs rather than three nouns—constitute the very process of analytic treatment. It is precisely their reciprocal dynamics that give rise to the transformations in patients through analytical work. The process takes place on two separate psychic scenes and, towards the end of his essay, Freud comments, with reference to working-through, on the different tasks that fall to patient and analyst:

> This working-through of the resistance may in practice turn out to be an arduous task for the subject of the analysis and a trial of patience for the analyst. Nevertheless it is a part of the work which effects the greatest changes in the patient and which distinguishes analytic treatment from any kind of treatment by suggestion.
>
> (Freud, 1914g, p. 155)

I would posit that the ethical value implicit in these technical passages resides here: if *working-through* is the way in which the experience of the analytical treatment—nourished by transference—becomes the object of subjective appropriation on the part of the patient, this can only happen if a certain degree of dissymmetry between patient and analyst is maintained. Whether we take into account the moments of symmetrization, which are given and which often bear important transformative impulses, or whether we make the most of the space and the transitional phenomena fostered by the analytic situation, nevertheless, it is my view that the presence of two distinct psychic spaces and two partly different psychic functioning regimes is not renounceable.

Of itself, the analytical method is based on a strong element of symmetry between analyst and patient, with evenly poised attention the analogue of free association. But there is a second fundamental rule that is just as powerfully symmetrical between patient and analyst, which is that the analyst must have been in analysis her/himself. Such elements, internal to the method, each of them entailing technical aspects, risk pushing in the direction of a symmetrization of the analytical relationship, preventing the establishment of the intermediate elements, internal to the method and thus each with relevant technical aspects, preventing the establishment of that asymmetrical space that alone permits the unfolding if the patient 's fantasy world, as it is connoted transferentially.

Working-through temporality leaves the analyst uncertain about if and what the patient is elaborating is, in itself, a barrier to the ever-present temptation of wanting to understand too much. The analyst is left on hold, in the uncomfortable position of "not knowing," and with only the main-tenance of the method as reference point during the treatment. Even Freud seems, in his clinical cases, to be affected by this overly anticipatory atti-tude towards the patient: in discussing his role as an analyst working with patients, the advice he offers to analysts is also directed at himself.

One aspect that has been greatly developed by clinical practice over the course of time is that of elaboration on the part of the analyst: the elabo-ration of countertransference may be considered the complement, though only in part, of the patient's *working-through*. It is my view that an all-en-compassing and too broad conception of what is meant by the term coun-tertransference does not, however, make sense of the specific quality of psychoanalytic listening that, by its very nature, is, to use Jean-Claude Rol-land's term, *a kind of working-through* listening (Rolland, 2006). According to this view, countertransference is instead an obstacle to *working-through* listening, and the need for the analyst to treat it self-analytically is some-thing quite different from listening to one's own associations, at all levels where they occur.

There is, therefore, no phenomenal evidence for *working-through*: the ef-fects may be seen indirectly over the course of the analysis and, as Freud is the first to point out in his essay, among the elements that can foster it, but not the only one, is the lengthy duration of the treatment.

*

I have often been struck by a phrase repeated by many patients at a certain point in their analytical journey, using more or less the same words: "At the beginning ... when I came here ..." They then follow this up with a sort of revisitation of how they felt at the beginning of the analysis, how they per-ceived themselves to be, and how, in their opinion, things stood with them. It is as if, with this utterance, the past of the analysis reappeared and took on the quality of a memory: in seeing himself again through this activity of reminiscing, the patient feels different from how he was at the beginning, but above all—and this is the element that I would like to try to highlight—he feels that the "story" of his analysis has become established within him as "another story," one which runs parallel and adheres closely to the story of his childhood and adolescence as he has constructed it over time.

"At the beginning ..." is a formula that seems to situate this time in the distant past, and this sense of distance from the starting point is a very spe-cific aspect: it is as if the starting point took on something of the quality of the beginning of time, a time outside of time about which it is possible to think anew without, however, attributing to it any objectivity. By being able to think about it and being able to perceive it, a before and an after is established. The analysis takes place in the more or less long-ago time of the beginnings, without, it seems to me, either the patient or the analyst knowing which unconscious processes have been activated. We work, step by step, on the fragments that gradually emerge, as Freud affirms when he writes that "... the analyst gives up the attempt to bring a particular moment or problem into focus. He contents himself with studying whatever is present for the time being on the surface of the patient's mind ..." (1914g, p. 147).

It is certainly possible to think of the reorganization that takes place during the analysis with reference to the Ego. It is in this sense that Loewald (1971) highlights the transformations during the analysis of every type of repetition in terms of activity/passivity.

I would suggest that such a perspective, which seems to me to concern the question of how the process of subjective appropriation of precisely what is experienced in the course of the analysis comes about, may be linked to the idea that we can think that the construction of a memory produced by the analysis—and therefore by the force of transference—has made it possible for lasting and mainly unconscious memories to be inscribed upon it.

Loewald tends, in his paper, to emphasize the capacity of patient's Ego to reorganize, in an active and creative way, that which has been experienced in a passive way during infancy and has reappeared with the force of repetition: "... repetition compelled by unconscious forces which have remained outside, removed from, the ego organization" (*ibid.*, p. 61). Moreover,

> The patient is not merely to be made aware of the existence of such contents in his psyche, but he is asked, implicitly if not explicitly, to own up to them as his wishes and conflicts and defences. To re-experience them as psychic activity of a non automatic nature.
>
> (*ibid.*)

In Loewald's perspective, the entire process turns around transference interpretations.

Based on my clinical experience, it is my opinion that such an understanding of how repetition compulsion can be transformed is revealing of the end result of a long process that is certainly, but not exclusively, based on the interpretative activity of the analyst, and accompanied at all times by the mutative potentiality of *working-through*, on the part of the patient, and *working-through listening* on the part of the analyst.

The combination of these activities, their length and their silent presence, can enable the patient to create a "memory of the analysis."

This memory, which we might define as a sort of conscious–unconscious neo-formation, also necessarily implies a further aspect: that of oblivion. Oblivion plays an important role in freeing the patient from the encumbrance that may be constituted by the transferential elements, which have contributed to its formation. The analytic transference is such because it can be interpreted and, in part, liquidated: the repression must take on its function again, otherwise there is a strong risk that the transference, in particular the transference on the analyst (as an) object, occludes spaces of possible further transformation.

I believe that in considering working-through, which is active throughout the entire course of analysis, it is important to observe how the reactivation of the repression is functional to the transformative process. If we consider psychic transformation of repetition compulsion in terms of enlargement of the Ego without taking into account the role of reactivating repression, we miss out on what is probably one of the most significative aspects of transformation in analysis.

The memory of the treatment, which we can see taking place at a certain moment in the analytic process, becomes a sort of new subjective story. This story will be deformed and organized by a memory that bears all the hallmarks of an effective repression. It will become a reminiscence and will acquire the qualities of the preconscious. The patient will be able to have recourse to it as something that belongs to him/her, and to which he/she can have access, while it continues to preserve a considerable degree of deformation, even beyond the end of the analysis.

*

Maria is the patient who allowed me to understand these passages in a very specific way; what had brought her to analysis, at an age no longer young, was an alienating condition so deep that no aspect of her life was free.

Her family, a traditionally Catholic one, lived in an old house in the village square: the church was at the center of the village as it was in Maria's education, as well as in that of her sister and brother.

Her father and his family were so devout that, even to the people of the village, they seemed somehow "weird." The father had decided his two daughters' destiny: they had to become nuns. Both succeeded in escaping their fate, even if in a different way: for her sister the conclusion was a tragic one, because she died young of a metabolic disorder, having developed a serious condition of obesity; however. she did marry and give birth to two daughters.

As for Maria, she opposed her father's dictations, defying him on an intellectual level, studying philosophy and abandoning religion. But her entire emotional life, her intimacy, her relationships and life projects came to a standstill as she spent her entire adolescent period imprisoned in an orthopedic plaster bust, due to a serious form of scoliosis.

She stayed at home, for years, in an isolated condition and a state of extreme suffering: she emerged from this state through meeting a "therapist" and his group of disciples with whom she associated for years.

It was not a difficult task to understand intuitively, from the preliminary talks we had together, when she came to see me asking for an analytical therapy, that the figure of the therapist and his group of followers were a replica, a rather exact one, of her family environment.

Her deep psychic suffering went together with a total inhibition of her sexual life: the sexual act was avoided; she was terribly afraid of it. I would say sexuality was, for Maria, inconceivable.

In *Beyond the Pleasure Principle*, Freud wrote that the death drive must be linked before pleasure's principle can be established, and this was certainly the case with Maria's initial psychic condition: in her, what Pontalis called "the principle of agony" (1988, p. 97, English translation, 2014) had imposed itself.

I was not so surprised that Maria had, in adolescence and in her adult life, repeated the unconscious scenarios that had determined her psychic history, but rather that she had, somewhere, maintained a sufficient libidinal reserve to feed her search for "something else," because this seemed to me to be her demand for analysis: something different from what she had ever experienced, even if she had no idea of "what" it could be.

I would like to mention here recent observations made by Olga Pozzi, commenting on *Beyond the Pleasure Principle*: "In a word, one could conclude that, although we can pay respect to the imposing 'close-up' devoted to Thanatos, the most serious (important) innovation introduced by Beyond the Pleasure Principle consists in in introducing Eros" (Pozzi, 2020).

Eros will remain in a latent state during the long years of Maria's analysis, becoming present and active on the analytical scene only around the final period.

The therapist and the group of disciples were a sort of totalitarian universe where private life, working activity, and what was called "therapy" were overlapped and simultaneously present in an extremely confused way.

What was left uninjured as an intimate psychic space was a poor thing and her moving away from that world (significantly, this happened at the beginning of her analysis) left Maria in a precarious psychic condition to the extent that she was not able to find her way about in the external world when she was alone.

Many times, over the years, I have wondered whether it was a question of eliminating what had allowed the compulsion to repeat to impose itself and to get the better of the pleasure principle, leaving the patient to deal with the work of "synthesis" and reconstruction, or whether it was not necessary to give as much attention to the construction–reconstruction of her subjective past. And if the compulsion to repeat had prevailed, what a weight to give, in analysis, to the elements of external reality so powerful that they imposed themselves and provoked protective reactions of survival, because this vital stake was at the core of Maria's analytical demand.

I am referring again to Pontalis, who expressed himself very explicitly on this point: "…. it seems to me that we must not prevent ourselves from acknowledging, in one way or another, the patient that reality has ferociously beaten, that we recognise the violence that has been done to him" (Pontalis, 1988, p. 117, translated for this edition, English translation, 2014).

If the patient has never been able to know, to experience, anything other than what unconsciously makes him always encounter the same scenarios, despite the attempts made to find other ways, the analytical experience becomes the "new world" to discover and meet for the first time.

Analysis was, for Maria, a totally new world that she could experience in many regards for the first time. While, during the initial years, the entire space of the sessions was occupied by the paternal *imago* and his replicas and by the group of siblings, slowly, imperceptibly, the maternal quality of the analytical frame and Maria's growing capacity to settle into it allowed her to appropriate it without being aware of this deep change. This process allowed her to get closer to the void, to the coldness and the distance of the mother, impossible to conceive up to that moment: a cold despair, encysted, unrecognizable had been imposed.

Maria: "... at the beginning, when I came here ... I didn't understand anything you said to me ... but I knew it was right ... I remember that I told you that before I died I wanted to know how the children were born ... of course I did, but I didn't understand the meaning ... I was like half-dead. Now I think ... yes, I had the life that I had ... but I did the analysis, that's what I felt, I don't know how, I had to do when I was 18 years old ... and I did it!".

Between those beginnings and now, this present time that has been recreated, a very long chronological time has passed: a duration that, to my great surprise, was hardly perceived by her. The long years of the beginnings had passed in a condition in which the passing of time was annulled; I found myself living a similar psychic state, but when it happened that Maria recounted, as if it were for the first time, a recollection, an event from the past, a dream already told, I woke up from that torpor that I did not know I felt.

Repetition, of which she was in no way aware, was the most recognizable sign, for the analyst, of her psychic life. Repetitive dreams and equally crystallized childhood memories characterized the work of analysis, which, however, never ceased to be invested with a vital stake before it became libidinal: the figure of the analyst as a libidinally erotically invested object was able to emerge slowly and over a long period of time from the treatment.

"In the beginning ...", in that time that Maria now perceives and of which she can also speak, having conquered another psychic place from which to be aware of, and think about, analysis, the analyst was a sort of life raft to which she remained firmly attached.

In this way, a memory of the treatment to which the patient will have access will be created and which will include the biographical memory as it was built up in the course of life, re-emerged during the analysis with the subjective sensation that it was always the same memories, always the same events. Memories, crystallized by repetition, will not be modified in themselves but they will take another place in a different net of memories, produced by analytical work. They will become innocuous memories and Maria will be able to test and feel this change in her psychic life.

A repetitive dream presented itself over and over again in the course of the analysis: the image was that of a sort of "procession" of cripples, sick, blind, lame, lepers or whatever, all holding hands and moving forward together. The patient watched, or was part of, the procession. This image caused her great distress and made her think of a dark Middle Ages in her familiar environment. I had seen a similar image during a trip to the south of the Indian continent: I felt I had been taken back in time and was almost incredulous at the scene. The work on this dream was long and lasted for years: each time it recurred, the patient seemed to measure her ability to put herself increasingly in an observer position until, after what would be the last appearance of this dream, I said to her, as if the expression had escaped me, "... ah, the funeral procession!" Neither the patient nor myself had ever referred to that dream image in those terms: the time had come to give it a funeral and Maria could let go and abandon the *imagines* to which she had remained masochistically attached.

Many years after the distant time of the beginning, Maria had a dream of transference: "I was with you in the same big bed—you got up—you had no problem showing off without clothes—you put on your dressing gown—what beautiful features! I was in contact with your nudity—I looked away—a big thing! I'm a bit ashamed, I have difficulty telling the story ... I feel it's about therapy, but there was no therapy in the dream ... You had a natural, light, simple, cheerful attitude.. the house was big, there was life in it ..."

It is not easy to describe here what it could mean for this patient to dream of the female figure, embodied by the analyst, in her nudity, the emergence of a representation of the female body in all its sensuality, full of tempered, mitigated sexual elements, able to act as an embankment to an excitement without representations, as it had been until then. The dream had been preceded by the new experience of being able to move in space, outside, without the fear of getting lost, without feeling a sense of depersonalization, alongside the re-emergence of the memory, repetitively present in analysis, of her as a little girl, an autoerotic moment that excited her and then left her, sitting on the floor, alone and with a vague sense of guilt. Following this memory was one much more upsetting, of her in kindergarten attacking, from behind, a little friend, standing over her on the floor, and taking off her panties. Both of these memories had been recounted several times: the powerful desire to strip the other child, which had already triggered a terrible guilt at the time, which lasted throughout her life ("I was already a neurotic and suffering child at the age of three, Doctor!") She now stood next to the analyst's nudity, a nudity from which she averted her eyes, nudity covered by a dressing gown: the repression of the contents that she had been driven into, leaves the field to more temperate libidinal representations, cheerfulness, naturalness.

The manifest content of this dream, and working on it for my part, reminded me of the expression "psychical coating," pointed out by D. Scarfone in his contribution to the Congress of French-Speaking Analysts (CPLF) in 2014 (Scarfone, 2015). An analyst's dressing gown, as appeared in Maria's dream, can cover up the "thing": surprisingly for me, repression is always active in the analyst's psyche! I found that Freud used this expression referring to Dora's "genital catarrh."

Singularly, my memory of this dream was partly different from the note I had written down: in the nudity of the analyst who she was looking at and from whom she looked away, the genitals were seen from behind, the vagina in particular. What had been established as my memory of the dream was, therefore, the transformation that I myself had operated, unconsciously, revealing in a more explicit way the representation of the place of the feminine and the maternal that, for Maria, had never had a psychic representation. It was a transformation that had most probably made its way along the course of the analysis and only became evident to me at that moment.

"Reproducing on the psychic plane" is a passage that necessarily implies the fulfillment of the symbolic processes that transform the drives, the excitements, into representations, that is to say, that allow the passage from thing presentation to word presentation (*Dingvorstellung-Wortvorstellung*), through the passage of presentation (*Darstellung*). In the analyst, the strong impact of the dream of transference gave rise to an unconscious movement of unveiling that could anticipate the necessary passage, for the patient, of the deeply repressed representation of the vagina: Maria had been able to avert her gaze from the female nakedness while the representation of the house, full of life, could emerge metonymically, favoring the removal of the most libidinally charged content.

Therefore, I believe that it is precisely working through and working-through listening, very evident in the case of this dream, that opposes repetition and allows the patient, in many cases for the first time, to "remember in the old way." In this case, the remembering will be libidinally invested and not persecutorily avoided and will have as objects new memories, produced by the reworking of the psychic events experienced during the treatment. I would be inclined to think that this function, which is activated by the particular conditions of the analytic treatment, is intimately connected with what we call the "maternal": starting from Freud's reference to the "patience" required by the analyst when he expresses himself in the brief final lines of his essay about the "physician's task." What is this "patience" if not an ability to wait, an ability to renounce an active, interpretative position on the part of the analyst who, from this point of view, has the task of ensuring that the psychic processes activated in the analysis develop? I do not mean maternal in the sense of *maternage* but a "maternal" that is psychic life itself, its mobility, the internal game between representations–affections and words, continually put into play by the transference of patient and analyst (Pontalis, 1988, p. 218).

If working-through, on the patient's part and, in a similar way, working-through listening, allows the psychic reworking that takes place during the analysis, the place that belongs to the analyst's ability to be "patient" seems to me particularly relevant. It is what allows the reconstitution, in the patient, of that house "full of life," of which Maria's dream is a meaningful representation if the analyst does not misunderstand the unconscious content of representations that are apparently so worldly with their sexual and impulsive content. In fact, these contents are a product of unconscious transformations that took place both in patient and analyst.

In my opinion, an analyst should avoid the risk that where "remembering in the old manner" could not develop, where the compulsion to repeat has taken on very considerable weight, the stakes on the vital level do not leave the sexual content in the shade.

References

Assoun, P.-L. (1997) *Psychanalyse*. Paris: PUF.

De Renzis, G. (2009) *Ripetizione e violenza*, in A. Garella & R. Musella (Eds), *Violenza e simbolizzazione*. Bari-Rome: la Biblioteca.

Donnet, J.-L. (2009). *The Analyzing Situation*. New York: Routledge.

Freud, S. (1905e). *Fragment of an Analysis of a Case of Hysteria. S.E.*, 7: 1–122. London: Hogarth Press.

Freud, S. (1914g) Remembering, Repeating and Working-Through. *S.E.*, 12: 147–156. London: Hogarth Press.

Freud, S. (1920g) *Beyond the Pleasure Principle, S.E., 18*: 7–64. London: Hogarth Press.

Loewald, H.W. (1971). Some considerations on repetition and repetition compulsion. *International Journal of Psychoanalysis*, 52: 59–66.

Pontalis, J.-B. (1988). *Non, deux fois non*. In *Perdre de vue*. Paris: Gallimard.

Pontalis, J.-B. (2014). No, twice no: An attempt to define and dismantle the 'negative therapeutic reaction'. *International Journal of Psychoanalysis*, 95: 533–551.

Pozzi, O. (2019). Qualche passo al di là? "Zoppicare non è una colpa". In *Notes per la psicoanalisi, 15*. 1920–2020 Al di là del principio di piacere I

Riolo, N. (2017). *Il metodo psicoanalitico*. In *Notes per la psicoanalisi*, n. 9, Rome: Alpes.

Rolland. J.-C. (2006). *Avant d'etre celui qui parle*. Paris: Gallimard.

Scarfone, D. (2015). *The Unpast. The Actual Unconscious*. New York: The Unconscious in Translation.

11 Acting-out and Working-Through

Josef Ludin

Working through is not so much a concept as a doing, like remembering or repeating. It was not given much thought in Freud's oeuvre, although it was soon apparent that it took up most of the time of the analytical process. Psychoanalysts are naturally more focused on pointing out an unconscious mechanism or a particular aspect of psychic reality, but they are more reticent about discussing how the many years of working through actually proceed. The process is obviously difficult to present. The many years it takes were also not originally intended and have emerged over time. Freud was not unaware that the length of analysis had been increasing and, as we know, at the end of his life he dedicated an exciting text to this theme of the terminability and interminability of analysis (Freud, 1937b), but it is astonishing that here, too, there was no question of working through. Even in this text from 1914, Remembering, Repeating and Working-Through, where, despite appearing in the title, it is only mentioned at the end of the text with a few lines.

If we assume that working through is primarily aimed at resistance[1], then this formulation references something essential about the long process, but does not say much about the background and anchoring of the resistance.

In this text under discussion, Freud speaks of remembering "an earlier situation" (Freud, 1914g, p. 147) and of "forgetting impressions, scenes and experiences" (*ibid.*). He believes that "the doctor uncovers the resistances which are unknown to the patient" and when "these have been got the better of, the patient often relates the forgotten situations and connections without any difficulty" (*ibid.*). What surprises us about this statement from 1914, a time when the seduction theory had long since been abandoned and the transference dimension had been recognized in its full effect? Freud obviously still seems to be on the lookout for "situations and connections" that could be uncovered. These, however, would have to contain something clearly identifiable and concrete, as suggested by the expression narrating "without difficulty." However, all clinical experience shows that these situations and connections may exist, but they are not the main problem of resistance in the cure. It is well known that narrating "without

DOI: 10.4324/9781003458340-11

difficulty" is rare. The effect of phantasy and drive activity described by the paradigm of infantile sexuality leads to distortions and to a subsequently (*nachträglich*) constructed memory and experience. Therefore, repeated interpretations from different perspectives are necessary for this defense to abate even slightly and to initiate a process of understanding. The compulsion to repeat is the most powerful resistance, but, as is well known, its full scope will not be formulated until 1920 with *Beyond the Pleasure Principle*. Here, it should be enough to point out that the defense is usually organized in such a way that it will reassemble, even if certain aspects have been breached successfully. We know that interpretations that initiate a process of understanding in the session are magnetically reabsorbed by the unconscious and that which was clearly illuminated in the last session has suddenly faded away. We still remember them, but their effect has either disappeared or been distorted. The length of the treatment indicates, then, that the unconscious problems are much more complex and cannot simply be linked to specified "*situations and connections.*"

In this text under discussion, repetition manifests in the form of acting-out and this appears to be of particular clinical and (currently) of theoretical relevance.

> We may now ask what it is that he in fact repeats or acts out. The answer is that he repeats everything that has already made its way from the sources of the repressed into his manifest personality—his inhibitions and unserviceable attitudes and his pathological character-traits.
>
> (Freud, 1914g, p. 150)

The question that arises is how we can think and experience this quite generally formulated statement clinically. Would it be possible that the *inhibitions* and *pathological character-traits* do not have to do with *forgotten situations* and *connections*, but connote everyday situations, in the sense of complex transference events, each of which would not necessarily have anything conspicuous in itself? Transferences do indeed take place ubiquitously and continuously, they "arise spontaneously in all human relationships" (Freud, 1910a, p. 51). The more intensive human relationships are, the stronger the transference processes. So, naturally, the most intensive transferences take place within the family complex. Freud says remarkable things about transference in this text. He says not only that it is a repetition of the forgotten past, but also that it is the main means of *curbing the patient's compulsion to repeat and turning it into a motive for remembering*, but also that it represents a *playground (Tummelplatz)*, an *intermediate region between illness and real life*, and that it is ultimately an *artificial illness* (cf. Freud, 1914g, p. 153).

As Freud points out elsewhere, these are *new formations, false connections* and *clichés* created in this intermediate realm—this *space of transition* and possibility (Winnicott, 1974). According to Freud, the person has acquired a particularity, creating a cliché that is repeatedly impressed anew.

The resistance that emanates from transference manifests itself primarily in acting-out, whereby Freud uses *acting-out* and *repeating quasi* synonymously here.[2] But how does one act-out in transference? We know this from observing children in their behavior towards their parents. Here, the transference is at work *in statu nascendi*: it will be distorted. The child's first lie is the prototype of a distortion in transference and it turns out that, in the further course of childhood, this acting-out develops into a dominant, but largely unconscious, form of defense. Why should it be any different in the analytical situation, where transference naturally comes to the fore? If we understand acting-out as a distorted form of memory, then, it should be added, its goal is primarily a defense against memory. I will come back to this.

The fact that something is repeated and impressed anew, that false connections are created, probably also has to do with the clinical experience

> that something is 'remembered' which could never have been 'forgotten' because it was never at any time noticed, was never conscious. As regards the course taken by psychical events it seems to make no difference whatever whether such a 'thought-connection' was conscious and then forgotten or whether it never managed to become conscious at all.
>
> (Freud, 1914g, 148)

This seems to me a fundamental psychoanalytical insight, and Freud adds something essential when he speaks of the dissolution "of thought-connections, failing to draw the right conclusions and isolating memories" (*ibid.*). We can add that this last formulation is the effect of distortion and deferred action, the expression of unconscious psychic work on memory.

Let us return to this *"narrating without difficulty of forgotten situations."* The psychic presence of the parents as the source of the transference between child and adult, certainly in the Ferenczian sense (Ferenczi, 1972) and as an expression of their own unresolved psychic reality, which manifests itself in largely unconscious abreaction, is often known to the child on a preconscious level and the repression status is not easy to determine. Their messages, imprints, fixations, and injuries certainly remain unconscious and unrecognizable in their effect. If the resistance refers to a repressed conflict which is actualized in the transference to the analyst, then the dissolution of connections is a mechanism via distortion and deferred action which follows an unconscious dynamic and results in the symptom.

A small vignette to illustrate

A patient grows up with his *"beautiful mother"* and his younger sister. There is a very distant contact to the father. The material circumstances in which he grows up are quite comfortable due to the mother's large inheritance. The mother is an art collector and wealthy, the father is a scientist and comes from rather modest circumstances. He is obviously very ambitious and in thrall to his superego. The patient is not only the glance in his mother's eyes, but also, later, has the impression that without her he could not create anything; she is the source of his creativity. The mother is very close to him into his adulthood. An oversized narcissistic bloating of self, which had already begun in early school years, was the result. And this despite the fact that, throughout the entire period of his childhood, he had repeatedly shown that he could barely satisfy basic school requirements.

Although very attractive and a great seducer, he does not create a stable attachment. His partners are always of exquisite and unsettling beauty. They fall devotedly in love with him, symbiotic dependencies and expectations arise, which then cannot be satisfied. The relationships break up more or less dramatically. What always remains is the ever-understanding mother, whose art appreciation and sensitivity is unsurpassed and who remains attractive and beautiful despite her age. He is always attracted by the figure of beauty and the beautiful. Beauty seems the real goal, as in art. After his narcissistic ego was initially confirmed in his studies and he received recognition and perhaps some admiration, there followed a period of strenuous work, effort, and discipline, in short: of drive renouncement, which, in his case, meant above all disavowing his grandiose narcissistic self and here he fails. This is where his *inhibitions and unserviceable attitudes*, his *pathological traits* come to the surface. He sinks into melancholic self-doubt and fantasizes about the ideality of beauty and purity and his need to believe. The father's world is a world of achievement and threatening to him, he returns to that of his mother. He sees the reason for his lack of creativity in the distance to his mother, the distance the analysis (i.e., *I*) imposed on him. As he cannot create anything in the distance to her, he feels desperate, his longing for the father, clearly evident in the first phase of the analysis, now changes in his dream images; he finds the father and any closeness to him repulsive and frightening.

Basically, we could say that the patient was flooded with indigestible impressions as a child. A flooding with drive-cathected impressions is perhaps the most fundamental theory of traumatization of a still fragile ego. For the tenderness of the growing child, the parental worlds—both psychic spaces—were noisy, drive-laden conglomerations of their psychic realities, consisting mainly of narcissistic and superego introjects. Even before the child can discover his own drive conflicts, as Ferenczi has already taught us, he is exposed to the massive drive conflicts of the parents.[3]

So, when Freud speaks of *forgotten situations and connections*, we could say that our protagonist grew up in these situations and connections. In those multiple situations of everyday experiences and events, any single one of which was not necessarily an 'event,' could, therefore, not be remembered "without *difficulty*." They can, we could say with Freud, never be forgotten because they were never conscious, and moreover there was a *dissolution of connections*, a *misjudgment of sequences* and an *isolation of memories*. To work through here means nothing more than to identify this dissolution of connections, the misunderstanding of sequences, and the isolation of memories in their respective situations, to take the messages from the everyday life of the cure and to bring them to consciousness from different perspectives. Strachey spoke of a knot, in which he said:

> Giving non-transference interpretations is indeed like trying to untie a knot in a rope that forms a self-contained ring. You can easily undo the knot in one place, but it will automatically close again at the same moment in another part of the circle. One cannot really loosen the knot unless one holds the ends of the rope in one's hand, and in the given situation this is only possible through a transference interpretation.
> (Strachey, 1937, p. 72)

In this text, he sets himself apart from the Freudian technique of interpretation in favor of the so-called transference interpretation, which he called "deep interpretation." Regardless of this distinction, it is a good illustration, emphasizing the dialectic of repetition and interpretation at the very core of working through. If the psychoanalytical process, as I see it, is, among other things, a learning process—certainly in the sense of Bion's "learning from experience"—then repetition is an essential principle of this learning. In our work it is innately expressed in the ritual of recurring sessions lasting for years. The movements of what is spoken during a session are never identical and yet often variations of the same things that occupy the subject recur and claim his or her psychic reality. For weeks and weeks, the analysand can talk about the one conflict and the one theme over and over again and yet in ever different ways. Then that subject dries up without being "cured," his activity exhausted. Our interventions also vary and respond to the different versions of what is being said. These are the everyday demands in the efforts of working through.

Oedipal inheritance

It is important to emphasize that working through often refers to thematic knotting, which preoccupies and distresses the analysand. At times, the contents remain unconscious and take on different forms of manifest expression, often in distorted form. These themes can then be identified as introjects that persecute the analysand. We cannot avoid the assumption that this has to do with the unconscious processing of the experienced. Martin Bergman spoke of the trauma of the parents as an "organising factor" (quoted from Bohleber, 2000, p. 814), that is, how strongly the subject unconsciously experiences fear and helplessness as inherited remnants of his parents and ancestors. We can ask ourselves why the "trauma of the parents" and not simply the psychic reality of the parents? The psychic reality is an inherited one, not in the sense of genetic inheritance,[4] but in the sense of a transmission of misunderstood messages, similar to the so-called enigmatic messages of Jean Laplanche. Freud spoke in his text "Constructions in Analysis" of the *"early history"* that the patient has forgotten (Freud, 1937d, p. 260). From today's perspective, we could say that these misunderstood messages are also in a direct line of inheritance from the respective parental superego constitution. In 1914, at the time of the text under discussion here, Freud had not yet envisioned the superego.

Inheritance is a term that had a very broad meaning for Freud, reaching, one could say, from biology to cultural tradition. Yet, he created a new form or expression of inheritance—in *Totem and Taboo* (1912–1913) and in *Man Moses* [*Moses and Monotheism* (1939)], as well as in many other writings—and it is the inheritance of the Oedipus complex. Wladimir Granoff, in his famous seminar of 1973–1974, spoke of "filiation," the genealogy of the Oedipus complex, and called it *"l'avenir du complexe d'Oedipe,"* literally, the future of the Oedipus complex. I took the liberty of translating this as the fate or destiny of the Oedipus complex. Given the extent to which Oedipal bonds are essentially discussed in their pre-Oedipal formulations nowadays, the fate of the Oedipal complex is hardly spoken of at all. Instead, there is talk of transgenerational transference, a term that does not necessarily place this process of transmission within the context of the Oedipal complex, although not explicitly excluded. Thus, in the texts on transgenerativity, fundamental categories of psychoanalysis such as distortion and deferred action no longer play a role.[5] Therefore, I prefer to speak of the fate of the Oedipus complex. This fate was negotiated by Freud in *Man Moses*: distortion herein becomes a *conditio sine qua non*. As is so often the case, Freud forgets parts of his own conceptualization: the idea of deferred action, which practically does not appear in *Man Moses*, is nonetheless essential for his construction.

As is well known, the feeling of guilt plays a major role in this fate. Our moral or even amoral ideas[6] are often a distorted form of inheritance. As deferred and distorted constructions, they are also an expression of a colossal resistance wanting to obscure all traces of the origin of these ideas. Hate, envy, resentment, fear, desire, which refer to the Oedipal figures (father, mother, siblings), we rightly understand as resistance against the recognition of infantile desires and their narcissistic fixations. The core of the resistance would consist then in the defense against the unconscious Oedipal fixations; the sovereign subject cannot admit that he has largely unconsciously submitted himself to this unshakable Oedipal monument and that its pre-eminence continues unrecognized. For the sovereignty of the subject, autonomy is indispensable; in his narcissism he considers himself independent, not really bound to or by anyone. He owes nothing to anyone.

To the extent that guilt, as the heir of misunderstood messages, mutates into unconscious guilt feelings, it generates complex forms of abreaction

that sometimes follow rational aspects and can more or less adapt to the reality principle. Their abreacting character can be seen in a sounding out and
crossing of boundaries and forbidden spaces, often observed in puberty or
adolescence. We regard this as an expression of normal psychic development. The unconscious feeling of guilt is, on the one hand, the motor of this
acting-out and, on the other hand, acting-out is the defense which solidifies
it. A vicious circle is created, similar to the one Freud spoke of in connection
with Dostoyevsky: the barbarians, "who murdered and did penance for it,
till penance became an actual technique for enabling murder to be done"
(Freud, 1928b, p. 177). This dialectic seems to address an essential dynamic
of acting-out from the sources of guilt.

Working through these resistances can only be achieved by restoring
their connections to the Oedipal heritage. Clinically, it will ultimately prove
to be a working through of the superego. Here, we would not be dealing
with the decline of the Oedipus complex, but with the partly unfathomable
meandering of its fate preventing its dissolution. They must be remembered and acknowledged so that the necessary work of mourning can be
done to overcome them. Psychic reality, with all its unconscious phantasies
stemming from infantile sexuality, draws its lines of projection and identification from the primary object relationships determined by the Oedipus
complex. The construction of the resulting memory subsequently created,
refers, I would say, in almost every session to this core complex of psychic
reality. This work forms the new, the analyzed ego. At least that is the claim
of Freud and the first generations of psychoanalysts.[7]

In "Remembering, Repeating and Working-Through," however, the Oedipal complex remains unmentioned,[8] the superego was not yet available
as a concept and narcissism was not yet or never really in Freud's clinical
sights. The resistances mentioned by Freud here, which are to be worked
through, therefore seem quite abstract and only comprehensible in their
abstraction. Clinically, however, the resistances are always concrete and can
be identified as figures of Oedipal or narcissistic fixations or as those of the
superego, where the two mainstays of psychic reality come together.

The introjects or the objects of working through

To return to our patient: in the literature, there have been various reflections on whether a trauma-generating experience would be an introject
or an identification, for example, with the aggressor. Sandler & Rosenblatt wrote as early as 1962: "Introjection means that the child behaves as if
his parents were present in their absence. It does not mean that the child
imitates its parents – that would be identification" (Sandler & Rosenblatt,
1962, p. 138). In a sense, the trauma causes the opposite of what one would
expect from identification. The ego regression leads to a return of the oral
defense mechanisms of early childhood. So, through the mechanism of introjection,[9] the fusion with the maternal primary object is always preserved

in secrecy and can be made available to the psyche at will. By incorporating the traumatising psychic object to a certain extent, it is apparently also rendered harmless, but, in reality, the psychic activity of the introjection cannot be overcome because the unconscious Oedipal threat has not been eliminated. In this sense, introjects can be perceived as misunderstood messages, as an incorporation of false links. Certainly, also as misunderstood sexual messages, but still more as a fixation on an idealized object that could not be abandoned in the course of development and where the reality check is unconsciously refused. Sooner or later, the idealization of the parents is given up in favor of "more" reality in the course of a reasonably successful resolution of the Oedipus complex. The narcissistic dimension of these introjects seems to be more dominant than their drive dynamic component.

Especially in the case of this patient, the physical closeness to his "beautiful mother" had been mentioned repeatedly. The fear of narcissistic depletion is tangible. The introjects are the guarantor of the libidinal cathexis of narcissism. With Winnicott, we could say that the clinical fear of breakdown is of a breakdown that has already been experienced, but that it is impossible

> to remember something that has not yet happened, and this thing of the past has not happened yet because the patient was not there for it to happen to. The only way to 'remember' in this case is for the patient to experience this past thing for the first time in the present, that is to say, in the transference.
>
> (Winnicott, 1974, p. 104)

If we follow Bela Grunberger (1988), we can assume that the resistances are based on two figures: on the one hand, the Oedipus conflict, which Grunberger rightly understands, with Freud, as a father complex, in other words as a castration complex, where the figure of the father becomes the guarantor of reality.[10] On the other hand, on the narcissistic fixations that form as a defense, the source of which is to be seen as the desire for a conflict-free space, the imaginary maternal space. Despite the fact that we can regard the early maternal bond as anything but a conflict-free space, Grunberger nevertheless describes the dichotomy of psychic reality between an imaginary idea of a reality that is distant from castration and a reality that threatens with castration. Avoidance of reality and, thus, avoidance of conflict, he regards as an avoidance of the threat of castration emanating from the father.

The false

The imaginary idea of a reality beyond the castration complex is expressed clinically, among other things, in the figures of idealization, or in what Janine Chasseguet-Smirgel so aptly called the *malady of ideality*. Since the castration complex cannot be recognized, this all-too-human malady manifests in a fixation on what she calls the "false" (Chasseguet-Smirgel, 1987, p. 102ff). The concept of the "false" is both interesting and complex. Similar to the "false self," it presupposes the "authentic" or the "true". As easy as a "false self" can sometimes be clinically grasped, the "true self" is less easy to paraphrase or not at all. The term also appears in what Freud called the false connection as a characteristic of transference. It, too, assumes a correct linkage. Since the analyst in the transference mutates to the guarantor of reality, a great responsibility is imposed on him. He must develop a kind of instinct for what is right in the false and what could be false in the right. If one assumes that the inner world of a subject is often engaged by "false" object cathexes, by false connections, then many forms of collective, familial, or individual imaginary worlds can easily be identified as a "fixation" on such objects. They can also be identified as distortions of infantile wishful thinking. On a collective level, the most manifest forms of these are ideologies of a racist, anti-Semitic, religious–pagan, or political nature. In clinical reality, however, these are not so much striking manifestations; rather, everyday figures whose narcissistic core often goes unrecognized: "Without my mother's presence I cannot be creative." The patient seemed convinced of this. This could be read as a private myth, as an introject of misunderstood messages, ultimately as a seduction. And it might even be that the patient lives it as real and believes it a physical and psychological experience. This is no different with collective ideologies, that is, collective false objects. They, too, are constantly formed through the personal experience and perspective of the subject, which means socially staged and transformed into an empirically *false experience*, since their core purpose is to avert the conflict of reality, that is, real experience. The idealizations and fixations on false objects are controlled by superego impulses that structure the defense. The destructiveness so often described is an attack on everything that challenges the established defense. Clinically, we are dealing more with self-destructive parts, sustained by feelings of guilt and masochistic fixations, than with a xeno-aggressive defense. The latter appears more frequently in clinical and social psychiatry and in crime.

But the fixation on false objects and on idealizations, hidden forms of idealization filtered through the superego and articulated as "high goals, ideals, intellectual and psychic demands" often conceal the acting-out that they set in motion. They cannot easily be recognized as repetition, although they do represent a mode of repetition. The patient, Freud says, "reproduces it not as a memory but as an action; he repeats it, without, of course, knowing that he is repeating it" (Freud, 1914g, p. 150).

But (psychic) acting-out is not necessarily an action in the true sense of the word either; it is, according to Freud, "his way of remembering" (Freud, 1914g, p. 149f), repeating something in the transference because the transference is "itself only a piece of repetition, and that the repetition is a transference of the forgotten past" (*ibid.*). And Freud adds the following: "not only on to the doctor, but to all other aspects of the current situation" (*ibid.*).

These last words underline the extent to which acting-out in transference is such a crux. For it is culturally, socially, and clinically the most important form of resistance, especially in a modern age where "doing," "resisting," and "activity" of any form are, to a high degree, positively connotated, where the performative speech act is not only criticized but has come to inflationary significance. Psychoanalysis becomes, on the one hand, a bulwark against this acting-out; it is one of its fundamental principles to remember and not to act-out, but, on the other hand, psychoanalysts themselves are given much opportunity (e.g., in their institutions and publications) to open new avenues for acting-out, in the best case sublimated, in the worst case careerist. As if abreaction as resistance were the devil's work from which not even the analyst himself could escape.

> The longer an analytic treatment lasts and the more clearly the patient realizes that the distortions of the pathogenic material cannot by themselves offer any protection against discovery, the more consistently does he make use of the one sort of distortion which obviously affords him the greatest advantage—distortion through transference. [Freud thought so a few years before the text to be discussed here, 1912].
> (Freud, 1912b, p. 103)

The "distortion through transference" must be understood here as a manifestation of acting-out. However, this is precisely what happens not only in clinical situations but is also omnipresent and determines our social and cultural reality. Particularly institutional contexts, such as political parties, universities, churches, etc., are predestined to become the focus of distortions by transference and the acting-out hidden in it. But family is the institution *par excellence* for psychic reality. In the history of psychoanalysis, this acting-out in transference has led to destructive divisions. Even the group-analytical experiences, proposed by various institutions to contain this acting-out, are clearly not able to do what they promise. There seems to be no reasonable antidote against acting-out and distortion in transference, which would herald the dawn of the "terminability" of analysis. It is not for nothing that Freud, in his letter to Oskar Pfister on 5 June 1910, said that the transference was "indeed a cross" (Freud, 1980, p. 37). Working through lightens the burden of that cross; it poses the question of the terminability and interminability of the analytical process and, hence, its limits and possibilities. These questions accompany the analytical process from its beginning to its end.

Notes

1 Freud distinguished (Freud, 1926d, p. 159) between five forms of resistance: Repression-, Ego-, Transference-, Id- and Super-Ego-resistances. Of course, it must be said that, in clinical reality, the forms of resistance are interrelated and not always easy to distinguish.

2 I suppose that when Freud spoke of *"Agieren,"* he initially meant a "doing," an "action," a motor, verbal, or a psychic reaction in the sense of what he initially called *abreaction*. Something that evades remembering and gives expression in a repetition.

3 Laplanche has expanded this idea, developed by Ferenczi in his text on the confusion of language between adults and children, most strongly and incorporated it into his theory of translation.

4 We must not forget that Freud made heredity/inheritance also in the genetic sense responsible for psychic reality. And we can certainly follow him in this, even when leaving the fields of psychoanalysis proper. There is no question scientifically, I think, that there are genetic predispositions for personality, character, and psychic reality. In particular, something as basic as mood or libidinous fixations have biological preconditions. But their fate is rarely determined only biologically.

5 Transgenerational transference is a term from research on the consequences of the Shoah on the second generation. In the course of the last 20 years, this term has been separated from Shoah research and applied to the general transference from generation to generation.

6 Freud expresses it with the following famous sentence: "If anyone were inclined to put forward the paradoxical proposition that the normal man is not only far more immoral than he believes but also far more moral than he knows, psychoanalysis, on whose findings the first half of the assertion rests, would have no objection to raise against the second half" (Freud, 1923b, p. 52)

7 I assume that the objective of the analytical process has undergone a transformation, supported by the various tendencies of object relationship theories as well as the emerging narcissistic theories. Classical psychoanalysis, which was ego-psychologically oriented, was suspected of overemphasizing the father principle, ego structuring, the castration complex, and the drive and reality conflict. Interpretation was at the center of the analyst's activity. It now has been moved to the background, being classified as too intrusive, "phallic", patriarchal, masculine. The father principle, so central to Freud, was viewed with suspicion and the mother–child relationship came into focus. Countertransference became the most important technique.

8 Freud brought the Oedipus complex to its final formulation rather late, and yet he sometimes seems to "forget" it in an astonishing way, such as in this text we are discussing. This observation would require an extended discussion, which cannot be done here.

9 Freud spoke of the differentiation between introjection and identification, especially in *Group Psychology and the Analysis of the Ego* (1921c). He refers here to Ferenczi's 1909 text, Introjection and Transference. Shifts occur that transform the inner objects into misunderstood or even enigmatic objects. In identification, this kind of displacement does not happen, or only to a small extent. In it, primarily an exaltation takes place, an idealization.

10 Freud often speaks of the father complex. Grunberger accentuates this reading by understanding the Oedipal complex as the confrontation with the father instance. The father is the cause of the conflict triggered by the Oedipus complex, so the phantasm of his murder is inherent in the conflict. He is the guarantor of reality to the extent that the bond with the mother is an illusion and must be abandoned.

References

Bohleber, W. (2000). Die Entwicklung der Traumatheorie in der Psychoanalyse. *Psyche*, 54: 797–839.

Chasseguet-Smirgel, J. (1987). *Das Ichideal. Psychoanalytischer Essay über die Krankheit der Idealität*. Frankfurt/M. Suhrkamp.

Ferenczi, S. (1972). Sprachverwirrung zwischen den Erwachsenen und dem Kind (1933). In *Schriften zur Psychoanalyse* (pp. 303–313). Frankfurt/M: Fischer.

Freud, S. (1910a). Five Lectures on Psycho-analysis. *S.E.*, *11*: 3–55. London: Hogarth Press.

Freud, S. (1912b). The Dynamics of Transference. *S.E.*, *12*: 97–108. London: Hogarth Press.

Freud, S. (1912–1913). *Totem and Taboo*. *S.E.*, *13*: 1–161. London: Hogarth Press.

Freud, S. (1914g). Remembering, Repeating and Working-Through. *S.E.*, *12*: 147–156. London: Hogarth Press.

Freud, S. (1923b). *The Ego and the Id*. *S.E.*, *19*: 3–66. London: Hogarth Press.

Freud, S. (1926d). *Inhibitions, Symptoms and Anxiety*. *S.E.*, *20*: 77–174. London: Hogarth Press.

Freud, S. (1928b). Dostoevsky and Parricide. *S.E.*, *21*: 175–196. London: Hogarth Press.

Freud, S. (1937c). Analysis Terminable and Interminable. *S.E.*, *23*: 211–253. London: Hogarth Press.

Freud, S. (1937d). Constructions in Analysis. *S.E.*, *23*: 257–269. London: Hogarth Press.

Freud, S. (1939a). *Moses and Monotheism*. *S.E.*, *23*: 3–137. London: Hogarth Press.

Freud, S. & Pfister, O. (1980). Briefe 1909–1939. Zürich: Ex Libris.

Granoff, W. (2001). Filiation. L'avenir du complexe d'Œdipe. Paris: Gallimard.

Grunberger, B. (1988). *Narziss und Anubis*. Munich: Verlag Internationale Psychoanalyse.

Sandler, J. & Rosenblatt, B. (1962). The Concept of the Representational World. *Psychoanalytic Study of the Child*, *17*: 128–145.

Strachey, J. (1937). Zur Theorie der therapeutischen Resultate der Psychoanalyse. *Internationale Zeitschrift für Psychoanalyse*, *23*(1): 68–74.

Winnicott, D.W. (1974). Fear of Breakdown. *International Review of Psycho-Analysis*, *1*: 103–107.

12 The Mark of Psychoanalysis: Working-Through in Freud and Today

Elias Mallet da Rocha Barros
and Alberto Rocha Barros

What is psychoanalysis in its essence? What distinguishes it from other modalities of psychological treatment, psychodynamic investigation, and other intellectual attempts at modeling the mind?

"Talking cures" have existed throughout human history in many different shapes and forms (Zweig, 1931; Entralgo, 1958; Jackson, 1999). And psychoanalysis itself developed against the wider backdrop of the emergence of a new concept of self and mind (Solomon, 1988; Makari, 2015); the exploration of unconscious forces in art, philosophy, and psychology (Nicholls & Liebscher, 2010; Ffytche, 2012; Kandel, 2012); and the rise of dynamic psychiatry in many guises (Ellenber, 1970; Burns, 2014). Psychoanalysis was *one* among many different (and sometimes competing) paradigms striving to give a rational account of human nature, the workings of the brain and the dynamics of the mind.

Psychiatric nosology was also undergoing significant changes in the beginning of the twentieth century. Emil Kraepelin had revolutionized psychopathology with the 1893 edition of his famous *Textbook in Psychiatry*, which went through a number of editions up to 1927 (Shorter, 1997, pp. 99–109; Hoff, 2015), Eugen Bleuler coined such terms as "schizophrenia," "ambivalence," and "autism" between 1908 and 1911 (Kuhn, 2004), and Karl Jaspers had published his immensely influential *General Psychopathology* in 1913 (Bormuth, 2019). This was a fertile time of searching for a more rigorous understanding of mental disease and for the reasons behind psychological suffering.

Throughout this period of the emergence of these diverse strands in philosophical psychology, dynamic psychology, and dynamic psychiatry, the problem was fourfold: (I) finding a *model* of how the mind works and of how mind and body are intertwined; (II) proposing a *conceptualization* of psychological disease (a theory of the nature of psychopathology and how it arises); (III) finding a *method* to access another person's inner world and psyche with some degree of "objectivity" in order to examine it and act on it; (IV) developing a *theory of therapeutic technique* to alleviate symptomatology, an account of how and why a certain method/technique operated

DOI: 10.4324/9781003458340-12

effectively. Psychoanalysis itself was born against the background of this scientific atmosphere.

The psychoanalytic movement suffered a number of schisms between 1910 and 1913, losing the support of such members as Alfred Adler, Eugen Bleuler, and Carl Jung (Schwartz, 1999, pp. 93–129; Makari, 2008, pp. 239–292). It was a turbulent period and the time was ripe for a summation of the core tenets of psychoanalysis. Between 1911 and 1915, Freud writes a series of papers on technique infused with a "conciliatory and genial rhetoric" (Gay, 1988, p. 305) and with the aim of producing a handbook or textbook on the general methodology of psychoanalysis (*ibid.*, pp. 292–295). The book never came to fruition, but the papers intended for it will become known as "Freud's papers on technique." Perhaps their slimness and economy are due to the fact that they were topics meant to be expanded on in the book that never came to be.

"Remembering, Repeating and Working-Through" (1914g) belongs to this group of papers and to this climate of defining the nature and boundaries of an emerging field. It was written in this time of important shifts within the psychoanalytic movement itself and during an age of richly diverse theories on the nature of the mind. It was natural for Freud to strive to find ways to clearly identify the nucleus of psychoanalysis, its distinguishing mark.

We mentioned above how the general blueprint for psychodynamic theory and psychotherapy depended on a model of the mind, a conceptualization of the nature and reasons behind psychological suffering, the discovery of a method to access another person's inner world with some degree of confidence ("objectivity"), and the delineation of a theory of psychotherapeutic technique. By 1914, many of these elements are in place within the Freudian system and Freud, in lieu of the 1910–1913 splits, had every reason to establish a bedrock of concepts all "psychoanalysts" could agree on. His topographical frame of reference (1900–1923; cf. Sandler *et al.* 1997, pp. 55–161) offered a model of the mind based on how the psychic apparatus manages the turbulent inner world of instinctual drives and their representatives. Free association, dream interpretation, and transference interpretation (among others) constituted a "royal road" (*the* method) to access the remote regions of the psyche. In "Remembering, Repeating and Working-Through," Freud will briefly fill in the last few pieces of the puzzle by stating the broad outlines of his theory of psychopathology and his theory of technique.

Freud's theory of nosology is organized around the notions of "forgetting," "repressing," "resisting," "repeating," and "acting out." Let us select a few passages from "Remembering, Repeating and Working-Through":

...forgetting is mostly restricted to dissolving thought-connections, failing to draw the right conclusion and isolating memories.

... experiences which occurred in very early childhood and were not understood at the time...

... we may say that the patient does not *remember* anything of what he has forgotten and repressed but *acts* it out. He reproduces it not as a memory but as an action; he *repeats* it, without, of course, knowing that he is repeating it.

The patient brings out of the armoury of the past the weapons with which he defends himself against the progress of the treatment.

We have learned that the patient repeats instead of remembering.
(All passages are taken from Freud, 1914g,
pp. 149–151; original italics)

For Freud, psychological suffering, inner confusion, and mental pain arises from failures in knowledge and understanding; from a breakdown in accurate apprehension of experience; from the incapacity to think out or think through situations; from misunderstandings and the impossibility of comprehending certain experiences; from the tendency to reenact and repeat what has remained dormant, undigested or misrepresented; from a perverted *use* of "history" as "weaponry". In one sentence: we suffer due to the "*the dissolving of thought-connections*." This is quite a unique take on psychopathology.

And what about his theory of technique? Freud opens the essay with an overview of how psychoanalytic technique evolved since its inception stating: "The aim of these different techniques has, of course, remained the same. Descriptively speaking, it is to fill in gaps in memory; dynamically speaking, it is to overcome resistances due to repression" (Freud, 1914g, pp. 147–148).

"Fill in the gaps of memory" shouldn't be understood literally here. It means (according to our proposed reading) a reweaving of lost thought-connections, a retrieval of the complexities of context, a reawakening to new ways of understanding past and present experience, a renewed effort to digest and metabolize our emotional lives, learning to let go of the past and not reenact it as an attack-and-defense system.

"Remembering," for Freud, is a constant rescanning and reconstruction of the past. A constant ebbing and flowing of our personal history in which we reacquaint ourselves with what happened to us while also reshaping and retelling our subjective narratives. This "remembering-and-forgetting," this "telling-and-retelling," are attempts to make the familiar unfamiliar and the unfamiliar familiar, in order to reprocess psychic experience. The literary critic Robert Shattuck proposes that Proust also viewed this work of memory in a "therapeutic" light:

I believe it is best to approach the reading of Proust as if it were a kind of long-term cure, or an initiation to unfamiliar mental and psychical movements evolved by another culture. A steady, leisurely pace, without the tension of fixed deadlines, serves the best. Certain habits of thought can thus be laid aside as others are slowly acquired. It may take months, even years. The *Search* creates a season of the mind outside temporal limits.

(Shattuck, 1974, p. 33)

The parallels with the psychoanalytic project are quite striking.

Freud writes: "Not only *some* but *all* of what is essential from childhood has been retained in these memories" (Freud, 1914g, pp. 148).

Freud is suggesting that nothing is truly lost in our recollections. Because all that is essential has somehow been preserved. The mind constantly strives to produce an account of its complete and global life cycle. But both the mechanism of safeguarding (holding fast to a version of the past) and the mechanism of excluding unwanted or unnecessary memories (brushing aside, forgetting, repealing, excising, splitting off) can be either healthy and conducive to psychic change and progress, or unhealthy and conducive to stagnation or regression.

And how is the healthy path achieved/selected? It is here, we suspect, that the critical concept of working-through plays a significant role.

Freud closes the 1914 essay by highlighting how the concept of *working-through* is precisely what sets psychoanalysis apart from other psychodynamic methods:

This working-through of the resistances may in practice turn out to be an arduous task for the subject of the analysis and a trial of patience for the analyst. Nevertheless, *it is a part of the work which effects the greatest changes in the patient, and which distinguishes analytic treatment from any kind of treatment by suggestion.*

(Freud, 1914g, pp. 155–156, our italics)

Yet, despite this exalted phrasing, Freud touches upon the idea of working-through only briefly in this paper and in later writings, "and in each case almost in passing" (Sedler, 1983, p. 75). He introduces what appears to be a critical concept with an almost excessive economy and laconism. The paucity of Freud's remarks might have "contributed to the obscurity in which the process of working-through has been shrouded" (Novey, 1962, p. 664).

In the 1950s and 1960s there was an impression that "working-through" was a rather neglected or overlooked concept. Phyllis Greenacre, in an oft quoted paper, wrote:

The process of *working-through* has held positions of varying importance and significance in the development of psycho-analytic therapy. Just at present one hears it referred to relatively little, and as a specific principle in technique it does not attract much attention.

(Greenacre, 1956, p. 439)

A few years later, Samuel Novey would write in a similar vein: "The principle of working-through is a relatively neglected area of study in psychoanalysis. The paucity of literature on this subject, already noteworthy, has become even more evident in recent years" (Novey, 1962, p. 658).

But things have significantly changed since those days. A cursory search on pep-web.org yields thousands of results and one finds working-through being conceptualized in a number of different ways.

In an excellent overview of how working-through has been conceptualized in psychoanalysis, Sandler, Dare, and Holder write:

> For Freud, 'working-through' represented the work entailed, for both analyst and patient, in overcoming resistances to change due primarily to the tendency for the instinctual drives to cling to accustomed patterns of discharge. Working-through represented analytic work that was *additional* to that involved in uncovering conflicts and resistances. Intellectual insight without working-through was not regarded as sufficient for the therapeutical task, as the tendency for the previous modes of functioning to repeat themselves in accustomed ways would remain.
>
> (Sandler, Dare, & Holder, 1992, p. 177)

But psychoanalysis isn't written in stone, and psychoanalytic authors, after Freud, embraced very different takes on what working-through entails.

Otto Fenichel notoriously perceived it as a "special kind of interpretation," in other words, an activity of the analyst: "The process that requires demonstrating to patients the same thing again and again at different times or in various connections, is called, following Freud, 'working-through'" (Fenichel, *apud* Sandler, Dare, & Holder, 1992, p. 178).

Irma Pick, in "Working Through in the Countertransference" (1985) also emphasizes working-through as something the analyst is required to do, but, instead of viewing it as a *technique*, she conceptualizes it as a psychodynamic process which takes place *within the analyst's internal world*, thus revolutionizing the concept in a extremely creative way and (perhaps) radically changing it from what Freud had in mind:

> … every interpretation aims at a move from the paranoid/schizoid to the depressive position. This is true not only for the patient, but *for the analyst who needs again and again to regress and work through.* I wonder whether the real issue of truly deep versus superficial interpretation resides not so much in terms of which level has been addressed, but *to what extent the analyst has worked the process through internally* in the act of giving the interpretation.
>
> (Pick, 1985, p. 158, our italics)

Others have postulated that working-through does not describe *a technique employed by the psychoanalyst nor a process occurring within the analyst,* but that it chronicles *an effort and struggle experienced by the analysand.* For example, in his *The Psychoanalysis of Elation* (1950), Bertram D. Lewin considered working-through: "as being the acceptance and assimilation by the patient of the truths discovered by interpretation and free association" (Lewin *apud* Novey, 1962, p. 661).

Walter Stewart, following this reasoning, writes:

> In spite of the obvious fact that analysis is a cooperative effort involving both analyst and patient, surprisingly *few articles explicitly focus on the patient's contribution to this effort. The concept of working-through was, I believe, intended to deal with this aspect of the analytic process.* This can be seen from Freud's statement that the 'working-through of the resistance may in practice turn out to be an arduous task for the subject of the analysis and a trial of patience for the analyst.
>
> (Stewart, 1963, p. 474)

On the same page he also wrote,

> The doctor has nothing else to do than to wait and let things take their course, a course which cannot be avoided nor always hastened.
>
> These sentences clearly emphasize that in the analysis there are times when patience, not activity, is required of the analyst, and that *the burden of work belongs to the patient.* In contrast to this view, most analytic papers are written as if the patient's efforts could be ignored, and further suggest an almost mystical belief in the power of the "correct interpretation." This attitude may be a reflection of the medical concept of the doctor-patient relationship and even a residue of the early hypnotic technique. It may also reflect the temptation toward grandiosity in the analyst or a hidden anxiety concerning the therapeutic efficacy of analytic treatment.
>
> (Stewart, 1963, pp. 474–475, our italics)

Although insisting that working-through takes place in transference, in the analyst–analysand dynamic, Mark Sedler also privileges that it is within the analysand's mind that the process takes place (see the phrases we highlight):

> ... in the midst of the transference, at its origin and limit, and *independent of the efforts of the analyst,* working-through names a battle to be fought and a labor to be done which the neurosis has, for so long, only served to postpone. *This is the struggle within oneself;* it is the labor of *transformation* that makes possible the rejection of the neurotic encumbrance and its symptomatic trappings in favor of a novel and

presumably healthier mode of life. (…) *working through names that aspect of the process which the analysand shall ultimately hold most dear, for it signifies his own triumph – and not ours [i.e. the analyst's] – over the clandestine operations of neurotic life.*

(Sedler, 1983, pp. 74–75 and pp. 96–97, our italics)

For other analysts, working-through is more of an all-encompassing concept, that covers the whole analytic process. For them, the expression is almost shorthand for what psychoanalytic clinical practice *is*. Charles Brenner states:

> … working-through is not a special kind of analysis. It is ordinary, run-of-the-mill analysis, as we know it today. Nor is it the analysis of one or another component of psychic conflict. It is the analysis of psychic conflict in all its aspects, now one and now another.
>
> (Brenner, 1987, pp. 106–107)

And René Roussillon writes:

> In the practice of psychoanalysis, the concept of working-through is a fundamental one (…) It is a fundamental concept and perhaps even *one that defines the specificity of psychoanalytic practice,* insofar as, much better than any other, it differentiates psychoanalysis from the kinds of psychotherapy based on suggestion; Freud himself emphasized this element. Although it appeared as long ago as 1914, at a time when the overall conception of psychoanalysis was focused on recovering forgotten memories – so that it could now almost be seen as a somewhat outdated way of looking at psychoanalytic practice – *it has travelled through the years and remained a feature of the various models and conceptions of how psychoanalysis is carried out.*
>
> (Roussillon, 2010, p. 1405, our italics)

Going in a different direction, we can also recall how Freud has a certain tendency to fashion terms which contain the idea of "work" (*Arbeit*) as a morphological component. The notion of "dream-work" (*Traumarbeit*) comes to mind, as does the range of words associated with psychical "working out" or "working over" (*Verarbeitung, Bearbeitung, Ausarbeitung*) (Laplanche & Pontalis, 1967, p. 125 and pp. 365–367). Sensing that working-through (*Durcharbeitung*) might be profitably explored when connected to this semantic group, one of the authors of this article (Elias Mallet da Rocha Barros) published a paper investigating these resonances:

> I suggest that the dreamwork described by Freud does not limit itself to the work that transforms latent thoughts into manifest dream contents by use of condensation, displacement and consideration for

figurability. It also comprehends a process through which meaning is apprehended, built and transformed in an expressive non-discursive level, based on representation through figurative/pictorial images. In this process fresh symbols are created that widen the capacity of the person to think about the meanings of his/her emotional experiences. I would like to conjecture that the working-through function of dreams is performed by a process of progression in formal qualities of the representations made available by dreaming in the form I have called affective pictograms mainly in response to interpretations.

(Rocha Barros, 2002, p. 1085)

So, *what is working-through*? A technical instrument in the analytic clinical toolkit (a technique employed by the analyst)? An internal dynamic process that should be elaborated within the analyst's internal world? An overcoming of resistances? An effort, labor or struggle that happens within the patient? Part and parcel of other processes, such as "dream-work" and "psychical working out?" These are quite different, though not necessarily irreconcilable, conceptions of working-through.

Apparently, it is very hard to pinpoint precisely what working-through means. This might seem daunting and a little confusing. But this is very common in psychoanalysis, with some writers fearing that many psychoanalytic concepts are always under the constant threat of slipping away into a "Tower of Babel" (Viñar, 2017, p. 40). Other analysts prefer to imagine that psychoanalytic theory allows for a range of applications of a given concept. Joseph Sandler, for example, has written an interesting paper in which he speaks of the "flexibility" or "elasticity" inherent to psychoanalytic concepts, which tend to cover "a number of dimensions of meaning" (Sandler, 1983, p. 43). We should note that this is no cause for alarm. Philosophy itself has the same relationship to some of its central concepts: the notion of "substance" or of "the self" in one philosophical system will be radically different than in another and philosophy is *more the richer for it*. Ludwig Wittgenstein's idea that the semantic range of certain words and concepts is loosely held together by a mere "family resemblance" might be useful here (Wittgenstein, 1953, paragraphs 65–67). It is not always possible or desirable to dissolve concepts into their elemental parts or fundamental constituents. The reach of certain notions is sometimes highly varied with zones of vagueness and ambiguity (Baker & Hacker, 1980, pp. 189–208). Craving for a fixed reference or for a rigid and clear-cut definition of "working-through" might be deeply counterproductive since psychoanalysis is continually reinventing itself and reevaluating its concepts: "Words and sentences, like people, must be allowed a certain slippage" (Ogden, 1997, p. 3).

Perhaps the crucial element around which all the different concepts of working-through gravitate towards is this idea that whatever it is and however we conceive (or reconceive) of it, working-through is that "part of the work which effects the greatest changes in the patient, and which distinguishes analytic treatment from any kind of treatment" (Freud, 1914g, pp. 155–156). In other words, instead of asking ourselves what the concept of working-through *is*, we should ask ourselves what *kind* of concept it is. Psychoanalysis, in its long history, has assembled a wide vocabulary to speak of mental change and psychic evolution: working out, working through, talking out, transformation, insight, symbolic progression, elaboration etc. Working-through is a distilled formulation of these various ideas, it labels what goes on *uniquely* in a *psychoanalytic* session (and only in psychoanalytic sessions). It indicates the Shibboleth of psychoanalysis, its distinguishing mark.

To understand this, it is perhaps interesting to revisit how unique psychoanalysis is. On the one hand, psychoanalysis emerged as a medical specialty and structured itself around a medical model, a theory of psychopathology and a clinical technique for symptom remission or relief. Yet, writers like Donald Meltzer have been astute in noticing that there is another trend running through psychoanalysis as it was in the process of shaping itself. Meltzer pinpoints this revolutionary shift to Freud's writing *Leonardo da Vinci and a Memory of his Childhood* (Freud, 1910c). Meltzer writes:

> I believe the Leonardo paper is the beginning of a new attitude in Freud to psychoanalysis as *something that investigates the whole person and his whole life*. From that point of view, the pathography – *the attempt to describe a whole person and his whole life* – is really a very important effort on Freud's part.
>
> (Meltzer, 1978, p. 63; our italics)

This shift in Freud's conceiving of psychoanalysis is accompanied by a shift in style: "The literal and mechanical quality of the earlier models has given way to imaginative, near poetic, and vital images and models in the later writings" (Meltzer, 1978, p. 14).

Jonathan Lear is also razor-sharp in capturing how psychoanalysis and the psychoanalytic tradition distinguishes itself from other modalities of psychotherapy in its global attention to "the whole person and his/her whole life," that is, to the human condition as such:

> Freud is a deep explorer of the human condition, working in a tradition which goes back to Sophocles and which extends through Plato, Saint Augustine, and Shakespeare to Proust and Nietzsche. What holds this tradition together is its insistence that there are significant meanings for human well-being which are obscured from immediate awareness. (...). In misunderstanding these strange meanings, humans usher in catastrophe. (...) ... psychoanalysis is the most

sustained and successful attempt to make these obscure meanings intelligible.

(Lear, 1998, pp. 18–19)

Humans are meaning-making and self-interpreting animals inserted in complex cultural webs. The advent of psychoanalysis was not merely the emergence of a new psychotherapeutic technique, but the establishment of "a new discursive space" (Makari, 2008, p. 123). The historian of science and philosophy G.E.R. Lloyd has written a number of works in which he compares how rational endeavors to understand the nature of the world and the human condition were carried out in ancient Greece, India, and China (Lloyd, 2002, 2012, 2014). All these societies produced sophisticated strategies for rational inquiries into human nature and the natural world, but Greece created a unique diction through which to carry out these endeavors, besides something which we could recognize as scientific discourse, namely, *Greek philosophy* (Rovelli, 2023). The strangeness and uniqueness of Greek philosophy is analogous to us to the strangeness and uniqueness of psychoanalytic discourse, and this is what George Makari means when he writes about the revolutionary nature of psychoanalysis ("a new discursive space"): it came about as a singular blend of psychiatry, the life sciences, psychology, psychobiography, anthropology, sexology, the humanities, and the arts. A new register to speak of the human condition.

We invite readers to keep these things in mind when approaching "Remembering, Repeating and Working-Through." If one reads it too literally, the essence of its radical nature will be missed.

If working-through is indeed shorthand for the work of psychoanalysis as such, its distinguishing mark, and if it accommodates a range of meanings, how would we view it today? Restrictions of space demand brevity of us.

In the first place, contemporary psychoanalysis has taken further steps towards revolutionizing the notion of a "psychoanalytic encounter" by stressing a much more dialectical dynamic between analyst and analysand (Ogden, 1994; Ferro, 1999): "Analysis is not simply a method of uncovering the hidden; it is more importantly a process of creating the analytic subject who has not previously existed" (Ogden, 1994, p. 47).

The examination of a whole life and the exercise of revisiting one's personal history has become more complexly blended between the psychoanalyst and the analysand. The discussion between "working-through" happening on the side of the analysand or on the side of the analyst has perhaps become less pressing.

In second place, contemporary psychoanalysis has laid increasing stress on the notion of symbolism, representation, and reverie (Rocha Barros, 2000, 2013; Rocha Barros & Rocha Barros, 2015, 2016; Civitarese, 2013; Levine *et al.*, 2013; Brown, 2019; Busch, 2019). For some schools of thought emphasis has shifted from a more straightforward view of representation and symbolization (a one-to-one equation) to a more complex take in which the *expressive aspects of symbolization* have become critical (Rocha Barros, 2000). This means that not only is *remembrance* vital, but also the *way* or the *form* through which reacquaintance with oneself occurs is centrally important.

Robust and healthy working-through personal history in the psychoanalytic session demands a number of steps: (1) the apprehension and/or recollection of lived experience with an appropriate affect, tempered by context; (2) the healthy processing and metabolization of experience through which the nurturing and constructive elements are retained while the toxic elements are expelled; (3) the development of a rich and expressive repertoire of symbols to capture experience in plastic and malleable ways; (4) the insertion of represented and symbolized experience in broader symbolic networks that allow us to revisit the story of our lives through different angles and prisms, and through different symbolic lenses.

The above is perhaps an all too brief summary of what the general contours of "working-through" look like to us today. It is the notion that signals out what psychoanalysis is and what it does. Psychoanalysis is unique in exercising a deep exploration of the subjective symbolic world of analyst-and-analysand and: "despite all its extravagant flaws, psychoanalysis remains the most nuanced general account of interior life we possess" (Makari, 2008, p. 5).

References

Baker, G.P. & Hacker, P.M.S. (1980). *Wittgenstein: Meaning and Understanding (Essays on the Philosophical Investigations)*. Chicago, IL: University of Chicago Press.

Bormuth, M. (2019). Karl Jaspers. In G. Stanghellini *et al.* (Eds), *The Oxford Handbook of Phenomenological Psychopathology* (pp. 96–103). Oxford: Oxford University Press.

Brenner, C. (1987). Working Through, 1914–1987. *Psychoanalytic Quarterly, 56*: 88–108.

Brown, L. J. (2019). Notes on Memory and Desire: Implications for Working Through. In *Transformational Processes in Clinical Psychoanalysis: Dreaming, Emotions and the Present Moment* (pp. 189–201). New York: Routledge.

Burns, T. (2014). *Our Necessary Shadow: The Nature and Meaning of Psychiatry*. New York: Pegasus Books.

*Busch, F. (2019). *The Analyst's Reveries: Explorations in Bion's Enigmatic Concept*. New York: Routledge.

Civitarese, G. (2013). *The Necessary Dream: New Theories and Techniques of Interpretation in Psychoanalysis*. Routledge, 2018.

Ellenberger, H.F. (1970). *The Discovery of the Unconscious: The History and Evolution of Dynamic Psychiatry*. New York: Basic Books.

Entralgo, P.L. (1958). *The Therapy of the Word in Classical Antiquity*. New Haven, CT: Yale University Press, 1970.

Ferro, A. (1999). *The Bi-personal Field. Experiences in Child Analysis*. London: Routledge.

Freud, S. (1910c). *Leonardo da Vinci and a Memory of his Childhood. G.W.* 10: 126–136; *S.E.,* 12: 145–156. London: Hogarth Press.

Freud, S. (1914g). Remembering, Repeating and Working-through. *G.W.* 8: 128–211; *S.E.,* 12: 147–156.

**Freud, S. (1918[1914]). *From the History of an Infantile Neurosis* (The "Wolf Man"). *G.W.* 12: 29–157; *S.E.,* 17: 1–122. London: Hogarth Press.

Ffytche, M. (2012). *The Foundations of the Unconscious: Schelling, Freud and the Birth of the Modern Psyche.* Cambridge: Cambridge University Press.

Gay, P. (1988). *Freud: A Life for Our Time.* New York: Norton.

Greenacre, P. (1956). Re-evaluation of the process of working-through. *International Journal of Psychoanalysis, 37:* 439–444.

**Greenson, R.R. (1967). *The Technique and Practice of Psychoanalysis Vol. 1.* New York: International Universities Press.

Hoff, P. (2015). The Kraepelian Tradition. *Dialogues in Clinical Neuroscience, 17*(1): 31–41.

Jackson, S.W. (1999). *Care of the Psyche: A History of Psychological Healing.* Yale University Press.

Kandel, E.R. (2012). *The Age of Insight: The Quest to Understand the Unconscious in Art, Mind and Brain from Vienna 1900 to the Present.* London: Random House.

Kuhn, C. (2004). Eugene Bleuler's Concepts of Psychopathology. *History of Psychiatry, 15*(3): 361–366.

Laplanche, J. & Pontalis, J.-P. (1967). *The Language of Psychoanalysis.* London: Karnac, 1973.

Lear, J. (1998). On Killing Freud (Again). In *Open Minded: Working Out the Logic of the Soul.* Cambridge, MA: Harvard University Press.

Levine, H.B., Reed, G.S., & Scarfone, D. (Eds) (2013). *Unrepresented States and the Construction of Meaning: Clinical and Theoretical Contributions.* London: Routledge.

Lloyd, G.E.R. (2002). *The Ambitions of Curiosity: Understanding the World in Ancient Greece and China.* Cambridge: Cambridge University Press.

Lloyd, G.E.R. (2012). *Being, Humanity, and Understanding.* Oxford: Oxford University Press.

Lloyd, G.E.R. (2014). *The Ideals of Inquiry: An Ancient History.* Oxford: Oxford University Press.

Makari, G. (2008). *Revolution in Mind: The Creation of Psychoanalysis.* New York: Harper Perennial.

Makari, G. (2015). *Soul Machine: The Invention of the Modern Mind.* New York: Norton.

Meltzer, D. (1978). *The Kleinian Development: Part 1: Freud's Clinical Development.* Strath Tay, Perthshire: Clunie Press.

Nicholls, A. & Liebscher, M. (Eds) (2010). *Thinking the Unconscious: Nineteenth-Century German Thought.* Cambridge: Cambridge University Press.

Novey, S. (1962). The Principle of "Working-through" in Psychoanalysis. *Journal of the American Psychoanalytic Association (JAPA),* 10: 658–676.

Ogden, T.H. (1994). *Subjects of Analysis.* London: Karnac.

Ogden, T. H. (1997). *Reverie and Interpretation: Sensing Something Human.* Northvale, New Jersey & London: Jason Aronson.

Pick, I.B. (1985). Working Through in the Countertransference. *International Journal of Pyschoanalysis,* 66: 157–166.

Rocha Barros, E.M. (2000). Affect and Pictographic Image: The Constitution of Meaning in Mental Life. *International Journal of Psychoanalysis, 81*(6): 1087–1099.

Rocha Barros, E.M. (2002). An Essay on Dreaming, Psychical Working Out and Working Through. *International Journal of Psychoanalysis, 83*(5): 1083–1093.

Rocha Barros, E.M. (2013). Dream, Figurability and Symbolic Transformation. *Psychoanalysis in Europe (The EPF Bulletin), 67*: 107–120.

**Rocha Barros, E.M. & Rocha Barros, E.L. (2011). Reflections on the clinical implications of symbolism. *International Journal of Psychoanalysis, 92*(4): 879–901

Rocha Barros, E.M. & Rocha Barros, E.L. (2015). Symbolism, Emotions and Mental Growth. In: J. Barossa, C. Bronstein, & C. Pajaczkowska (Eds), *The new Klein–Lacan: Dialogues* (pp. 235–254). London: Karnac.

Rocha Barros, E. M. & Rocha Barros, E. L. (2016). The Function of Evocation in the Working-through of the Countertransference; Projective Identification, Reverie, and the Expressive Function of the Mind-Reflections Inspired by Bion's work. In: H.B. Levine & G. Civitarese (Eds), *The W. R. Bion Tradition: Lines of Development, Evolution of Theory and Practice over the Decades.* London: Karnac.

*Roussillon, R. (2010). Working through and its various models. *International Journal of Psychoanalysis, 91*: 1405–1417.

Rovelli, C. (2023). *Anaximander and the Nature of Science.* London: Allen Lane.

Sandler, J. (1983). Reflections on Some Relations Between Psychoanalytic Concepts and Psychoanalytic Practice. *International Journal of Psychoanalysis, 64*: 35–45.

Sandler, J., Dare, C., & Holder, A. (1992). *The Patient and the Analyst* (revised and expanded edition). Routledge.

Sandler, J., Holder, A., Dare, C., & Dreher, A.U. (1997). *Freud's Models of the Mind: An Introduction.* London: Karnac.

Schwartz, J. (1999). *Cassandra's Dream: A History of Psychoanalysis.* New York: Viking Press.

Sedler, M. (1983). Freud's concept of the working-through. *Psychoanalytic Quarterly, 52*: 73–98.

Shattuck, R. (1974). *Proust.* Glasgow: Fontana/Collins (Fontana Modern Masters).

Shorter, E. (1997). *A History of Psychiatry: From the Era of the Asylum to the Age of Prozac.* Wiley.

Solomon, R.C. (1988). *Continental Philosophy since 1750: The Rise and Fall of the Self.* Oxford: Oxford University Press.

Stewart, W.A. (1963). An Inquiry into the Concept of Working-through. *Journal of the American Psychoanalytic Association, 11*: 474–499.

**Thompson, M.G. (1994). *The Truth About Freud's Technique: The Encounter with the Real.* New York: New York University Press.

Viñar, M.N. (2017). The Enigma of Extreme Traumatism: Trauma, Exclusion and Their Impact on Subjectivity. *American Journal of Psychoanalysis, 77*(1): 40–51.

Wittgenstein, L. (1953). *Philosophical Investigations.* The German text, with an English translation by G.E.M. Anscombe, P.M.S. Hacker, and Joachim Schulte. Revised 4th edition by P.M.S. Hacker and Joachim Schulte. Wiley-Blackwell, 2009.

Zweig, S. (1931). *Mental Healers: Mesmer, Eddy, Freud.* Pushkin Press, 2013.

Index

Note: Page numbers followed by n refer to notes.

For Product Safety Concerns and Information please contact our EU
representative GPSR@taylorandfrancis.com
Taylor & Francis Verlag GmbH, Kaufingerstraße 24, 80331 München, Germany

www.ingramcontent.com/pod-product-compliance
Lightning Source LLC
Chambersburg PA
CBHW071415290326
41932CB00047B/2977

9 781032 602479